METHODS OF TEACHING ELEMENTARY SCIENCE

METHODS OF TEACHING ELEMENTARY SCIENCE

By

Ghanta Padma Tulasi

M.Sc. M.Ed., Ph.D.

Lecturer in Science

M.M. College of Education

Vijayawada–520 010 (A.P.)

General Editor

Dr. Digumarti Bhaskara Rao

M.Sc., M.A., M.A., M.Ed., Ph.D.

Reader

R.V.R. College of Education

Srinivasa Nagar Colony

Guntur–522 006

Andhra Pradesh

India

DISCOVERY PUBLISHING HOUSE

NEW DELHI-110002

ISBN: 978-81-7141-871-8

Methods of Teaching Elementary Science

Published by:
DISCOVERY PUBLISHING HOUSE PVT. LTD.
4383/4B, Ansari Road, Darya Ganj
New Delhi-110 002 (India)
Phone: +91-11-23279245, 43596064-65
Fax: +91-11-23253475
E-mail: discoverypublishinghouse@gmail.com
sales@discoverypublishinggroup.com
web: www.discoverypublishinggroup.com

Printed at:
Infinity Imaging Systems
Delhi

Foreword

Teacher education is quantitatively marching ahead towards quality education. The central and state governments through the NCTE and the Directorates of School/Higher Education are rendering their legitimate service in improving the quality of teacher education by formulating and implementing various academic policies and educational programmes. Along with these policies and programmes, the teacher educators and the prospective teachers teaching and studying in teacher education institutions need good curriculum and quality books.

The methods of teaching each subject play a pivotal role in enhancing the efficiency of their practitioners. Identifying the very importance of the methods of teaching and the quality of books, a series of books on the methods of teaching different subjects have been developed by experienced teacher educators for the benefit of teachers in making in teacher education institutions. Thanks to the authors.

Valuable suggestions for the improvement of these books are welcome from fellow teacher educators, prospective teachers and other academicians involved in the arena of teacher education.

The authors and the editor dedicate this series of books on the methodology of teaching to Mr. Tilak Raj Wasan, Proprietor, Discovery Publishing House, New Delhi, for taking up this commendable task of publication to meet the felt needs of teacher education faculty and clientele.

Dr. Digumarti Bhaskara Rao
Research Director in Education
Nagarjuna University
br_digumarti@rediffmail.com

Preface

The movement of modern education in India is almost two century old. It has come of age now. Over the decades, great educationists have contributed towards the development and evolution of education, as a discipline. Thus, education in India has been enriched a lot.

As a result, the Indian education system can be placed at par with any advanced education system in the modern world. In fact, education is a vast sea and Teachers' Training is a stream in it. So, it makes it essential that the responsibilities of the faculty members are focused on the task of providing better training to the future teachers, for their better learning and proper development. And this responsible exercise can only be undertaken, if the trainers are equipped with all the needed skill and knowledge of the subject, they are supposed to teach. Hence, it becomes essential for making adequate provisions, for each course to the teacher-trainees. Methods of Teaching are very important for the successful training of teachers and for their career in future.

In order to provide all related material in one cover, here is this book, on this important subject. Of course there are several books on the subject in the market, but, every book has its own style and way of presentation. Similarly, the present one, too has its own merits and advantages.

During the course of the preparation of this book, the undersigned has done his best for the accomplishment of the job. He would be pleased and feel contented, if this book is acknowledged, as a textbook and a reference tool for the teachers and students, alike.

Author

Contents

1

Introduction

Learning is a life-long process. It brings about a permanent change in the behaviour of an individual. The process of learning for school children should be so planned that learning becomes a joyful activity for them. We are all aware that each individual is different from other and hence needs different type of treatment. The children who come to us in primary schools pass through different phases of development. Even in the same class the children are at different stages of development. It is very necessary for the teacher to know the stage in which a child is to make his/her instructional process more effective. The different stages of primary school children, as identified by Piaget are as under :

(i) Pre-operational Stage

(ii) Concrete Operational Stage

(iii) Formal Operational Stage

The identification of stages would not only help to bring about an improvement in the instructional process, but at the same time would also help the curriculum developers to remove those concepts from the text books which are really difficult for the children of that stage to understand. Thus it would also be useful in curriculum development. Therefore "Research Studies on the Cognitive Development of Indian Primary School Children in Science Concepts were conducted by Siddiqi (1975-77).

Why these Research Studies? UNICEF Assisted Science Education Programme (SEP) was started in the Union Territory of Delhi in July 1970. NCERT developed new science programme, 'Science is Doing' which was introduced in 40 Delhi primary schools as a pilot project. Then this programme was used in all the 1800 primary schools of Delhi. The programme consisted of:

(1) Class I-V Science Syllabus

(2) Class III-V Science Textbooks

(3) Class III-V Teachers'Guides

(4) Primary Science Kit, and

(5) Primary Science Kit Guide

(6) Two 16 mm Films-'Science is Doing' and 'Primary Science Kit'.

It looked that this programme was adopted as such without taking into consideration the cognitive development of primary school children, classroom conditions and teachers' background.

In October 1974 a National Seminar was organised at NCERT to discuss the primary science programme and make some changes if necessary. Siddiqi attended this seminar as the Incharge of SEP in the Union Territory of Delhi. During the discussion in the seminar, Siddiqi quoted the research findings of the studies on Cognitive Development of Primary School Children conducted at Florida State University (FSU), USA where he participated in these studies as a research fellow (1970-73) and worked with Jean Piaget in November 1970, where he came as visiting professor.

"According to these findings only 5% population of primary school children was formal operational and the remaining 95% children were either pre-operational or concrete operational and therefore they were unable to understand Science and Mathematics concepts without working with concrete objects. Similar results could possibly be expected for children in Indian primary schools. Therefore working with concrete objects or doing experiments was thought to be a very important part of primary science education. Therefore it was recommended that those concepts for which working with concrete objects was not possible should be deleted from 'Science is Doing' textbooks. Also those concepts which were not compatible with the cognitive level of children at certain age (class) level should be deleted, or shifted to the next higher classes where the children could understand them.

Majority of the educators who participated in the National Seminar on primary science education did not agree with Siddiqi. Their main objection was that these studies were not conducted on Indian children. This was one of the main reasons why these studies were conducted.

Several primary science texts were available that time in the market based on the NCERT Primary Science Syllabus. They were mostly content oriented. Though 'Learning by Doing' is accepted as the best way of learning science, yet 'reading a textbook' and 'listening to the teacher when he reads the book' were very much in use in the primary science classes. It looked that curriculum developers, textbook writers, apparatus designers and teachers had generally gone about their work without taking into consideration the Cognitive Development of primary school children for whom the materials which they produced were intended. Therefore it was thought that these studies would be interesting and useful for the primary science teachers, curriculum developers, science supervisors, teacher educators and those who were interested in research in science education.

2

Scope and Nature

The Scope

We teach and learn science for various reasons :

1. Science is fundamentally concerned with exploring the physical world through the three fundamental areas of Science Physics, Chemistry and Biology. Physics and Chemistry together is Physical Science. The physical and biological world is of fundamental interest for man and man has a basic motivation to understand and control the physical and biological world in which he lives.
2. We live in a scientific and technological age and no citizen can function effectively in a developed society without a basic scientific literacy (like what is happening in the immediate environment of a child i.e., EVS) and certain elementary skills (Science Processes). Every citizen needs to live a healthy life with proper sanitation and clean surroundings (what is included in primary EVS—Science). The knowledge and skills required by a modern householder in dealing with electrical gadgets, plumbing, and human first aid may be cited as some justification for teaching science to all the children in schools.
3. Science has provided so many aids for the good life—from bicycle to jet aircraft, antibiotics to heart surgery, radio to

coloured television, from satellite to multi-TV channels, and fertilizers to plant growth hormones. The priority which the developing countries like India are giving to basic science education for public health and agriculture can clearly be seen.

4. Science develops power of thinking, reasoning, curiosity, open mindedness and ultimately develops scientific attitude or scientific temper.
5. Science is used for the welfare of society by a body of men and women when they are specially trained for science-based vocations in industry, research and teaching.

All this shows that there is a great scope of teaching science in schools at all levels including primary.

The Nature

What we teach in science is CONTENT—facts, theories, laws, principles, concepts. Now the question arises 'What is Science'? Science is a way of describing and explaining some aspects of the world around us. To the extent that a lot of human efforts have already been expended in developing such explanations. Our children do not have to start from scratch. A large and ever-increasing body of scientific knowledge (i.e., science content) already exists, and evidently part of the task as science teacher is to pass on some of it to the children. But this is only the part of the job, for science is also a package of science processes by which we increase our knowledge of external world (or science). Teaching science implies involving our children in investigation, so that they become "Scientists for the day". There are science facts, theories, laws, principles, concepts : (i.e., science content) and also a way of working with some processes (i.e., science processes), which together constitute the subject 'Science'. Thus science is not just content, Science is content + processes. This shows Science has a dual nature.

1. Science is content
2. Science is processes

Structure at Primary Level

If we look at what a child has in his immediate environment, it is "he" himself— his living body. The child belongs to family, and family lives in the house. The house is in the neighbourhood which also has the school. The school, the neighbourhood and the house are on the earth, and the earth is a part of universe, the sky. Thus Structure of Science at Class I-II level may be a package of seven units :

1. Our Body 2. Our Family 3. Our House 4. Our Neighbourhood 5. Our School 6. Our Earth 7. Our Sky

Every unit has a lot of science in the child's environment to be taught in Classes I and II.

Similarly in Classes III, IV and V, EVS (Science) may also be structured in Seven Units :

1. Living Things
2. Human Body, Nutrition and Health
3. Materials and their Properties
4. Air, Water, Weather and Seasons
5. Force, Work and Energy
6. Soil and Crops
7. The Earth, its Natural Resources and the Sky

These units may further be divided into sub-units :

(i) 13 in Class III,

(ii) 12 in Class IV, and

(iii) 15 in Class V.

Impact on Environment

Man, ever since he appeared on the surface of the earth, became a part of his environment. Awareness of his physical environment was not something new for him. He observed and enjoyed nature. Today he no longer thinks of nature as a personified being. Man thought himself to be a master, not a slave, and he started utilising his environment resources to meet his ever-increasing wants for a better living. But now, he has trespassed too far, to the extent of causing serious ecological and environmental imbalances.

Population explosion is a worldwide problem. Our special and unique planet 'Earth' is very dear to us. It is special and unique from other planets due to the fact that it has climate and specific factors (air, water, food-plants and animals) to support life. The life started on the earth in the form of uniceller organisms about 300 million years ago. Men is comparatively a newcomer to the earth. Men came into existence only 200 million years ago when the earth was already inherited by plants and animals.

Men stepped into the world with a negligible population. The growth of human beings was very slow. It was in the lag phase for thousands of years till the 17th century. By 1665 the population has only grown to 545 million.

World Population Trend

Year	*World Population*
1665 A.D.	545 million
1850A.D.	1121 million
1950 A.D.	2400 million
1970 A.D.	3000 million

The lag phase was not due to the small birth rate but it was due to high death rate. The world human population entered the exponential phase only in 18th century and still continuing. Between 1665 and 1850 the population shot up considerably, practically it doubled. This doubling took place only in about 200 years, whereas the doubling of population in early history required more than 2000 years. But during the period of 1850 to 1960, it again doubled in only 110 years. This shows that world population is not only increasing but rate of growth is also increasing.

Population explosion is the worldwide phenomenon, but position of population trends in India is the worst. In the early 20th century the population of India was 238.3 million, with birth rate 49.2/1000 and death rate 42.6/1000. But now when we have entered the 21st century the population increased from 238.3 million to 930 million (became 4 times more), birth rate decreased from 49.2/1000 to 32.7/1000 (became 1.5 times less), and death rate decreased from 42.6/1000 to 14.8/1000 (became 3 times less).

Advancement in Science (agriculture and medicine) has decreased the death rate due to starvation, malnutrition, disease and epidemic etc. Industrialization, better storage and distribution of food have also decreased the death rate. More and more people are living longer, reaching reproductive age and producing more children. Therefore the rate of growth of human population is growing so fast. With national and international developments in public health and medicine death rate in India as well as all over the world has declined. It is primarily the decrease in death rate rather than increase in birth rate that has led to the increase in population explosion. Science has given methods for decreasing birth rate. The 20th century, 1.5 times decrease in birth rate is due to these methods which are being used by Indian couples, but not by all the couples. If all the couples cooperate and use these methods, the birth rate will further decrease and when birth rate becomes equal to death rate, population will no more increase.

More population needs more food and more land. Our land is limited. Therefore our forests are being cut. Indiscriminate cutting down of forests has led to the extinction of many a species of flora and fauna. Deforestation has also led to soil erosion (top soil good for crops) which in turn has caused floods. Inspite of modern technologies soil erosion and flooding are on the increase. Deserts are also expanding. As a result of increased industrialization the percentage of carbon monoxide and sulphur dioxide is increasing in the atmospheric air, causing air pollution. And when we breathe in polluted air we suffer from various kinds of diseases. Untreated industrial wastes and city garbage disposed of in the rivers (which flow to oceans, seas and gulfs) are toxic to marine life. Ganga water is now no more safe drinking water, man has made it polluted. Besides "Air Pollution", and "Water Pollution", there is one more pollution "Sound Pollution" due to overpopulation, which is disturbing our lives.

This is the impact of science on environment. Now the men after going too far in exploiting the environment has come to realize that the time has come to take the remedial measures. And so, not only India, but the whole world is concerned about it. This is just the beginning that we have realised many follies in the large scale application of science and technology in terms of a net environmental damage. And now we will use science again to rectify the follies (like application of science and technology in a better way which would not affect the environment adversely) and to enable more people (as those who are already born will live on this planet for years to come) to live on this planet in conditions which do greater justice to the dignity of man.

The Importance

Now when we have entered in the 21st century, we cannot survive without science. We use science all the time without thinking that this is science. We have our body all the time with us. Every part of it, external or internal, has some science behind it. If we know the functioning of each part, we can do something to keep it healthy. Some of the body parts always work, even when we sleep. Our heart and pulse are beating since we are born. How many times your heart beat from the time you were born till now? To keep your body healthy you need nutritious food—carbohydrates and fats, proteins, vitamins and minerals. We need clothes to cover our body. Clothes and houses protect us from cold, heat, rains, hails, snow fall and fog. We get our food from plants and animals. We get salt from sea water. Some clothes are also made of man-made fabrics. We build different kinds of houses. In our houses, we have natural as well as man-made material. Our kitchen is full of science. It has cereals, oils, pulses, water, utensils, cooking gas and so may things. When we need something we go for shopping. Many things are made in factories. When we are sick, we go to the Doctor's clinic or the hospital. There we get the latest medical technology for our treatment. If we want to go from one place to another, close, far or very far we have different means of transport. We can travel on land, in water and in air. We have nine planets and 32 satellites. The Sun gives light and heat to all of them, and so to our planet 'earth' and our satellite 'moon'. Moon like other satellites is natural. Moon is no more a far object, man has landed there several times, and has sent messages to earth. From the moon they saw that the earth is round and earth is also in the sky. Now we have not only natural satellites but many artificial satellites in space. How useful they are for us. Thus look "how important is science for us."

Scientific Method

Our environment is full of objects—living and non-living. Human beings, animals and plants are living things. Mountains, rivers, oceans, air, water, stars, planets and satellites are non-living things. There are thousands of things like these in our environment. Man has learned much about them, and still he is learning. For learning something he needs and uses some methods. One of the methods, mostly used is scientific methods, in which he uses some science processes to learn something for the things around him. Science processes like observing, classifying, using numbers, measuring, using space—time relationships, communicating, predicting, defining operationally, formulating hypotheses, interpreting data, controlling variables, experimenting and inferring are some of the best techniques (Science process) to learn about science by scientific method. At primary level when using scientific method, at least four steps may be used—*Problem, Hypotheses, Experiment and Conclusion*. For how to use these steps let us see the following example.

Example

Suppose we want to enable our students to find out whether air around us has weight or not. Then students may be asked, "Does air have weight"? This is *Problem*. Then based on their experiences some students will say : (1) Yes, air has weight, and some students will say (2) No, air does not have weight. These are two Hypotheses formulated by students. Then students may be asked to find out experimentally which hypothesis is right and which hypothesis is wrong. They will take a spring balance and a football bladder. They will weigh the bladder empty with the help of the spring balance and then again after filling air into it. They will see the second reading of the spring balance is higher than the first reading. From this experiment they will reach to the conclusion that 'Air has weight'. Thus almost all the science in the environment could be learned by students by scientific method.

Scientific Attitude

Some time back in a symposium some science experts, science educators, DIET's science faculty, science teachers and DIET's trainees met in a Delhi DIET to discuss the topic, "Scientific Attitude and its Development". They discussed the following questions.

1. What is scientific attitude?
2. How can we recognise whether or not particular person has scientific attitude?
3. How is scientific attitude developed?
4. What is scientific temper?
5. How can we recognise whether or not a particular person has scientific temper?
6. How is scientific temper developed?
7. What is the relation between scientific method and scientific attitude?
8. What is the relation between scientific method and scientific temper?
9. What are the similarities between scientific attitude and scientific temper?
10. What is the difference between scientific attitude and scientific temper?

The following is the summary of discussions—the report of the symposium.

Characteristics of a Person having Scientific Attitude

(i) One who makes decisions and solves everyday problems by scientific method, has scientific attitude.

(ii) One who does not believe what other people say unless he is convinced that what people are saying, has scientific attitutde.

(iii) One who is open minded, searches for truth, solves problems objectively, has spirit of inquiry, believes in cause and effect relationship has scientific attitude.

Difference between Scientific Attitude and Scientific Temper

Almost the same qualities were quoted for a person who has scientific temper. It looks there is no difference between scientific attitude and scientific temper.

Scientific Attitude and Scientific Temper

Thus the operational definition of Scientific Attitude or Scientific temper as follows :

Scientific attitude or scientific temper is that which compels a person to show the following behaviours :

— making decisions and solving everyday problems by scientific method

— not believing what other people say unless convinced what other people are saying is correct

— openmindedness

— searching for truth

— solving problems objectively

— having spirit of inquiry

— believing in cause and effect relationship

Development of Scientific Attitude or Scientific Temper

Once the characteristics of a person having scientific attitude or scientific temper identified, and scientific attitude or scientific temper operationally defined, it was finally suggested that in order to develop scientific attitude or scientific temper, start doing and practicing the same things which a person having scientific attitude or scientific temper does.

Generating Knowledge of Environment

Science has contributed a great deal to our modern life. The teaching of science is more than a skilled exposition of facts, theories and inventions. The method of acquiring such knowledge is of paramount importance. We should try to develop in our pupils scientific attitude or scientific temper.

Science comprises a vast field of human knowledge almost any part of which would suitably exhibit the application of scientific method.

In generating scientific knowledge we must keep two things in mind:

(a) To have any hope of success we must create and maintain interest in science among pupils. Pupils are most interested in the things around them and the happenings which they experience.

(b) Every citizen should have scientific knowledge which may be seful to him and to the nation.

The pupils should learn their science by performing experiments successfully by absorbing instructions. They will understand the importance of scientific method and develop lively, personal interest that will survive beyond school days.

The science which we teach must have social relevance. Once interest is awakened, the subject can be amplified and extends through demonstrations by audio-visual aids and by carefully planned visits of places of scientific interest like factories and so forth. The descriptive approach should not replace the experimental approach. These, however, provide the background knowledge that makes the scientific pattern of modern life more intelligible.

At the elementary (primary and upper primary levels) stage inductive method is usually preferred. This has basically four stages:

(a) Introduction, directing attention to objects and phenomenon within the experience of the pupil (feeling the surrounding objects pertaining to the experiment).

(b) Collection of already known facts.

(c) Formulation of definitions and conclusions.

(d) Application to every day and experimental problems.

At the primary stage the spirit of wonder and inquiry should be kept alive. The child should be given appropriate scope for activity.

At the senior and senior secondary levels, deductive method (to deduce particular results from the laws) is more useful. At this level children grow older. Their interests change and their experiences widen. At this level more systematic work in physical and biological sciences is required.

There are a few other methods which are as under :

Heuristic Method–Here children rediscover everything by their own efforts. The child is not to discover, but there has been a two way discussion between the teacher and the class which leads to the development of ideas necessary to arrive at a useful conclusion.

Historical Method–This is good for the exposition of the more important theoretical concepts but for a normal science lesson it takes too long; the class gets bogged down in a mess of detail that is subsequently discarded.

Biographical Method-This is sometimes useful as it creates interest in the child as sometimes he tries to project himself into the life of the original discoverer to experience his success and frustrations.

Opportunism–To cite an example, if children are working in the garden and they collect some caterpillar, teacher can ignore it or throw it away, kill it or collect it in a jar and study. This is good for studying the life history of an insect. This free method of teaching by accepting the challenge of opportunity as it comes, makes great demands on the teacher who needs greater insight and broader knowledge.

Social, Cultural and Ethical Aspects

Science is an organised and experimentally verified knowledge, produced due to inventive attitude of human thinking. The study of scientific concept includes observation, experimentation, hypotheses, conclusion etc. and aimed to search truth. It is a creation of human spirit, just as much as religion, art or literature and is an essential part of humanities. The basic or biological needs which man shares with animals such as food, sex, territory, self-preservation and play are integrated and fused with various social, cultural and ethical needs for happy survival.

The process of transferring scientific knowledge from one person to another, may be teacher to student, is influenced by various social, cultural and ethical aspects of the society in which they live. As we know that a man belongs to two worlds—world of things and world of experience, world of facts and world of faith, world of matter and world of mind, world of sense and world of spirit. Thus the primary business of education is the unification of these two worlds in each individual. Thus the process of scientific study cannot be separated from these aspects. The effectiveness of processes involved in transferring scientific knowledge cannot be achieved fully without proper understanding and even integration of various social, cultural and ethical aspects of society. The indepth relationship of these aspects with science is popularly termed as social, cultural and ethical aspects of science.

As it is understood, the society is made up of individuals and people. The relationships between these individuals are governed by already established social conventions such as behaviour towards other members, nature and natural resources. The need of developing emotional health together with mental and physical health including subtle consciousness among the people is very important in establishing a happy social life. The emotional system of human is managed by exercises of concentration (dhyana), relaxation and self-awareness (kayosarga), auto-suggestion (bhavna), breath regulation (pranayama), and yogic postures (yogasanas). These have to be strengthened by science teaching.

The culture is a fragrance of a society and helps in understanding social set-up of society. It includes ways of making living, language, religious beliefs, dress, political organisation and other aspects of life. Culture can be observed through art, family life, music, dance, ways of spending leisure, placement of household things in house, etc. It changes with political, economical, social, geographical, climatic and religious aspects of life.

The ethic is a nature or permanent character of physical and social phenomenon and includes customs, temperament, character and way of thinking of the society and individual. The concept of goodness, justice, happiness, conscience, source of power, moral feelings etc. comes under ethics. Ethics is an ancient and interesting branch of philosophy and a scientific discipline studying morality. Emergence and development of ethical thinking proceed parallel in identification of abstract moral norms. It is normative in character and provides recommendations on the choice of particular pattern of behaviour. These may be philosophical ethics, scientific ethics, professional ethics, cultural or even social ethics.

As the education is aimed for integrated development of personality through attitudinal change and behavioural modifications, the importance of social, cultural and ethical aspects in science teaching cannot be ignored. The values like sense of duty, self-dependence, truthfulness, freedom from fanaticism, human equality, co-existence, patriotism, mental equilibrium, patience, honesty, compassion, modesty, self-discipline, friendliness, will-power, etc. has to be developed through our science education.

For developing and strengthening various social, cultural and ethical aspects of science the teaching has to be based on ancient widsom and modern scientific theories. It should emphasise individual attention, guidance and frequent cross-examination of children about right methods. There is an urgent need to assess the efficacy of exercises from time to time so as to develop internal abilities, positive attitude and high standard of human behaviour.

Part and Parcel

Science and Technology are the inseparable parts of our life. It is a sequential and systematized way of understanding the world and making new inventions and discoveries. Science helps in solving various problems related to our daily life. Today each and every aspect of human life is related with science or its practical form i.e., technology. So we can say that science has a very wide scope. It has dual nature—content and processes. It has a great impact on environment. We cannot survive without science. In ancient times, the knowledge of science was limited only to a special group of people. Its reach was not for all. But today science is for all. So its content matter at primary school level must be structured in such a way that it is related to environment and the daily life of the children. Special attention is also needed in case of selection of teaching methods. Science should be taught by scientific method which can develop scientific attitude or scientific temper. This method has four steps statement of problem, hypotheses, experiment and conclusion. This method is also useful in solving our daily life problems. Other methods of generating the knowledge of science are Heuristic method, Historical method etc. The social, cultural and ethical aspects of science cannot be denied. All aspects of social life are based on science. Science takes care of our culture and also helps in developing the same. Thus for developing and strengthening various social, cultural and ethical aspects of science, the science teaching should be based on ancient wisdom and modern scientific theories.

Questions

1. What is the role of science education?
2. Write five important aspects of the content of 'Science for all'.
3. What are the four important steps of scientific method?
4. With the help of an example, explain how will you use scientific method in your teaching-learning process?
5. Explain the five stages of inductive method.
6. List different methods of teaching science. Which method would you like to adopt for your classroom teaching?
7. What are the reasons for teaching science at school level?
8. What are the scope, nature, structure and importance of science?
9. What is the impact of science on environment?
10. What is scientific attitude or scientific temper? How can it be developed?

3

Role of Teacher

At primary level Science has an important place in curriculum. This subject has two main parts—social studies and science.

In classes I and II these are taught as an integrated course, EVS (social studies and science).

In classes III, IV and V these subjects are taught as EVS social studies and science.

For giving Science an important place at primary level, EVS Curriculum is based on certain objectives to be achieved. Unfortunately the way the curriculum is made, it has different meanings to different people. For teachers, students and parents textbooks themselves are curriculum. For paper-setters perhaps just the syllabus is the curriculum. For NCERT, Curriculum is a package of some instructional material. This package includes Syllabus, Textbooks, Teachers Guides, Science Kit, Kit Guide and Evaluation Material. The curriculum package sometimes also has some 16 mm films or video tapes related to the teacher training. But curriculum should be so developed that it should have the same meaning to all the people who use it—teachers, parents, students, book writers and paper-setters.

After the curriculum is developed, and the textbooks along with other instructional material are written, it is the Role of Teacher to see how he can use it in his teaching-learning process.

During your Practice Teaching you will teach EVS to primary classes (I-V). Then you will see EVS Primary Curriculum, and use it in your teaching. You will also know 'what to teach', 'why to teach, 'what you teach', 'how to teach', 'why to teach the way you teach', and 'how to find out that children have learned (understood) what you taught them'.

So after the EVS Curriculum is in your hands, it is upto you how best you transact it. As a Science teacher you will have different roles to play for Curriculum Transaction.

Teacher's Responsibilities

Planning for Curriculum Transaction

The Science teacher has several roles to play in Curriculum transaction like.

- identification of concepts, sub-concepts, and concept-mapping,
- writing the objectives in behavioural terms.

In Science text books sometimes the contents are given in such a way that it appears as they have been written for a specialist. It does not appear to be developed for the children. Sometimes the content is beyond the understanding level of the children. Therefore children either start memorising it without understanding or start skipping the classes. Thus they lose interest in learning Science. Therefore the content in the text books should be presented in such a way that the children are able to understand it, and they need not memorise it without understanding. For each class the content should be compatible to the cognitive level of children. If it is important to include a particular topic, it should be included in a higher class where the children could understand it. But if such a content is already there in the text books, the teacher should thoroughly analyse it and plan what previous knowledge is to be given to the children, and what should be the sequencing of the content when teaching. This should be done keeping in mind the principle from '*SIMPLE to COMPLEX*'.

Identification of Concepts, Sub-Concepts and Concept-Mapping

After identifying the content to be taught, the teacher is to do 'Concept Mapping' i.e. Sequencing of concepts and sub-concepts of the content. This will enable the child to understand it better.

Example of Concept-mapping

The UNIT-1 of Class IV EVS (Science) 'LIVING THINGS' can be divided in five concepts, and sub-concepts as shown below:

Concept 1—The main source of food for human beings and animals are plants.

Sub-concepts

- some plants give us eatable seeds called grains like wheat, maize, corn etc.
- sugarcane is the stem of the plant.
- grass is used as food by grazing animals.

Concept 2—Plants and animals are useful to man in different ways.

Sub-concepts

- oil can be obtained from the seeds of some plants,
- some plants are used for obtaining medicines, perfumes, gum, rubber, paper and cotton,
- some plants, leaves, flowers and fruits can be used for decoration purposes, and some plants with thorns can be used for fencing purposes,
- from some trees wood is obtained for building purposes and for fuel,
- from some plants we get useful fibres,
- plants and trees help in protecting the soil from soil erosion by water and wind,
- the dead parts of the plants are used as fertilizers,
- the waste materials excreted by some animals are used as fertilizers,

- some animals provide us with wool,
- some animals are used for farming,
- the skin of some animals is used for making leather. Note: This concept may be divided into two parts :
- plants are useful to us,
- animals are useful to us.

Concept 3—Different parts of the plants have different functions.

Sub-concepts

- roots keep the plant fixed to the soil, plant absorbs water and minerals from the soil with the help of the roots,
- water and minerals reach different parts of the plant through stem,
- green leaves manufacture food by taking water from roots, carbon dioxide from air and energy from the sun,
- some plants bear flowers which develop fruits and seeds.

Concept 4—For the growth of plants and for their reproduction, dispersal of their seeds is necessary.

Sub-concepts

- when many seedlings develop at one place, only a few of them are able to survive,
- some seeds have hair or wings which help them to float in air,
- some seeds get dispersed when fruits burst,
- when pulp of a fruit is eaten, it is thrown, this helps in the dispersal of the seeds inside the fruit,
- some seeds have thorns or hooks on them, through which they get stuck to the animal's body and thus get dispersed to far off places,
- some seeds get dispersed through water.

Concept 5—Plants and animals should be taken care of.

Sub-concepts

- plants should be protected from excess heat, cold and continuous shade,
- plants should be watered and manured properly at regular intervals,
- walking on plants (grass) stops their growth,
- for domestic animals proper sheds should be arranged.

Note : Similar to the above given example the teacher should divide the content to be taught by him in his class in concepts and sub-concepts. This will help the child in understanding the content more easily. His interest in content learning will increase, and he will pay more attention in understanding rather than memorising.

Writing Objectives in Behavioural Terms

The education department develops the draft curriculum. This makes the teacher unable to understand what he has to teach and upto what depth, the examiner is unable to understand what he has to examine or test, and the student is unable to understand what he has to study. The main reason behind this is that the objectives of education are not well defined. If the objectives are written properly and clearly, then the curriculum will have the same meaning to the teachers, parents, students, textbooks writers and the paper-setters. The teachers will know what they have to teach, students will know what they have to study, and the examiners will know what they have to examine. Hence the objectives should be very clearly stated. The best way of writing the objectives very clearly is to state them in behavioural terms. How to state objectives in behavioural terms, and what key words to be used in behavioural objectives have been also discussed in this book.

Examples

Some of the objectives of class IV—UNIT-1 : 'LIVING THINGS' may be stated in behavioural terms as given as follows :

- observes the things in his environment and classifies them in Living and Non-living,
- observes and describes similarities and differences between the animals and plants,
- recognises and names the parts of a plant,
- observes and describes the function of various parts of a plant,
- classifies plants on the basis of their size, life span and seasonal growth,
- recognises some important uses of plants, trees and animals,
- recognises some harmful insects and weeds,
- explains the need for protecting and taking care of plants and animals and describes some of the easy ways in which this can be done,
- participates in school plantation programme and appreciates its importance.

Note: Objectives written in such a way are also called Learning Outcomes.

In this way writing the objectives in behavioural terms for other Units is one of the main roles of a teacher. Beside this, there are some other very important roles of a teacher, which are given below

Teacher as an Organiser

Planning or Organisation

'I heard and I forgot. I saw and I remembered. I did and I understood'. You must have heard this saying. This is directly indicating how EVS (Science) should be taught. This signifies the importance of 'Learning by Doing'. Thus the role of a science teacher as an organiser can be divided into the following steps :

- selection of activities
- selection of materials, and
- organising activities.

Selection of Activities

At primary level the children are not very experienced. They need more guidance at each step. They can work mostly under the guidance of their teacher. Thus the role of the teacher as an organiser, is to select proper activities keeping in mind the content, concepts and sub-concepts. For one sub-concept there may be one or more activities. For selection of activities the teacher should keep the following points in mind :

- these should be according to the interest of the children,
- these should be according to the availability of time,
- only those activities should be selected for which the material can be made easily available,
- only those activities should be selected which could be performed easily in the existing classroom / school / environmental conditions,
- only those activities should be selected which can be done by children's direct purposeful experiences,
- activities should be according to the age, interest and mental level of children,
- activities should be according to the content being taught.

Example

One of the sub-concepts of class IV Unit 'Living Things', is 'roots keep the plant fixed to the soil, and the plant absorbs water and minerals from the soil with the help of roots',

For this sub-concept, the following activities may be selected:

Activity-1

Ask the children to pull out some plants from the soil. Then ask them to replant them in the soil, and again pull out. Interact with children with the following type questions :

- While pulling out the plants, in which case did you apply more force?
- Why more force was required in the first case?

From this it should be inferred that the roots keep the plants fixed in the soil.

Activity-2

Take a plant, and keep it in a glass containing coloured water, after washing its roots with water. Let the children observe it after one hour. They will see the coloured water reached leaves through stem. Leaves became coloured. Cut the stem of the plant and see it through a magnifying lens. They will see coloured water made the stem also coloured.

From this it should be inferred that plant absorbs water and minerals from the soil, and they reach the leaves through the stem.

Selection of Materials

For teaching certain concepts, after the selection of activities the selection of materials and arranging them for activities is the main role of the teacher. If a field trip is arranged, then selection of materials to be taken from the school, and the materials to be collected from the environment is also very important role of the teacher.

Example

For the above activities, the following materials are required:

Some plants rooted in the ground (soil), glass tumbler, water, colour, plants with roots like Gulmehdi or any other soft plant.

Organising Activities

After selection of material for selected activities, the next role of the teacher is to organise these activities. For this—

- the teacher should have full knowledge of the activities,
- while performing activities discipline should be maintained along with Learner-Learner Interaction; Teacher-Learner Interaction; Learner-material interaction, and Teacher-material interaction (here material interaction means working with the activity material). With these interactions silence is impossible. Here discipline means

that these interactions should be so controlled that neighbouring classes are not disturbed.

- all children should participate and help each other when doing activities,
- care should be taken that children take interest in doing activities.
- children should be guided if the teacher sees that they are not going on the right path when doing activities,
- children should be guided, (if needed) for taking out the right.

Teacher as an Activity Facilitator

Planning or Teaching

As an activity facilitator, the science teacher has to play some very important roles Like—

- introducing the topic
- questioning technique
- conducting group activities
- teacher-student relations
- classroom management

Introducing the Topic

For making Teaching-Learning process easier, the teacher should relate the topic with the previous knowledge of the children, when introducing the topic.

Questioning Techniques

Questions before the lesson, during the leasson and after the lesson, should be to the point and well-sequenced. This will give an ample opportunity to the children for Teacher Learner interaction. This will make the children more interested in learning, and they will be able to understand what is being taught to them more effectively.

The teacher should keep following points in mind while asking the questions:

- questions should be based on 'simple to complex principle',
- children should be encouraged to ask questions,
- language of questions should be simple,
- children should be motivated to answer the questions in their own words instead of using the bookish language,
- some questions should be close ended which have single answers, some questions should be open ended which may have more than one answer, e.g., 'What will happen if........' type questions are open ended questions?
- all children should be involved to answer the questions.

Conducting Group Activities

After introducing the Topic, the conducting of the group activities (4-5 children per group) with the help of available material inside or outside the class, is the next important role of the teacher. There is no set method of how to conduct the group activities. It all depends upon the teacher, the existing classroom and outside environmental conditions. But the teacher should know some key points :

- When teaching skills like reading a thermometer, reading a spring balance, setting the photosynthesis experiment for the first time, the teacher should use Teacher Centred Approach.
- When teaching concepts like temperature, weight, photosynthesis, the teacher should use Child Centred Approach.
- Do not give the readymade answers to the child. Let us find out.

Example

If you want to teach the concept 'air has weight' to the children, do not say 'Air has weight, let us find out'. instead ask, 'Does air have weight'? (Problem)

Some children will say

(i) Yes, air has weight.

Some children will say

(ii) No, air does not have weight.

These are two Hypotheses. Now we are to find out which of the two hypotheses is right. For this children should know the Weighing skill by a spring balance (This you are to teach beforehand by Teacher Centred Approach).

Now the children can do the experiment themselves—weighing empty football bladder, and air filled football bladder.

And after the experiment children will reach on a Conclusion that Hypothesis—1 is right. Air has weight.

This is Scientific Method for conducting the Group Activities. It has four steps :

1. Problem
2. Hypotheses
3. Experiment
4. Conclusion

Step-1 is Teacher Centred. Teacher gives the problem. In Step-3, teacher already taught the children 'skill of weighing by spring balance', by Teacher Centred Approach.

Now Steps-2, 3, 4 can be done by children themselves by Child Centred Approach.

Thus when conducting group activities children may be involved in finding concepts on their own by Scientific Method.

Teacher-Students Relations

For making the teaching-learning process more interesting and pleasant, teacher-students relationship will be an asset. Children have full faith in their teacher. The teacher should see that each child is being given equal importance. He should have sympathetic attitude with all the children. All the children should be equally involved, and they should accept the teacher as their Guide.

Classroom Management

When conducting group activities, the classroom should be so managed as all the children are fully involved in activities without disturbing any one. The following few points may be taken in mind for classroom management:

- The class should be divided into small groups (4-5 children per group).
- Some activities may be carried out with the whole class, with good demonstrations. Care should be taken that all the children are fully involved and are clearly observing, using all their five senses (seeing, hearing, smelling, tasting and touching).
- Sometimes activities can also be organised by dividing the class in peer groups.

Teacher as Moderator

Sometimes during teaching some Discussions are involved. Primary school children are too small to lead discussions. If it is so, the teacher should lead Discussions and they see that children are involved in Learner-Learner Interaction. If the class is divided into small groups discussion may be more effective. If children are doing group activities, or the teacher is posing Open Ended Questions, Discussions may be very interesting and effective.

During Group or Class Discussions the teacher should not give his own opinion or readymade answers, unless he sees that children are going out of track. If it is so the teacher should tackle the situation very tactfully, and bring back the children on the right track. This is Moderation. Thus the teacher instead of fully or partly involving himself in Discussions, he should Moderate Discussions.

When children are involved in Group Activities or Class Activities, sometimes the children are unable to sum up the outcomes of activities, as the primary school children are young and not very much experienced. If such a situation arises, the teacher should tackle it very tactfully, and enable the children to sum up outcomes of activities.

Teacher as a Guide

Planning for Remedial Teaching and Environment Programmes

Providing proper guidance to the children is an important role of the teacher. At Primary level children do not have sufficient experiences in how to learn.

For learning EVS at this level, these children need more guidance of the teacher. The teacher should proceed by taking all children together even if they are slow or fast learners. Slow learners should be given Remedial Teaching. Fast learners should be given Enrichment Programmes.

'Helping Slow Learners' needs more attention of the teacher

Firstly the teacher should recognise the slow learners. This he can do by observing them in the class, how far they are involved in activities, how far they are able to ask and answer questions, how far they are able to understand what is taught to them in the class.

If the teacher knows why a particular child is slow learner, he can also help him (child) out so that he no more remains slow-learner.

The various reasons for the slowness of the child may be :

Physical Reasons : Weak physique, illness, breathing problem, visual problems, hearing problems, stammering.

Mental Reasons : Defect in previous education, lack of curiosity, lack of interest, lack of ability to concentrate.

Emotional Reasons : Lack of confidence, language problem, social maladjustment, shyness.

School Environment : Peer groups relationship, teacher-student relationship.

Reasons Related to Family : Parents being over-ambitious, poverty, having too many brothers and sisters, being step-children, lack of interest on part of parents in their children, parents being less educated or illiterate.

Note : Slow learners take more time to understand things. Once they understand, they always remember.

'Peer Group Learning' is another challenge or a teacher

Some children in a class have some common interest. They become close friends, and form a group called a peer group. Peer groups want to stay together. Some teachers don't like it. They want to break these groups. Some teachers, when dividing children into small groups for group activities, do not disturb these peer groups, and encourage these peer groups to do group activities in their peer groups. It has been seen that most of the time such teachers are quite successful, and these peer groups do a lot of learning in their peer group activities.

You also try this experiment. Identify the peer groups in your class. Involve them in group activities in their own peer groups. Handle them very tactfully and see how far they are successful for their effective learning.

Integrated Course

In classes I and II the curriculum has social studies and science as an integrated course, while in classes III, IV and V the curriculum has social studies and science as separate subjects. Though in EVS curriculum development, primary school teachers have a negligible role, yet its transaction is entirely in their hands. For effective EVS curriculum transaction a science teacher or a teacher teaching science has various roles to play. He/she is to act as an organiser, activity facilitator, moderator and guide. How effectively a primary school teacher can perform all these roles, has been discussed in this chapter. In EVS (Science) curriculum there are some skills and some concepts.

Skills should be taught by Teacher Centered Approach, and concepts should be taught by Child Centred Approach. Concept mapping after identifying concepts and sub-concepts facilities the teacher for effective teaching, and enables children to understand easily. If the curriculum is based on objectives stated in behavioural terms, the teacher knows what to teach and evaluate, students know what to learn, and textbooks writers know what to write in textbooks. If a teacher teaching science is a good organiser, it will facilitate him/her in selecting science activities, selecting material for science activities, and organising science activities. As an activity facilitator the teacher very effectively will introduce the topic. He/she will use a very challenging questioning technique. He/she will conduct group activities with pleasant teacher-student relations, and a good classroom management. As a moderator the teacher will lead group and class discussions, moderate discussions whenever needed, and will help children in summing up outcomes of activities. As a guide the teacher will help slow learners with remedial teaching and fast learners with enrichment activities, as well as he/she will motivate peer groups to learn more science even in their groups.

Questions

1. Why does in classes I and II EVS curriculum have social studies and science as an integrated course, while in classes III, IV and V it splits in two different courses—EVS (Social studies) and EVS (Science)?
2. What is the role of primary teacher in EVS curriculum development?
3. Give four roles of a teacher teaching science for effective transaction of EVS (Science) curriculum.
4. How should we teach skills?
5. How should we teach concepts?
6. What is concept-mapping? How can it help to teach EVS (Science) effectively?
7. How objectives stated in behavioural terms, help teachers for effective teaching and objective evaluation?
8. What a teacher teaching science will be able to do if he/she is a good
   (a) organiser
   (b) activity facilitator
   (c) moderator
   (d) guide

9. How will you recognise slow and fast learners in your class? How will you teach them EVS (Science)?
10. What are various reasons which make a child a slow learner? If you know these reasons what will you do so that the child is no more a slow learner?
11. Select a topic from Classes III-V. Write down its concepts, sub-concepts and activities.

4

Teacher Training

Most of you are B.Eds. You have learned how to teach science at senior secondary, secondary and upper primary levels in B. Ed. But you are not trained in how to teach Science at primary level. ETE (Elementary Teacher Education) Science course discussed in this book is a specialised course for teaching of science at primary level. Two things what you learned in B. Ed. are different from what is taught in ETE Teaching of Science Course at Primary Level—Psychology of Primary School Child, and Primary Science Teaching Methods. In this book the latest issues of Primary Science Teacher Education are discussed. Go through the list of contents, and you will exactly know what more you need for being an effective Primary Science Teacher, and then read what you need. This will be your self orientation as an In-service Primary Science Teacher.

Primary Science Teaching

We do a number of activities in the classroom, while teaching primary science. But before that we should prepare ourselves to answer the following relevant questions.

1. (a) What we teach in primary science?

   (b) What should we teach in primary science?

   (c) Why should we teach, what we teach in primary science?

2. (a) How we teach primary science?
   (b) How should we teach primary science?
   (c) Why should we teach, the way we teach primary science?
3. (a) How we evaluate learning in primary science?
   (b) How should we evaluate learning in primary science?
   (c) Why should we evaluate, the way we evaluate learning in primary science.

Discuss, Discuss, Discuss. What you do, and Why you do; What you do, How you do, and Why you do the way you do; you know.

What you should do and why; how you should do and why; find out from this book. Then Do, what you found, and you will enjoy teaching primary science and your students will Enjoy their science classes and science learning.

Primary Science

What we teach in Primary Science is content. But Science is not just content.

Science = Science Content + Science Processes. Therefore we should also teach Science Processes when teaching Primary Science along with science content, as Science has Dual Nature.

1. Science is Content
2. Science is Processes

We are to decide "what to teach in Science", before we start Teaching Science at primary level. For this we should ask ourselves 3 Questions.

1. Do primary students need it?
2. Can primary students understand it?
3. Will primary students enjoy it?

If we get the answers of all the 3 Questions "Yes", we should teach it, otherwise not. But sometimes that Content is in Primary

Science Course, you will have to teach it. Empower yourself and send your recommendations to the concerned authorities.

Now we cannot survive without learning Some Minimum Science. Most of our Primary School Children leave their studies after passing Class V. They do not join upper primary school. But they will need some minimum science throughout their lives. So we should select that minimum, asking the above 3 questions to ourselves. What you selected is minimum levels of learning (MLLs) in primary (2.5, 2.6, 5.11), from the Maximum (2.4 and 5.4, 5.5, 5.6, 5.7, 5.8, 5.9, 5.10).

Now compare the Minimum with the Maximum. Do you find any difference? Can you say for the Minimum, we should teach it because

1. Primary Children need it
2. Primary Children can understand it
3. Primary Children will enjoy it

If "yes", fine. If "no" what you think, you should do? Discuss.

What we teach in primary science should be compatible with the cognitive level of children, so that they should understand, and not memorise without understanding. If there are some concepts in the primary science course, which are not compatible with the cognitive level of primary school children, then what will you do? Discuss. If you teach these concepts, will they understand or will they memorise without understanding?

How should we teach science to primary school children? Various methods of teaching science are given in this book. Which of these methods are you using in teaching primary science in your classes? Why? Which of these methods are you not using? Why? Which other methods are you using? W... Why? Name them. Are you using Lecture Method and Lecture-cum-Demonstration Method for teaching Science to primary school children? Are these methods going on well, or are you feeling some problems when using these methods in teaching science to primary school children?

When you select a method for teaching primary science, ask yourself ...r 2 Questions.

1. Can primary school children understand what you teach in science by this method?
2. Will primary school children enjoy learning what you are to teach in science by this method?

If you get the answers of both these Questions "Yes", go ahead otherwise change over to some other suitable methods for teaching primary science.

"How we teach primary science" should be compatible with the cognitive level of children, so that they should understand and not memorise without understanding.

Learning science is understanding science and not just memorising without understanding. If primary school children are not understanding science by one method, other methods may be tried out. Sometimes you will have to use different methods for different groups of children in the same class, so that all types of children in the same class may understand what you teach in primary science.

Methods and Approaches of Teaching

Various methods of teaching science to primary school children are given below. You are to choose the right method/methods to teach a particular science topic in your primary class.

1. Discussion or Interactive Approach
2. Activity Approach
3. Teacher Centred versus Child Centred Approach
4. Child Centred Activity Based Teaching Learning Approach
5. Conceptual Appoach
6. Process Approach
7. Integrated Approach
8. Environmental Studies (EVS) Approach
9. Scientific Method
10. Problem Solving Method

11. Project Method
12. Inquiry Approach
13. Lecture Method
14. Demonstation Method
15. Lecture-Cum-Demonstration Method

Interactive Approach

When teaching science by lecture method or lecture-cum-demonstration method, if students are involved in discussion (interaction) they are in a much more better situation of learning science. As discussed under lecture method, the teacher should not lecture continuously for more than a very limited time so that the teacher should not lose the concentration of their students. For this he can do a change of activity, and discussion (interaction) is one of the several activities in which students can be involved very actively. So by using lecture-cum-discussion method some of the disadvantages of the lecture method can be taken care of.

Similarly when lecture-cum-demonstration method is combined with a well directed discussion (interaction), it may prove to be a successful teachnique of teaching science.

In our schools lecture method and lecture-cum-demonstration method are most commonly used. If we add "discussion" or "interaction" into it, these methods may come out to be much more effective.

There may be four types of interactions. (i) Teacher-Learner Interaction (TLI) (ii) Learner-Learner Interaction (LLI) (iii) Teacher-Material Interacton (TMI) (iv) Learner-Material Interaction (LMI)

When teacher is lecturing, TLI may be initiated. When children are discussing in small groups, like tutorials, LLI may be initiated. When teacher is demonstrating, he is using some teaching aids (material). He can use TMI along with TLI for more effective teaching. When children are doing some experiments in small goups, LMI will be of better use along with LLI and TLI.

Project Method

The Project Method involves investigation, discovery and finding out something which was not known to the student before. An investigation is much more than the repetition of a standard experiment. Here the student is to decide what experiments are necessary and how he is going to carry them out. He may have to design his own apparatus, if that is not available in the laboratory. He has to search for the appropriate principles, laws, formulae, apparatus and data; and originate solution to a problem. The student will act like a scientist.

This method involves the steps of scientific method :

1. Problem
2. Hypotheses
3. Testing of hypotheses by experiments
4. Collection of data
5. Interpretation of data
6. Conclusion

This is the least used method of teaching science in our schools. In USA, Canada and UK teachers try to cover a part of syllabus by this method. In this method a group of students select a problem in consultation with their teacher, and then through discussion develop the plan of action and design the type of equipment needed to carry out the experiments to reach the conclusion. Students thus are trained in science processes and scientific method.

Some Science problems to investigate are given below. Primary School Children will have fun when investigating the solutions of these problems by Scientific Method.

Identification of a problem for an investigatory project sometimes becomes a problem by itself for students. They ask the teachers and look into the available literature. But the problems can be identified if one asks some questions from himself. Some ideas are given below. Students can be given practice to identify such problems. Some of these problems are simple and can be solved very easily, others can take longer, and need well designed procedures.

What Will Happen, if?

Ink is boiled; coloured water is frozen; food colouring is placed on a potato, an apple..., fish are placed in water coloured with food colouring; popcorn is planted in soil; a leaf is ironed with a steam iron; guppies are raised completely in the dark; you put a rubber band around an ice cube and allow it to melt; you freeze a pickle, an orange; insects such as ants, beetles, butterflies etc. are exposed to only blue light, red light, ...; you try to get a spider to make a web inside a large jar; various insects in containers are placed in a refrigerator for an hour, a day; you try to grow a water plant in salt water; the leaves of a plant are pulled off and then the plant is placed in soil; seeds are planted in different types of soils; some plants are watered with salt water and others with sugar water; seedlings are exposed to different colours of light; a salt water fish is gradually introduced to fresh water; different types of seeds are planted in the same hole; solutions of different concentrations are compared in terms of evaporation rates; a fresh chicken egg is frozen.

Butterflies

Are Butterflies attracted to flowers by scent or colour; can it be said that one butterfly visits only one species of flower; how high can a butterfly fly; how long can a butterfly survive; how long is each stage in the life cycle of a butterfly, i.e., from egg to adult; what is the nature of the colouring matter on the wings of butterflies?

Detergents

How do detergents in water affect the growth of green plants, how are the life spans of small fishes influenced by the presence of detergents in water?

Magnets

Can animals detect a magnetic field; is the growth of plants affected by a magnetic field; does the presence of magentic field affect the formation of crystals?

Science is Fun

(a) *Air guns.* What are the muzzle speeds of the various air-guns available in the market; to what height and how far can a gun project its shots?

(b) *Bow and arrow.* What are the relationship among the size, shape and mass of arrow and bow?

(c) *Bicycles.* How is the strength of the wheel related to the spokes; how fast can one drive a bicycle; how is the air pressure in the tubes related to the speed?

(d) *Water.* How is water taken from wells, rivers, lakes, sea, rains, etc.? Compare fresh water samples of water from different sources and places, with distilled water.

Setting and Maintenance of an Aquarium

In a primary science an aquarium can be used in many ways. Many basic principles of science can be taught through an aquarium. It could be used as a project for students. They should be given responsibility to maintain it, in the process they will be able to learn many things. Also the aquarium can supply various living organisms like plants, snails, snail eggs, fish and even micro-organisms to be used throughout the year.

Setting of an Aquarium : All the necessary things should be collected as described below. Responsibility can be given to different students.

Aquarium Tank: Tanks of various sizes are available commercially, can be purchased from an aquarium shop with other supplies, 24 x 12 x 12 inch (1 inch = 2.5 cm) is a reasonable size tank. Place available for keeping an aquarium should also be kept in mind while deciding on the size of the tank. Aluminium frame tanks are nice to look at and easy to handle. Some other containers like big rectangular jar, big wide mouthed bottles can also be used as containers for setting an aquarium.

The tank should be cleaned very thoroughly before setting the aquarium. Sides can be rubbed with few folds of newspapers, detergent should not be used for cleaning aquarium. In case it is very necessary to use detergent washing should be very thorough not to leave any remains of detergent. Otherwise it may affect the fish and other organisms.

Substratum : At the base of the tank about an inch (2.5 cm) of sand, pebbles or badarpur is required as a substratum for fixing the plants, hiding the dirt and filth, providing the plants with nutrients and a place for burrowing the animals. Sand or other material used for substratum should be washed into many waters to remove all the dirt. The water should be clean after settling down the substratum. Water should be poured by putting a beaker (or any other container) or thick layer of newspaper to prevent rolling of the substratum.

Water : Spring water or ordinary tap water can be used. Tap water should be left for one or two days before putting the animals. It is advisable to keep the aquarium covered to check evaporation. Water level should be upto the top to avoid salt marks on the sides of the glass.

Plants : Many submerged water plants can be used in the aquarium. Water plants are used as a source of oxygen and also food for fish, they may also be used for various experiments in the laboratory.

Vallisneria (water lily) is an ideal aquarium plant. A coiled variety of this is called cork screw vallisneria looks very pretty in the aquarium. Other nice aquarium plants are Cobomba, Limnophila, Synnema, Lemna (duck weed). Too many plants should not be fixed in the aquarium as they hinder the penetration of light. If plant growth is too much some plants should be removed from the aquarium.

Place for Keeping the Aquarium : Aquarium should not be kept in direct sunlight but at a place where diffused light is coming from a window. If sufficient light is not available artificial light should be fixed on the cover. Two 40 watts bulbs or a fluorescent light will be suitable. Most of the aquarium fish are sensitive to temperature, an electric heater preferably with a thermostat may be fixed in it, temperature should be kept around 75°F—78°F [C = 5/9 (F—32)].

Fish : There are many varieties of tropical fishes available in the aquarium shops. Some common ones are guppies, mollies, sward tail, zebra fish, fighter, angle fish, gold fish. Angle fish are hard to keep as they do not tolerate much fluctuations. Gold fish usually are not kept with other varieties. If small gold fish are there they may be tried out to be kept with others. Suggestions should be taken from the supplier for the combination of fishes.

If fish are collected from a pond or lake they may slowly be acclimatised and gradually be transferred to the aquarium water. Some snails and small cattish can be kept as scavengers.

Food for Fish : Various fish foods are commercially available which can be purchased from the aquarium shops. Dried and crushed shrimps also make good food for them. Overfeeding is dangerous for the organisms. Small amount of food can be given on alternate days depending on the number of fish in the aquarium. Feeding schedule can be fixed by the class. Unutilized food start decaying and disturb the balance of the aquarium.

Once the aquarium is well established, the plants start growing giving new leaves and roots, develop runners. Fish like guppies, black mollies and few others give live births. The loaded fish should be separated, there should be enough plants for hiding the babies. The mother should be removed after having the babies for protection purposes. If thought provoking questions are asked many things can be learnt from an aquarium.

Lecture Method

This is one of the most popular methods of teaching in our schools. This is a teacher centred method, and the students are just passive listeners most of the time. Very few teachers allow questions during the lecture, though some of them give some time to their students to ask questions after the lecture. Many students forget their questions by the time the lecture is over. So their questions remain unanswered. Teachers talk most of the time without using any teaching aid, though some of them use blackboard. For them the lecture method is talk and chalk method. Sometime the back benchers cannot even read what is written on the black-board.

Students take notes of the lecture, and slow writers miss many points.

Research studies have been made on what actually happens in classrooms where teacher is teaching by lecture method. "Step into a classroom and what do you hear? The chances are better than 60 per cent you will hear someone talking. If someone is talking, the chances are that it will be the teacher more than 70 per cent of the time. The teachers talk more than all the students combined."

"The teacher is the main actor 85 per cent of the time." "Pupils receive recognition, praise and encouragement only 1-2 per cent of the time." "We want to encourage our pupils to learn to express themselves fluently, yet on average there are two speeches by each pupil each day in class, and the mean length of these is 8.4 words."

"Students dislike lectures. In an adult education class those who had heard only 15 minutes of a radio talk could score 41 per cent of a factual recall test while those who listened to the 30 minutes of the lecture could score only 25 per cent on the same test. In other words, the second period of 15 minutes proved to be far less productive as it reduced the listener's ability to recall the first 15 minutes. It may be due to fatigue set in which students lost the concentration. The span of concentration seems to be less for the child than the adult. Children switch their attention rapidly from one subject to another."

It implies that the teacher should not lecture continuously for more than a very limited time, say 15 minutes with an average secondary school class. After that a change of activity, to practical work, watching a film, writing or working in small groups, or discussion could be submitted.

Lecture Method alone in Primary Science Classes will not work. Integrate with it Teacher-Learner Interaction (TLI), and Learner-Learner Interaction (LLI) to make it effective for primary school children.

Demonstration Method

Demonstration means 'to show'. In lecture method, the teacher just talks but in demonstration method he also shows and illustrates certain phenomenon and applications of abstract principles through demonstration of experiments. Demonstrations provide concrete experiences to students. Demonstrations may also include use of films, slides, overhead projector.

While using the demonstration method the teacher can :

1. provide significant, rich and worth-while experiences to students enhancing their power of observation.
2. illustrate abstract ideas in concrete form.
3. co-ordinate science lesson with practice.
4. pose a problem to students and gather their hypotheses based on their experiences.
5. provide concrete experiences for the solution of a problem.
6. add additional demonstration after its review, if considered necessary.
7. do those demonstrations which are dangerous for students to perform themselves.

Characteristics of a Good Demonstration

1. It should be clearly visible to all students, even to the back benchers.
2. It should be pre-tested so that it may be convincing, striking and clear-cut.
3. Children should also be involved.
4. Results should not be known to students.
5. If there are more than one demonstration in a lesson they should be well-spread.
6. In a demonstration only one idea should be taken at a time. Too many ideas in one demonstration may confuse the children specially the young ones.

Some Key Points to be Noted

1. For large scale demonstration, the teacher must spend a good deal of time in thinking and devising experiments

to make principles quite clear, and in showing various types of experiments necessary to clarify the numerous difficult concepts of the science course.

2. The teacher should carry out the experiment in such a way that the students should learn how to carry it out by themselves.

3. When carrying out demonstration experiments the teacher should make sure that everything is in order before the lesson begins. He should be certain that the demonstrations will prove his points. The table should be well illuminated either by day light or by electric lights. The background should preferably be white or black so that the apparatus and other materials are clearly visible.

4. The teacher should see the general order and tidiness of the demonstration table. Nothing looks worst than a demonstration table littered with books and other material not to be used. The demonstration table should have only apparatus and materials relevant to the lesson.

5. In this method students are placed in a passive role which may be frustrating or boring for them unless the teacher involves them in thinking behind the experiment and in the manipulation.

This problem can be minimized if the demonstration is assembled ready for action before the lesson and there is every expectation that it will work. Demonstrations need to be rehearsed. For effective demonstration the following questions should be kept in mind :

(a) Is the apparatus clearly laid out from where the students view?

(b) Do instruments have large enough dials to be read by all the students in the class?

Overhead projector has made it possible to modify some demonstrations so that they are more easily seen and students can take readings and plot graphs while demonstration is proceeding. Under such conditions the teacher can involve their students in making predictions, speculations about causes, and thinking of ways of testing ideas.

Lecture-cum-Demonstration Method

This is a method generally used by our primary science teachers. Students cannot learn science either by lecture or by demonstration used in isolation. Even most effective demonstration cannot guarantee learning in primary science. This may also be true for the lecture-cum-demonstration method. It can succeed when lecture is based upon concrete experiences of the students' environment and a demonstration focuses them into scientific phenomenon, while discussion between teacher and students goes on in a permissive atmosphere. Demonstration method when combined with a well directed discussion is a successful teaching technique. It can be modified by allowing limited students participation and by problem solving at times. It fits well into the regular method of uniform class procedure for all students but does not permit of very wide individualization. If widely individualized and modified, it approaches to a method usually called the problem solving or project method.

Through contrived situations in this method students themselves form concepts. Therefore lecture-cum-demonstration method should achieve and the advantages of both lecture and demonstration methods, and minimise their disadvantages. Lecture-cum-demonstration method though widely used in our science classes has a limited role in the teaching-learning process. This is because all students do not participate actively.

To make this method more effective to teach science to primary school children, all the four interaction should be integrated with this method.

1. Teacher-Learner Interaction (TLI)
2. Learner-Learner Interaction (LLI)
3. Teacher-Material Interaction (TMI)
4. Learner-Material Interaction (LMI)

Use of Teaching Aids

Use of teaching Aids is very important part of Primary Science Teaching. As most of the primary school children are either Concrete Operational or Pre-operational and only a very small percentage is Formal Operational, primary school children will not understand science without use of teaching aids, and they will memorise science without understanding. Learning is understanding, and not memorising without understanding. Therefore a primary science teacher must learn selection and use of teaching aids when teaching science to primary classes.

Edger Dale Cone of Experiences : Selection of Teaching Aids.

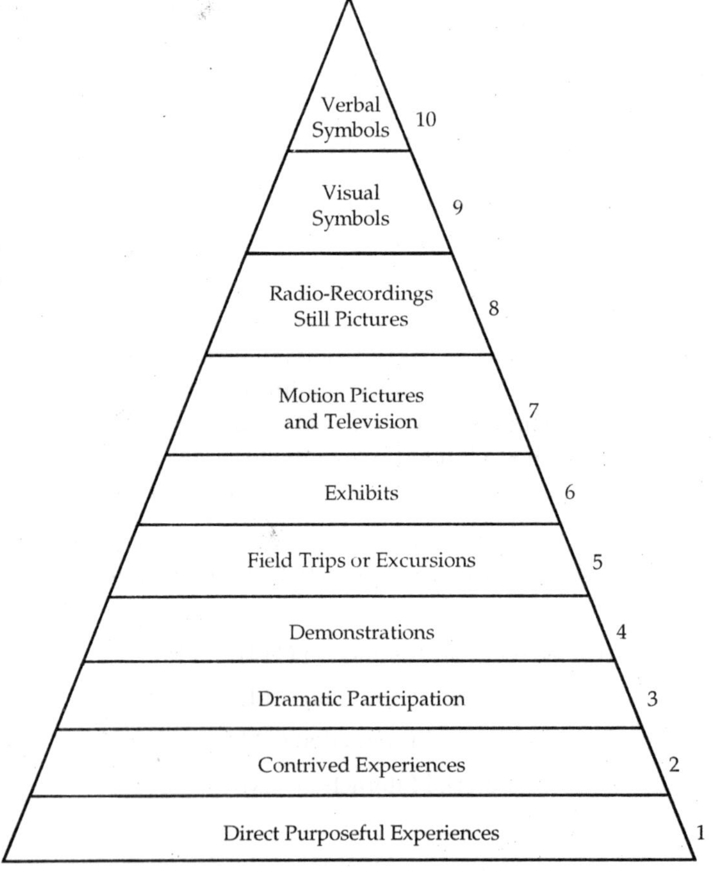

Fig.

Some of the teaching aids are more concrete in nature and some of them are comparatively more abstract. Edger Dale has arranged the various audio-visual aids in pictorial form which he called "Cone of Experiences".

This is a kind of visual aid to visualise and explain the inter-relationship of various types of audio-visual material as well as their position in learning process.

At the top of the Cone are verbal symbols which are most abstract and at the base are the direct puposeful experiences which are most concrete form of experiences. This is only a pictorial form where all sorts of aids and experiences are arranged in a Cone. The various bands of the cone representing various experiences and aids, should not be considered as rigid divisions or watertight compartments. They overlap and blend with each other. For example, you can be a viewer of an exhibit or a person who made it, you can observe a demonstration or can demonstrate it yourself. It is also not being suggested that the various aids and materials are arranged in the form; of their effectiveness but they are arranged from most abstract to most concrete. As a teacher we should also know that abstract ideas, concepts, or generalisations are not possible without rich meaningful concrete experiences. A primary science teacher has to pick and choose the aids according to the maturity levels of the students and the topic to be studied.

Direct Purposeful Experiences

The base of the Cone of experiences represents "direct purpose-ful experiences." Here the word 'purposeful' is very important. Every direct experience may not be very meaningful, therefore, it may not be purposeful. We have to see the direct experience in terms of learning outcome. In cases where the real things are too small or too big to comprehend, direct experiences are not very effective and therefore are not purposeful. For example, "structure of atom," "working of a factory," "water supply in a city" etc., can be understood better by some indirect experiences like models or charts, etc.

In teaching primary science many direct experiences can be given to the students for effective comprehension. Some examples are : observing real flowers, leaves, plants, insects; taking a walk through woods; going to the seashore and observing marine animals; setting and maintaining an aquarium, etc. In such cases learning is by direct participation.

The primary science teacher has to decide what direct experiences will be purposeful for his classes and then try to give them as many experiences as possible because direct and concrete experiences soon become associated with abstractions and help in developing more difficult concepts.

Contrived Experiences

Next in the hierarchy towards abstraction are contrived experiences. Examples of contrived experiences are static models, working models, specimens, dioramas, etc. Contrived experiences may differ from the original in size (big things are made smaller and smaller things are made bigger) and complexity. It usually is a simplified and edited version of the real thing, where the unnecessary details can be removed to make the learning clear. For example, a petroleum refinery is difficult to comprehend in a real situation but its model will be more meaningful. In the same way models of places where it is difficult or impossible to reach and see can give a clear idea, like models of globe, volcano, internal parts and systems of the body, bottom of the ocean, view of a forest, etc. Sometimes we imitate the whole natural habitat in the form of dioramas and keep in museums. Cut-away or half cut models are extremely useful in teaching internal structure of eye, ear, stem and root, etc.

There are some examples where nobody has seen the real things, the models are made on the basis of indirect evidences like model of atom, models of internal parts of human body. Here the whole concept is developed on the basis of these imaginary models.

While teaching through the models, teacher should give the idea of the real thing, regarding their size and complexity. All models are not correct reproduction of their originals, they are only simplified versions.

Objects and specimens are very common in primary science. These are also examples of contrived experiences. We collect rocks and soils from various places. Different kinds of plants and animals are collected; pressing, preserving and stuffing are done for storing and study purposes. The objects and specimens are taken from the real settings. They are samples of real things minus real settings. The specimens are collected and stored so that they are readily available for study purposes. Another most important advantages of objects and specimens which is not otherwise possible in direct experience is that they can be arranged into groups and classes.

Dramatic Participation

This has been placed on the third band of Cone of experiences. Dramatization means substitute for real experience of reconstruction of the original reality. There are many things we cannot possibly experience at first hand. There is a great value of dramatization in education. Students can participate in a dramatization or watch some kind of dramatization. Both are valuable experiences but participation is much more meaningful and closer to reality than only watching.

The question is "What is the scope of dramatization in primary science teaching?" Dramatic acts are quite popular in languages and social sciences. In sciences also the scope is not limited.

The films and videos made on the work of various scientists are only possible because of dramatization. Such films and videos are quite effective as such experiences are otherwise not possible.

Students of primary and upper primary classes participate in scientific dramatized act in schools, such activities are also brought to science fairs etc. Some very abstract and uninterresting ideas are taken for dramatizations, for example, different students act as various components of solar system with proper costumes, dialogues, songs, music and dance, and the abstract concepts become clear and leave a long lasting impact on participants and viewers; students act as various petroleum products and explain how they are formed and utilized like coal, petrol, vaseline, synthetic rubber and plastic etc. Functions of carbohydrates, proteins, vitamins and minerals can also be taught through dramatization.

It is also possible to use dramatization in classroom teaching where costumes are not necessarily required but different students can remember their parts and act out in the classroom.

An imaginative primary science teacher can think of many such topics which can be taught more effectively through such activities. Thus dramatization can become an effective teaching aid in teaching science.

Demonstrations

Demonstrations are quite familiar activities in primary science classes. In the Cone of experiences they have been placed on the fourth band from the base because it is essentially a process of observing. It differs from the first three bands, which are essentially doing. Demonstrations are used to show how something is done or not done. When demonstration is followed by doing on the part of students, it becomes very much meaningful.

Demonstrations are used to clarify ideas, and help to develop skills, processes and attitudes. They are not limited only to demonstrations through apparatus only. They can be used to clarify abstract ideas on the chalkboard, through slides or motion pictures also.

Demonstrations can be improved to a great extent if certain points are kept in mind while planning and doing a demonstration.

- Plan all steps of demonstrations in advance.
- Rehearse the demonstration before going to the class-room.
- Keep the demonstration simple as far as possible.
- Keep the students involved.
- Make it sure that all the students can see it.
- Outline various points on the board.
- Keep summarizing various steps.

Field Trips or Excursions

What is Field Trip or Excursion? A field trip or excursion is a planned visit to a point outside the regular classroom. It may be in the school, out in the community or it could be a long trip to far away places. Usually in field trips to places like visits to a factory, poultry farms, museums etc., we often see other people doing things. As spectators we are not involved but we directly watch it and get a first hand knowledge. Therefore field trip is an excellent bridge between the work of the classroom and the work of the outside world. The chief difference between a field trip and other educational experiences is that the students get their experiences in the field and not in the classroom. Because of its nature to be mostly observation it is kept on the fifth band of the Cone of experiences as less concrete than other experiences discussed before. But if the field trips are planned and arranged in such a way that they go beyond observation, for example of a sea-beach, on a pond where they can also touch, feel and collect things, it becomes a direct experience for them. Such a variation in the field trip indicates again how the bands of the Cone interlap and blend into one another.

Importance of the Field Trips

Excursions or Field Trips are of great educational value especially in primary science. The classroom is a limited place, bounded normally by four walls and meagrely equipped for the task or providing students with worthwhile experiences. The environment outside the classroom has no bounds; it has almost every conceivable situation that a teacher might wish to utilize. In school corridor students may study wiring system for supply of electricity to different rooms. On school grounds there may be various types of plants, birds, insects, different kinds of soil, sunshine and shadows, building materials, bicycles, scooters and cars. And just beyond the school boundaries lie the unlimited resources of community.

Contributions of an Excursion or Field Trip

(i) Field experiences are first hand experiences. They arise from direct learning situations. Sometimes they play the same role or even better in the learning of primary science as do experiments and demonstrations.

(ii) Field experiences tend to be much more meaningful and permit easier transfer of learning to solutions of real life problems.

(iii) Fieldwork if properly organized awakens many interests that classroom work cannot arouse. Fieldwork is the study of actual objects which stimulate more curiosity than to ideas. Out of almost any situation encountered in the field can develop into some challenging problems.

(iv) Fieldwork permits first-hand study of many things that cannot be brought into the classroom because of size and other inconvenience, e.g., it is only outside the class that the students can be acquainted with the flora and fauna of the area.

(v) Fieldwork permits a class to engage in activities that are too noisy or too violent to be used in the classroom, e.g., a model airplane, gasoline engine if demonstrated in the classroom would disturb the other neighbouring classes too.

(vi) Outdoors, students are able to work with large size materials, e.g., an iron piece pipe makes a more impressive lever than a routine stick and erosion is better demonstrated from a garden hose than with a tiny trickle from a yet drawn in a glass tube.

Some Special Experiences of Field Trips

Fieldwork brings students in contact with many objects. The observation and manipulation of object in the environment are bound to arise questions. Attempts to answer questions give rise to new problems.

Field trips can be used for review and drill. Ideas learnt in classroom can be better fixed in mind in actual situations, e.g., by visiting factories, the ideas of running a plant and the products manufactured can be better fixed in students' minds, or visiting a zoological park or a botanical garden, more abstract ideas about animal and plant life can be more clarified to students.

Difficulties Experienced in Arranging Field Trips

Lack of availability of good inventories regarding field experiences, school policies, and transportation problems create hurdles in arranging field trips. Therefore the teacher will have to take a key role if he wants to arrange the trip.

Procedure to Arrange the Field Trips

1. Survey of the place of excursion should be taken before going to the field trip, so that the teacher knows beforehand what their students are to see there; or relevant literature should be studied if places are far away.
2. Objectives of the field trips should be very carefully identified to make a field trip a success. If this is done teacher knows what lie is going to teach and the students know what they are going to learn there.
3. Permission from the authorities and parents of students should be taken well in advance.
4. Appropriate activities compatible to the identified objectives should be listed and given as well as discussed with the students beforehand.
5. If there is a need for transport and place to stay they should be arranged in advance.

Preparation of Students for Excursion

1. It is essential to brief students after arriving at the area. This should be as minimum as possible. A long lecture may deprive the students of an opportunity to explore the place.
2. Students should be divided into small groups appointing a group leader for each group. Group leaders may help in running fieldwork smoothly and quickly.
3. You as a teacher should be aware of the fact that there are slow as well as rapid learners. Activities and responsibilities should be so divided among the students as to be equally shared by both type of students without any feeling that they are slow learners or rapid learners.

4. Students should be made aware that there may be some difficulties like : (a) noise while visiting any working plant in a factory, (b) listening to the guide due to distance while standing around him, or (c) technical language used in explaining particular process; and they should try to solve such difficulties themselves as far as possible.
5. Students may be advised to take notes and draw diagrams, whenever they think it is necessary.

Teacher's Role

The teacher's role is very important for a successful field trip. Some of them are listed below :

1. Watches students closely and gives specific help as and when needed.
2. Recognises student's achievement.
3. Avoids frequent interruption in student's work but occasionally if it is justified.
4. Does not lecture while in field.
5. Avoids loud voiced comments.
6. Acts as a guide, resource person or consultant.
7. Does the relevant follow-up activities of the trip.

Follow-up Activities

Follow-up activities are very important in any kind of field trip, it may be a short trip just outside tbe classroom or a long excursion to various far away places.

Follow-up activities vary according to the nature of excursion. If the field trip is taken just outside the classroom in the school lawns to find the population densities of various species of plants, the follow-up activity will include the pooling up of data collected by each student or each group of students and discussion on the result. If the field trip is an observational trip to places like factories, mills or hospitals, discussion about what they have learned is important. Field trip can also be taken to study the fauna and flora and collection of specimens from seashore, hill stations or any other places. If such field trip is taken by the students follow-up activities will include pressing of plants, preservation of animals, drying of insects, classification and displaying of material. If proper care has not been taken just after or during the trip (in case of long trips) the materials collected cannot be utilized properly and go waste. Sometimes the students and teachers are quite enthusiastic while planning and taking the field trip, but forget about the material after the big excitement or do not do the follow-up activities properly, therefore, the field trip is not as effective as it should be.

In short we can say that follow-up activities should be planned according to the objectives of the field trip. Primary science teachers should plan their objectives for the field trip well and do the follow-up accordingly for better understanding.

The Exhibits

Kinds of Exhibits

There is a big variety of exhibits. Sometimes they are three-dimensional working models, sometimes a series of pictures/ photographs or pictures/photographs mixed with charts, models and real objects. But exhibits are essentially something one sees as a spectator. Usually one is not involved in handling any thing or working with the material. Primary science teachers take their students to show the science fairs where different kinds of exhibits can be seen. They are also of great educational value. Sometimes they may also influence the attitudes.

When primary school students are involved in making science exhibits, it becomes a direct experience for them. Investigatory science projects done by primary school students can be displayed as exhibits. Exhibits can also be used by the primary science teachers to teach primary science.

Museum

Museums are places where items and exhibits of knowledge are assembled, protected and studied. In big cities there are public museums of various kinds like art museums, history museums, science museums, and natural history museums etc. Here we are concerned with science and natural history museums. In our country there are not very many science and natural history museums.

But if they are available in your cities, advantage should be taken from them.

Mostly Science and Natural Histroy Museums (Science Museum in Bangalore, Natural History Museum in Darjeeling and New Delhi) have two functions : (i) presentation and display of the materials, and (ii) to work with classroom teachers on specific curriculum units. If this facility is given by the public museums, primary science teachers should take full advantage of such arrangements.

The other kind of museums are school science museums. Museum should not be considered as a collection of various items and objects. It is more than that, it must be viewed with an idea, a process, and an objective. Therefore science museums should not emphasize only on the product of science but due importance should also be given to science processes.

There is a big scope of displaying of specimens and objects collected by students. Models and projects made by students could also be displayed there. In fact development of museum can be taken as one of the school science club activities.

Motion Pictures and Television

Next on the cone towards little more abstraction comes the T.V. and motion pictures because we are only the viewers of these audio-visual aids. First we will discuss the motion pictures.

Motion Pictures or Films

It is not possible to learn everything by doing or first-hand viewing. We have to get some of our experiences indirectly, 16-mm films play a very important role in giving this indirect experience. Motion pictures present an abstracted version of the real events omitting unnecessary and unimportant details. They can dramatize events so effectively that we feel as though we are present at the reality itself. No other medium has brought so much information and scientific knowledge to the classrooms as the educational sound motion pictures.

There are various kinds of motion pictures. Here we are concerned with the educational films. Educational films include documentary and instructional films. Though some documentary films can be used in classroom teaching they are especially planned for classroom teaching purposes. On the other hand instructional films are specially planned to achieve certain educational objectives and are made in specific subject areas for teaching purposes. These films can be background films or direct teaching films. They help to promote to achieve a skill, an attitude or to convey certain facts, information, phenomenon or theory. As a primary science teacher you will be mainly concerned with the instructional films in science.

Though we are only spectators before a motion picture the learning outcomes are quite effective because of certain specific values of motion pictures.

For 16-mm films, 16-mm movie projectors are needed. Now video cassettes of 16-mm films are available, which can be seen on T.V.withV.C.P.orV.C.R.

For an effective use of films or video cassettes, preparation and follow-up are two very important steps to be taken by a teacher. Teachers should select the film or video cassette which goes along with the topic. The film or video cassette should be previewed and important points to be covered in the lesson should be outlined. It will be advisable to frame a few short answer questions. These questions can be given to the students before showing the film or video. During the follow-up activity unanswered questions and other important points should be discussed. Such activities help in coordinating the film or video with the topic. In the absence of such coordination sometimes the film or video becomes a wastage of time and effort.

The next point is to learn to operate the 16-mm film projector and V.C.P./V.C.R. which is not very difficult. Ordinarily only a few hours instruction followed by a brief practice results in satisfactory operation. Simple threading and operating instructions are given somewhere on the projector, which should be followed carefully. The possibilities of error should not discourage the teacher but it should be taken as a challenge. The thrill of this educational device will compensate for minor disappointments.

Television (School T. V. Programme)

Television has all the potentialities of motion picture with a little more concreteness because of the "on the spot coverage" and the nature of the TV programmes, as most of them are specially produced for a particular audience. This is more so for educational TV programmes. In many countries educational TV programmes include series of science programmes.

In Delhi the educational TV programmes started in General Science, Social Studies, Physics and Chemistry. Later Biology, Maths, Geography and Primary Science were also included.

TV presentation is only one part of the learning procedure. Preparation for the TV lesson or the pre-telecast activities and the follow-up or post-telecast activities by the classroom teacher are equally important without which the TV lesson may not be very much meaningful.

Pre-telecast activities will include the preparation by the subject teacher. Preparation will vary with class to class and also depend on the topic, the classroom teacher can see the topic of the TV lesson in advance from the TV booklet. During pre-telecast activities his job is to make the students ready to receive the TV instructions. He can ask motivational questions. If some background knowledge is needed it should be given at this time. The time-table is arranged in such a way that there are about 10 minutes before and after the actual telecast, usually the presentation is of 20 minutes duration and class periods vary from 35-40 minutes.

After the TV presentation follow-up activities should include clarification of points of doubts raised by students. Recapitulation questions should also be asked to see how much they have grasped. With little encouragement by the classroom teacher many activities can be followed by students as continuation of the TV presentation for better understanding.

Radio, Recordings and Still Pictures

Next stage on the cone of experiences after motion pictures is the number of those devices which can be called one-dimensional aids. We will take the scope of each in teaching science one by one.

Kinds of Still Pictures

Various kinds of still pictures can be used in teaching primary science. They include pictures, photographs, illustrations and 35 mm slides. These visual materials are of great importance in primary science teaching.

Pictures, photographs and "illustrations can be used without projection, 35 mm slides can be projected on the screen with 35 mm slide projectors. Therefore pictures can be divided into two kinds : (i) unprojected, and (ii) projected.

Unprojected Pictures

Photographs, illustrations and clippings of pictures from magazines and newspapers can be collected for teaching purposes. Pictures give a correct impression of the object of situation and motivate and enrich teaching. It is good to have relevant pictures on the walls of science rooms—pictures of great scientists and some of their apparatus, etc. Pictures can also be used in teaching for motivation, introduction, presentation or recapitulation as the need may be.

Pictures and illustrations with some theme can be displayed on a bulletin board.

Bulletin Board

It is a place for posting "bulletins," as the name suggests. Bulletin boards can be used in many different ways and as an effective "teaching device." Bulletin boards inside and outside the science rooms can be used for putting visual materials (pictures, illustrations) with relevant heading and some labelling for supplementing the teaching. It should be of scientific interest and importance. With proper teacher guidance and motivation bulletin boards can provide opportunity of developing creativity, responsibility and interest among the students. Other than displaying the pictures, photographs and illustrations, bulletin boards can also be used for displaying reports of science projects done by students, science news and cuttings from science magazines, collected and presented by them.

Projected Pictures

Projection of visuals have certain advantages. For example, projection magnifies the material, therefore, a bigger group can easily see it. It is somehow motivating, therefore, compels attention.

35 mm slide projectors are used in classrooms for projecting still pictures. They all are very easy to use, with little planning on the part of the teacher, teaching can be quite effective.

Opaque Projector or Episcope

The opaque projector projects and simultaneously enlarges material directly from original books, magazines, etc. All kinds of written, printed or pictorial matter in any sequence can be projected for teaching purpose. It can also project opaque thin objects like leaves, shells, sample of fabrics, butterflies, moths, etc.

Designs for posters, maps, pictures for displaying on bulletin boards etc., can be projected in the desired enlarged forms and then traced. The opaque projector, though has many unexplored possibilities, is not being used much because of its bulk, weight and requirement of a very dark room.

Educational Radio Programme

Educational broadcasts for schools in the AIR are regular features from the last few decades. These programmes include science lessons for students and teachers at various levels including primary. Teachers' programmes are on corftent as well as on methodology. Before the board examinations revision lessons on various science subjects are quite popular. These are given by experienced science teachers and educators.

The school broadcast is a separate unit of AIR in New Delhi. The unit tries to coordinate between various agencies to improve the effectiveness of the broadcasts. Meetings are held where people are invited from Directorate of Education, Delhi Municipal Corporation of Delhi, New Delhi Municipal Council and Delhi University to plan future programmes and give suggestions for their improvement.

Radio broadcast schedule in the form of a chart is printed and sent to the schools in the beginning of the year. (It can be obtained from AIR). Teachers can utilize the relevant boradcast in their classes. Radios and transistors are or can be easily available in the schools. If the teachers are conscious of the radio programmes, students can be benefited. Pre and post-broadcast activities will improve the effectiveness of the programmes as discussed in TV programmes.

Recordings

All the values of radio can be applied to recordings also. But the disadvantages can be eliminated like timing, administration and one way communication problems. Recordings from many sources can be utilised in the classrooms, like spool-tape records and cassette records.

Advantages of Recordings

(i) Recordings can become two way communication as it can be stopped, discussed and replayed wherever it is necessary, it can be controlled by us.

(ii) Recordings on cassette can be made in the school also. A commentary can be written and recorded on the available slides in your subject in the school for effective use and re-use.

(iii) Good radio programmes can be recorded and replayed in class whenever needed.

(iv) Scientific talks by eminent personalities can be taped and reproduced in the class.

Visual Symbols

Kinds of Visual Symbols. They include the abstract representation of real pictures. Various kinds of visual symbols used in communication are drawings, sketches, diagrams, graphs, cartoons, etc. They all can be projected on screen, and can also be shown on the blackboard or on the overhead projector.

Diagrams and charts etc., are part of everyday work for most of the primary science teachers. Almost all the primary science teachers use blackboard to show in the structure and happenings of various things in their subjects.

Commercially made charts are available in various subjects. Charts and other graphic aids are also made by various Governmental agencies. Central Institute of Educational Technology (CIET) of NCERT, New Delhi develops various kinds of graphic aids for school purposes. Charts are also made in schools by teachers and students and can be utilised in teaching science quite effectively.

Chalkboard. Blackboard now is usually called a chalkboard because of variations in colours. It is one of the very important but quite neglected aids of the classrooms. If it is properly used can become a valuable aid in teaching science.

It should not be taken for granted that you already know the use of chalk board, but the techniques should be learned and practised especially as a trainee teacher.

Importance of Chalkboard

(i) This aid is used with all other aids for better clarification, for example, the main points of a demonstration, planning and summarizing of a field trip, questions for a motion picture and so on can be written on the board.

(ii) It gives a concrete form to abstract and vague statements and ideas.

(iii) It helps in developing the skill of drawing a particular diagram.

(iv) It is less time consuming and comparatively cheaper.

(v) It can be used for some student's activities like quizes, competitions and discussions, etc.

(vi) Some chalkboards can be used for permanent outlines of maps, graphs, tables and other special materials where some filling up can serve the purpose.

(vii) If properly used chalkboard becomes an attractive point and holds students' attention.

Effective Use of Chalkboard

(i) Clean the board properly before using it.

(ii) Try to write neat and bold so that it is legible.

(iii) Do not write too much on the board. Start writing from top left hand. Give headings and sub-headings in the written summary.

(iv) If diagrams are used for referring or introduction, they can be made beforehand. If you want the students to draw the diagrams then it should be drawn in front of them and they should be asked to draw side by side. In the same way a complicated process should not be drawn beforehand, but it should be developed before them for clarification and better understanding.

(v) If necessary, some tools can be used to draw on the board.

(vi) Coloured chalks should be used for making complex diagrams.

Overhead Projector

Anything which is written or drawn on a chalkboard can also be projected by an overhead projector with some additional advantages.

An overhead projector projects photocopied black and white/ coloured transparencies of pictures, diagrams and tables etc. Coloured pens also used for writing and drawing diagrams on plain transparencies.

Verbal Symbols

This is the most abstract and one of the most important forms of experience we get and give to our students. Our job as a primary science teacher is to make sure that the various terms, ideas, words, principles and other abstractions in primary science used should be meaningful for students. The ideas and concepts which can be translated into verbal symbols come by getting other concrete experiences. Rich experiences gained by students help them to understand the verbal symbols meaningfully and therefore they can read and understand the science textbooks also. Ability to speak and read the word does not mean that one also understands the object, process or phenomenon.

If from the very beginning primary science is taught by reading books or abstraction only, students usually acquire the habit of memorising and accepting verbal formulation given by others. This is no way of teaching science.

Various kinds of experiences discussed on the cone of experiences from direct and purposeful experience to visual symbols, all help in the development of verbal symbols meaningfully. Then reading is not only the process of reproduction of verbal symbols but also involves a thinking process, which includes meaning of words.

Science textbooks and other reference books provide the most to the students, because all teaching is not possible by any one particular aid or experience. But the textbooks should be written in understandable vocabulary of that level. Sometimes in primary classes the language of science textbooks is much more difficult than the language in the language textbooks of that particular class. Another important aspect is also the style of writing and format. In writing and specially in teaching if references and examples are given from their environment and known things learning will be more meaningful.

Lesson Planning

Any activity well planned in advance comes out to be successful, so is the classroom teaching. If a teacher plans his lesson before-hand, he knows what he is going to teach, how he is going to teach, what teaching aids he is going to use, what questions he is going to ask, what questions students might ask, what objectives he is going to achieve and how he is going to evaluate that he has achieved his identified objectives. The answers of such questions make a lesson plan. For a beginning teacher it (lesson plan) may be a detailed script and for an experienced teacher it may be a small package of some teaching points in the written form or just in his mind. For a primary science teacher a lesson plan comes out to be very effective in science teaching.

It is advisable for a primary science teacher to select and organise in a logical sequence, the suitable material for classroom instruction. Where should he start today's lesson with respect to where he ended yesterday?

When teaching a certain primary science lesson, what questions should the teacher ask? Should the teacher answer all the questions raised by the students, or the students leave the classroom with some questions unanswered? When the teacher is discussing or demonstrating, should the student note down all the information, applications or uses?

There are several possible answers to the above questions. The teacher should give serious thought to such questions when developing his lesson plan, in order to arrive at an efficient and economical approach to teaching. The format of the lesson plan and the actual written material in it are not of great importance. The significant factor is that the lesson plans provide the primary science teacher with the opportunity of checking which of the suggested teaching methods are potentially most effective for achieving the identified objectives of the lessons.

Features of a Lesson Plan

The important features of what a lesson plan should contain are :

(i) Why should we teach this lesson (Objectives)?

(ii) What should we teach in this lesson (Content)?

(iii) How should we teach this lesson (Methods)?

(iv) How should we know that students have learned what we taught them (Evaluation)?

Steps Involved in Lesson Planning

There are many types of lesson plans which are as follows :

1. Preparation
2. Specific Objectives (written in behavioural terms)
3. Teaching Aids
4. Previous Knowledge

5. Introduction
6. Statement of Topic
7. Method (Presentation)
8. Recapitulation
9. HomeWork
10. Blackboard Summary

Art of Questioning

The art of questioning is also critical when teaching a lesson of science. We should not underestimate the importance of questioning skills increasing or diminishing student participation. We ask questions for a variety of reasons.

(i) To obtain feedback about the level of understanding in the class,

(ii) To know what they already know,

(iii) To promote thinking,

(iv) To draw attention to something,

(v) To provide the student with an opportunity to verbalize his ideas in a coherent way,

(vi) To give opportunities to praise and encourage a student, and

(vii) To act as a measure of class control etc. etc.

Remember

Your methods of teaching should :

- Make the students Think.
- Make the students Do.
- Make the students See.
- Make the students Say.
- Make the students Hear.

Enrichment and Remedial Primary Science Programmes

There are primary school children not of widely different ages but of widely different abilities in the same class. There are primary school children who are from different socio-economic backgrounds, who have different values and different outlook. There are primary children who require differentiated educational programme and services beyond those normally provided by the regular school programmes. These programmes can be enrichment programmes and remedial progammes.

Enrichment Primary Science Programme

Before discussing any enrichment programme it will be desirable to describe the students for whom these programmes are needed—enrichment programmes are needed for gifted children to fulfil their demands.

I. The gifted children have been defined in many ways. One acceptable version is gifted are those who by virtue of out-standing abilities capable of high performance and are identified by professionally qualified persons. They include all the following:

   (a) Talented. Those students who may be talented in one or few fields.

   (b) Intelligent. Students who score high on intelligent test (verbal or non-verbal), they may be with an IQ of 130 or above.

   (c) Creative. Creative children are intelligent, talented plus they have something extra; they are also productive thinkers.

   (d) Skilled. They are capable of performing better in psycho-motor abilities.

II. The gifted children can be identified by some of their beha-vioural characteristics.

In their Learning Characteristics, they :

(i) usually have advanced vocabulary for their age and grade level.

(ii) are keen and alert observers, usually see more to get a more out of a description and films etc.

(iii) read great deal on their own, prefer adult level books.

(iv) regarding Motivational characteristics, they :

(v) get easily bored with routine task.

(vi) are not easily satisfied with their own speed of products.

(vii) often pass judgement or events, people and things.

In their Creative Characteristics, they :

(viii) display great deal of curiosity, ask questions.

(ix) display a good deal of intellectual playfulness, manipulate ideas i.e., change and elaborate upon them.

About their Leadership Characteristics, they :

(x) are self-confident with children of their own as well as adults.

(xi) adapt readily new situations, are flexible in thoughts and actions.

Primary Science Programmes for Gifted Students

Some enrichment programmes which are used to fulfil the demands of gifted are described here.

1. Acceleration. It means skipping classes, it may be in one subject or more subjects or by some other means shortening the time spent on studies.
2. Special Grouping. Here the opportunity is given for special education in each homogeneous group based on abilities.
3. Enrichment Programmes. Special academic provision for various students.

Primary Science Talent Search Scholarships

Municipal Corporation of Delhi (MCD) and New Delhi Municipal Council (NDMC) education departments conduct PSTS contests for the students of MCD and NDMC schools respectively at two levels:

(i) Class IV students, and

(ii) Class V students.

MCD has only written tests. NDMC has written tests as well as oral tests on science practicals (Interviews). Those NDMC students who compete in written are invited for interviews. The selected students get scholarships.

You as primary science teachers should be in touch with these organisations. Get full information on the above mentioned contests for the talented, prepare your gifted students for these contests, and ask the SCERTs of your state for any guidance in this regard.

Remedial Programmes for Slow Learners

There are children in primary science classes who are not motivated to learn science. They are slow in learning than average students, they are weak intellectually and emotionally. They are also called backward children.

Backward Children are those having I.Q. below average, usually they are slow in learning. In our normal schools we are mostly concerned with border-line cases.

An acceptable educational definition of backward child is one who is not able to do the work of one year below. If a V class child is not able to do IVth class work he can be considered as backward.

It is also possible that a student is considered backward in one subject and not in others.

The enthusiasm of slow learners tend to be short-lived. Apart from a limited attention span within a lesson, there is a strict limit to the length of the time that a teacher can spend on any topic before it loses appeal. It is easier to teach those who want to learn science than it is to teach those who do not. This will be a challenge to teach science to slow learners. This challenge should be taken by science teachers not as a burden but with pleasure.

There are some skills and qualities to be developed in slow learners. They are as follows :

(i) The ability to communicate in speech and writing and to read with understanding.

(ii) The ability to make measurement and do calculations.

(iii) Capacities for thought, judgement, discrimination and enjoyment.

(iv) Responsibility for their work.

(v) An understanding of the physical world and the society in which they live.

(vi) A vocabulary for discussion of current events and issues in science.

(vii) An appreciation of the importance of personal relationship and the value of cooperative effect.

(viii) An ability to find out scientific information for themselves.

(ix) An awareness of the variety of ways in which leisure time can be used.

(x) Self-confidence, self-respect, and as realistic an idea of one's own capabilities and potential as is possible.

Virtually all these qualities can be fostered within the teaching of science, and it is thus important that one should think of education through teaching rather than of teaching science as an end in itself.

The same objectives could well be achieved through a study of different topics in science. When choosing science content to meet these objectives, the following questions should be kept in mind by the teacher.

(i) Is the material relevant? In other words, will the pupils see the material as useful to them either at the time they are in school, or after they have left school?

(ii) Is the material capable of being presented in an interesting way?

(iii) Is the material within the pupil's powers of comprehension?

In most of the Indian schools there is provision for a remedial period in the beginning or at the end of the school hours. Very few teachers are using this period for actual remedial work. Many a time teachers use this period to cover the course or to revise the course in a full class. This period should be utilised only for actual remedial work for the few students who have been identified as slow learners and actually need teacher's help.

The teacher has to be patient with slow learners, they need care and love. They develop hatred if they are not properly cared as they are emotionally weak.

Students can learn more if the teacher makes the learning "Child Centred" as far as possible. The students should be allowed to become active agents in the educational process.

A warm but firm hand, and a genuine concern is needed for slow learners. The teacher should praise the slow learners frequently. The teacher should help the students to achieve success. This will encourage them to work hard, and they will devote more time in studies. Thus they will be able to learn just about the same devoting more time what average students learn in less time.

Are You Ready to be a Good Science Teacher?

After completing your teacher training programme, this is the right time to ask yourself whether you possess the basic intellectual and personal qualities necessary to be a good science teacher. Do you have the attributes, such as integrity, drive, and a high sense of responsibility, which are valued in teaching specially science teaching. Besides these, there are special characteristics of successful and happy science teacher.

Checking the following questions may help you decide, how good a science teacher you are going to be.

	Question	***Yes***	***No***
1.	Do you enjoy reading and studying in science as well as in other academic areas?	....	....
2.	Have you been a good science teacher?	....	....
3.	Do you like working with students and other science teachers?	....	....
4.	Do you like to help your students?	....	....
5.	Do your students and other science teachers like to work with you?	....	....
6.	Could you enjoy and adopt to a career in which the subject is constantly and rapidly changing because of new discoveries?	....	....

7. Do you, on your own, sometimes do more work than is required by teachers?	....	....
8. Have you developed science projects and participated in science fairs?	....	....
9. Do you like to find answers to problems on your own?	....	....
10. Do you have a sense of humour?	....	....
11. Can you accept criticism and profit from it?	....	....
12. Do you consider that preparing students for living in the world of the future is a challenging job?	....	....
13. Are you developing the ability to read quickly and with comprehension and to express yourself clearly and interestingly in speaking and writing?	....	....
14. Are you in good health, both physically and mentally?	....	....

If you have thoughtfully checked YES for most of the above questions, you very likely would enjoy teaching science at any level, and you should read on to learn how you prepare for this type of exciting career.

Specialised Course

B.Ed. does not prepare teachers for teaching at primary level. ETE is a specialised course for teaching primary school children. So, if you are B. Ed. and teaching science at primary level LEARN at least TWO THINGS—Psychology of Primary School Child and Methods of Teaching Science at Primary Level. You should learn—what to teach in primary science and why, how to teach primary science and why, and how to find out that primary school children have learned (understood) what you taught them in science. There are several methods of teaching science at primary level. Every method is good for a particular situation. Practice them all. According to Piaget most of the primary school children are either concrete operational or pre-operational. They cannot understand science without teaching aids. So always use teaching aids when teaching primary science. Teaching Aids give concrete experiences for primary school children. Edger Dale has arranged teaching aids, from concrete to abstract, in a cone of experiences. It will help you in selection of teaching aids when you teach primary science. Lesson Planning will facilitate you when teaching science at primary level. So learn to do lesson planning when teaching science to primary school children. When you teach science at primary level, you will find some children who are gifted or slow learners. Identify them and give enrichment programmes to gifted and remedial programmes to slow learners. How good a primary science teacher you are? Find out. Then with some self-learning programmes in Primay Science Teacher Education, try to improve yourself, and one day you will be among the best primary science teacher of the country.

Questions

1. (a) List the three stages of cognitive development of primary school children.
   (b) How will this help you in what to teach and how to teach primary science to these children?
2. List 15 methods of teaching science at primary level in a sequence—the best method you liked as No. 1, and then others in order of your liking.
3. Why should we use teaching aids when teaching science to primary school children?
4. List 10 Experiences given in Edger Dale Cone of Experiences. Which of the experiences do you or will you like to use in your primary science classes?
5. Select a topic for a class I to V from primary science, and develop a lesson plan.
6. What will you do for gifted and slow learners when teaching science at primary level?
7. How will you find out how good a science teacher you are?

5

Methods of Teaching

In the teaching-learning of science, primary goal is the development of skills and attitudes for scientific investigation and also to understand the scientific concepts and generalisations. The teachers are concerned with developing sound patterns in the children's thinking generally attributed to scientists as 'scientific thinking'. It is, therefore, important for science teachers to look at what thinking is the process by which it develops, the conditions by which it is facilitated and finally, what the teachers can do to nourish and direct it.

Science and thinking with reasoning are like two sides of a coin. Both are extremely complicated processes and produce products. The raw materials in thinking are sensations, percepts, concepts, principles or generalisations which shape the products to be derived from processes of thinking. Further, the products of thinking are varied. They include conclusions, opinions, behaviours, actions, etc. Thus, any scientific teaching involves experimentation, thinking and generalised conclusion.

There are different methods or approaches of science teaching in relieving the ultimate objectives.

We shall briefly discuss those approaches and methods of teaching science in this chapter :

1. Conceptual Approach,

2. Process Approach,
3. Integrated Approach,
4. Child Centred Activity
5. Problem-solving Method,
6. Environmental Studies,
7. Activity Approach,
8. Scientific Method,
9. Teacher Centred Versus Child Centred Approach,
10. Inquiry Approach.

Conceptual Approach

In activities, a child gets the opportunity to touch (a doll), feel (a ball), taste (a biscuit), handle (a toy), smell (a flower) and so on. Such sensory experiences are caused by external environmental stimulations. These result in percepts. Percepts develop from impressions or awareness of sensations caused by an environmental stimulus which requires little interpretation. Percepts are primary factors in thinking which often initiate train of thought.

When percepts are recalled at some later time without the use of external stimuli, the memories and images are already formed. The percepts in the form of images and memories develop into greater abstractions called concepts. The concept is usually organised as a result of many related sensations, percepts and images with verbal symbols incorporated. If the child has distinguished apple from other fruits, he has applied the word 'apple' to a group of ideas which include the image and memories in the form of shape, colour, size etc. of the apple and he has developed a concept. In the concept formation there is an ascending level of abstraction of words for the concepts that emerge. For example, a simple observation of salt as it exists and its further related experiences lead to concept formation of higher ideas like cells, molecules etc.

Our senses shape and influence our perceptions. This process continues with awareness of a total situation breaking the situation down into separate parts, and then reconstructing these separate parts back into a clear pattern.

Thus from the above discussion it is clear that in the conceptual approach of science learning, the child understands through sensory-motor experiences. The teacher will do well to expose the child to practical activities which can give these experiences.

Concepts are understood well if taught by Child Centred Approach is also Child Centred. Therefore Scientific method is also an effective method for teaching concepts.

Process Approach

Another approach to science teaching employs a well known method called 'Process approach'. The word 'Process' is here synonymous with 'Scientific method'. The classical pattern of 'Scientific method' includes processes of observation, hypotheses, testing (experimenting), collecting data and reaching conclusion. It should be understood that there is no need to precisely follow this pattern in a necessarily ordered form.

In the process approach, the child adopts its own method. Given a problem and the opportunity to explore, the child will discover a heed for certain processes. The processes involve different actions which are later on linked to arrive at a logical conclusion.

The process approach envisages certain processes (skills) considered important in science. The processes which might be incorporated into each activity are listed below:

Observing—This is paying close attention to details that can be directly detected. For example, observing a white candle amongst many other coloured candles.

Classifying—Arranging into groups according to similarities and differences.

Using numbers—Counting, determining per cents, tabulating etc. are some methods employed in Science.

Measuring—Like determination of length, weight or volume etc.

Using space-time relationship—Recognising specified objects in relation to other within a specified time.

Communicating-Giving complete and precise information in the clearest form.

Predicting—Suggesting the outcome of further observation and/or testing, basing the suggestion on preliminary observation.

Inferring—This means reaching a logical deduction based on observed evidences.

Defining perationally—Defining on the basis of observation in own words.

Formulating Hypothesis—Developing an 'educated guess' to explain a wide variety of observations related to a phenomenon.

Interpreting data—Arranging or grouping information, data or principles so as to describe or explain a phenomenon.

Controlling variables—Testing the effects of one variable at a time to find the answer to a question.

Experimenting—Testing one or more variables in a carefully controlled situation and recording all pertinent data for later interpretation.

Integrated Approach

When we teach science, we teach 'concepts' and 'processes' both. If we teach temperature, we also teach how to measure temperature by a thermometer i.e., we teach reading a thermometer. Here 'temperature' is a 'concept', and 'measuring temperature' is a 'process'. If we teach weight, we also teach how to find out weight of a body by spring balance, i.e., we teach weighing by spring balance or reading scale of spring balance. Here 'weight' is a 'concept' and 'weighing' is a 'process'. If we teach photosynthesis, we also teach how to set up photosynthesis experiment and collect oxygen during photosynthesis. Here 'photosynthesis' is a 'concept' and 'setting up photosynthesis experiment' is a 'process'. Thus, when we teach science, we do not teach concepts and processes in isolation at least at primary level, but we integrate concepts and processes. Hence we use both the approaches (conceptual approach, and process approach) together i.e. at primary level we teach science by integrated approach. Conceptual Approach involves Child Centred Approach (CCA) and Process Approach involves Teacher

Centred Approach (TCA). Thus using both the approaches (Conceptual Approach and Process Approach) together is Integrated Approach for teaching Science.

Child Centred Activity

Approach Science teaching in the primary schools have a great role to play. It develops the child's attitude and skills for making wise decisions concerning his future. The present day society expects the citizens to have good scientific background and technological ability. Thus the children of the country are required to know and understand the operation of science in society effectively. The children have to be taught so they can recognise that nothing is fixed and the only basic factor of our universe is change. They should anticipate change and the inherent problems associated with it. Science, by nature, evolves and can build a better understanding of the processes of change. Elementary school science is needed by all children. Science and scientists play an important role in the democratic society. Our children, the citizens of future, need a realistic view of the scientist, his work so that may make valid decisions relative to the scientific enterprise.

For the five or six years before the child enters the classroom he has been involved in the interaction between himself and his environment. His experiences slowly help him to identify every object he comes across—like his pup, books, parents etc. A prime element in this slow, determined process is the sensation experiences by the child through smell, taste, touch, sight and hearing. These sensations make a life-long impression on the child.

At the same time that the child is learning about his newly acquired self, he is also developing concepts of the causation of events especially while viewing himself as the possible motivating force for events he knows that if he cries, mother will get worried and care for him. Repeated experiences convince him that he is capable of producing different effects through his different actions. His constant experience with natural elements like heat, cold, rain, light, darkness, thirst and other physical and biological phenomena reinforce his ideas about these concepts. It is all these preliminary experiences he carries when he first joins the school. The teacher is aware of this and the teacher is also aware that the child has natural tendency to have its child-like qualities. It will be active, inquisitive, playful and learn more and more through contact with environment. These above backgrounds form the basis of teaching science through Child-Centred Activity-Based Teaching-Learning Approach.

Normally in the learning process, active participation is preferred to a passive process like simply listening to the teacher. The learning situation, to be of maximum utility, must be realistic and meaningful to the learner and should take place within a rich and satisfying environment. The learning process proceeds most effectively when the experiences, materials and desired results are carefully adjusted to the maturity and background of the learner.

In the Child-Centred Activity-Based Teaching-Learning method, the teacher suggests activities and initiates certain questions. For example, the child is taken for a trip outdoors and the child is advised to observe the nature of the sky outside the building and from where the child can see in all the directions. Now the teacher should raise questions such as—

1. Is the day cloudy, partly cloudy or very bright and sunny? How do you know?
2. Is there breeze? In which direction do you think it is blowing?
3. Are there clouds? If so, how do they look like? Do they remind you something which you know already?
4. Are the clouds moving? Do you think it will rain? Such questions become thought provoking for the child.

Thus, in the child-centred, activity-based teaching-learning, an excellent progress can be made through appropriate involvement of the teacher in the perspective discussed above.

Problem-solving Method

In the methods of teaching science, there is another method which is very effective and it is called problem-solving method. Children, by nature, are very inquisitive and they have a tendency to explore. Through the self-exploration activity they learn many things. The children come with questions and problems. The teacher does not give the solution of the problem but guides in finding the solution.

Normally in the problem-solving method, the problem should be presented or posed by the students. But teacher can also pose a problem. After selecting the problem the students should solve the problem by study, experiments and discussions with the teacher's help and guidance.

While this method can be applied to the children of 5-8 years age group, it will be effective in 7-10 years age group because the power of understanding the significance of this method will be better with age maturity.

In any problem-solving method, it is imperative that the materials associated with its solution should be available. The students should be given a set time limit to solve the problem. This method may be a scientific method. In this, the students are active participants and the method develops the power of logical thinking in the students. If the problem is solved the students get excited, experience a great personal satisfaction and become eager to solve more such problems. Normally, the level of problem should be of their own standard and must be according to their individual intellectual level. The problem must be relevant, so that the interest of the students remains sustained. If a problem is of difficult nature, the teacher should play a very important supporting role. If a problem at initial stage remains unsolved, it becomes detrimental to students' interest. In such cases, it is advisable for the teacher to create and suggest problems which are of same magnitude as students' capacity to solve. This will build up the tempo of interest in students' mind.

The problem-solving technique is helpful not only as a method of science teaching, but will be useful even in solving day to day problems because the scientific temperament (temper) gets created. In tackling any problem in a scientific manner the following points may be kept in mind :

1. Know the objective of the problem and prepare a ground by surveying the related information.

2. Plan meticulously the procedure for attacking the problem.
3. Collect all information and data related with the problem.
4. Analyse the data and make inferences and conclusions.
5. Verify the whole process and ensure that the solution has been found.

It should be pointed out that the source of the problem does not always have to be a real situation in child's life. It is more desirable in the primary levels to deal with things with which the children are familiar.

As the science at the primary school level is aimed to help the individual to understand common phenomena in his environment, to apply the scientific thoughts in both personal and civic problems; and to appreciate the implications of scientific discoveries for human welfare. Then it must be followed by the children under the teachers' guidance keeping in mind the principles and every day activities at home and school.

Interest in the child's mind can be aroused by the actual problem solving process itself. The involvement of the child in actual planning, exploring, evaluating, observing, demonstrating and experimenting provides much interest and motivation. The excitement and suspense that can be so much a part of the process of problem solving provides an almost discovery approach to learning, which is generally missing in other classroom procedures. The classroom is a physical and intellectual environment for children as well as a knit social and emotional environment. As such, the teacher concerned with developing problem-solving skills should use these elements of the environment to the best advantage.

Environmental Studies

When we teach science, we use audio-visual aids, otherwise most of the children will not understand science. Our environment is full of audio-visual aids—natural and man-made, living and non-living. Some are materials like our own body, food and food items, water and other drinks, air and other gases, things inside the earth, on the earth and above the earth, things in the universe like sun and other stars, planets and satellites etc. Some are events, happenings or phenomena like lightning and thunder, wind and storm, rains and hails, fog and snowfall etc. If we use materials and phenomena of the environment when teaching science, learning science will be fun for children. Using materials and phenomena of the environment when teaching science is Environmental Studies (EVS) Approach for teaching science. EVS Approach may be integrated with any method or approach of teaching science.

Activity Approach

'Believe nothing because you have been told about it. Don't believe what your teacher tells you merely out of respect for the teacher'.

Who said this? When this question is put to Science teachers in seminars, the reply is 'some scientist'. Actually it is the statement of Lord Buddha.

Many times teachers teach and children do not understand. This is because children are conditioned in accepting and memorising what teacher tells them, without questioning and understanding.

In science there are many facts, principles, laws, concepts and skills, which children memorise without understanding. Have you ever thought why is it so?

Cognitive Development of Children

There are three types of children :

Formal Operational—They can understand science without activities.

Concrete Operational—They can understand science only if they do activities by their own hands.

Pre-operational—They can understand science if they do activities repeatedly by their own hands.

This is the way Piaget categorised the children. These are the children's cognitive stages of development.

Example

Siddiqis worked with Piaget at Florida State University (USA) in 1970 when he came as a visiting Professor. He went to the neighbouring schools to demonstrate how children at these cognitive stages look at things, think and response. There it was found that only 5% children at primary level (I-V) were at formal operational stage, the remaining 95% children were either concrete operational or pre-operational.

By using Piagetian tasks, Siddiqi conducted Research Studies on 1206 Primary school children in Delhi from all type of schools during 1975-77. The average interview time with each child was about 15 minutes. So it took about 300 hours to complete the task. It was found that only 4.4% children at primary level (I-V) were at formal operational stage. Even in Class V formal operational were only 9.4%, while concrete operational were 69.3% and preoperational were 21.3%.

Science is Doing

Generally in our primary schools, science is taught by teacher telling or book reading, and sometimes by demonstrating a few experiments. Children are not really involved in doing activities by their own hands. Teachers should also learn a lesson from the following saying:

'I heard and I forgot,

I saw and I remembered,

I did and I understood'

This is not just a saying. As hypotheses these were tested by Siddiqis and they were found correct.

If our objective is that the child may remember the content for some time. Lecture Method may be relevant without even using Audio-Visual Aids. If the objective is that the child may remember for longer duration, Lecture will not work. But Lecture-Demonstration will be more effective. Care should be taken that every child is able to observe what is being demonstrated using all the 5 senses (see, touch, smell, taste, hear).

But if the objective is that the child must understand then doing is the only method for pre-operational and concrete operational children. Teacher telling and even the Demonstrations are not going to work. The children will have to be involved in doing activities by their own hands.

Thus Activity-Based Science-Teaching is the only way of teaching science, if we want our children to learn science. Learning science is understanding science, and not just memorising.

A suggested list of 139 EVS (Science) activities (for Class III 35 activities, for Class IV 61 activities and for Class V 43 activities) along with 38 primary (III-V) EVS (Science) activities has already been given. These activities may be done when teaching science by Activity Approach.

For doing activities you need some material. You have lot of material in the environment. Besides you also have some material in your Primary Science Kit. You can also improvise some low cost and no cost teaching aids from the hand tools in your Primary Science Kit and Mini Tool Kit.

Scientific Method

Scientific Method is a Discovery Method. When teaching Science by Scientific Method, children do not verify the already known facts. Instead they are involved in finding out the solution of a problem.

Science can be taught by scientific method in four steps.

Problem : What does a child want to learn?

Hypotheses : What does a child think the answer would be? (These are predictions)

Experiment : How could a child tell the answer would be what he predicted (This is testing of hypotheses).

Conclusion : What do the results of the experiment show? Are the hypotheses accepted, rejected or need modification.

Scientific Method is a Child Centred Approach (CCA) of teaching science.

Merits

1. Children learn science on their own by Child Centred Approach (CCA) under the guidance of their teacher.
2. Children collect the evidence to prove or disprove the identified hypotheses.
3. Children learn to solve every day problems.
4. Children establish a healthy and favourable relationship with their teachers. They don't have to believe what their teachers say or teach, unless they are convinced that what their teachers are saying or teaching, is correct.
5. Children develop scientific temper or scientific attitude.

Demerits

1. This method is comparatively slow, long and time consuming.
2. There is too much emphasis on doing activities (practical work) which some children do not like. Though learning science by practical work is a joyful process, but for some children too much practical work becomes boring.
3. Most of the teachers are perhaps not able to teach science by scientific method, because they do not practise scientific method during their practice teaching, and they do not try scientific method when they become regular teachers.
4. All children are not capable to learn science by scientific method.

Teacher Centred vs Child Centred Approach

Teacher Centred Approach (TCA)—If we observe classrooms, we find it is the teacher who speaks most of the time, and the children either given no opportunity to speak or a very little opportunity to speak—ask questions or interact. This is a Teacher Centred Approach of teaching.

Example

In a study about 1000 primary (I-V) and upper primary (VI-VIII) classes were observed in all subjects and in all types of schools, and it was found that on an average 95% of the time teacher was speaking and 5% of the time the children were speaking. This is an example of Teacher Centred Approach of Teaching.

Teacher Telling, Book Reading Method, Lecture Method and Lecture Demonstration Method are Teacher Centred Approaches of Teaching. Teacher Centred Approach is a very effective method for teaching skills (processes). Reading a thermometer, reading a spring balance, making a slide and seeing it through a microscope, setting the experiment for photosynthesis etc. are all skills. Until a child perfectly learns a skill, the teacher is very much involved in telling the child "what to do" and "how to do". The teacher has to use Teacher Centred Approach for teaching skills, cooking, sewing, riding a bicycle, driving a scooter, a motor cycle or a car, repairing any machine, playing musical instruments, dancing, wearing a sari etc. are all skills. Teaching each of these skills, a teacher is needed who teaches these skills by Teacher Centred Approach.

Example

Reading a thermometer is a skill. According to a study primary school children and even primary school teachers not taught this skill by Teacher Centred Approach, generally read the thermometer wrong. If the reading was 46°C, they read 40.6°C. Then came the teacher to teach this skill by Teacher Centred Approach. He pointed at 40 and asked "What is the reading"? The child said "40°C". Then he pointed at 50 and asked, "What is the reading"? The child said, "50°C". Then the teacher asked, "How many marks are there between 40°C and 50°C"? When the child failed to answer, the teacher himself counted—1, 2, 3, 4, 5, 6, 7, 8, 9, 10. Then the teacher asked "How much is one mark?" Then the child replied "1°C?" (This is actually the least count of the thermometer which the child was not knowing, and therefore he reads 40.6°C instead of 46°C). Then the teacher asked, "How many marks is the mercury above 40°C?" And the child counted, "1, 2, 3, 4, 5, 6". Then the teacher asked, "Now tell, what is the reading of the thermometer?" And the child again counted, "41, 42, 43, 44, 45, 46", and then said, "Thermometer reads 46°C and not 40.6°C".

Now look at the approach, teacher used to teach the child to read the thermometer correctly. In this approach the teacher was more involved than the child, and therefore this is Teacher Centred Approach. Reading a thermometer is a skill. Therefore Teacher Centred Approach (TCA) should be used to teach skills (processes) to the child.

Child Centred Approach (CCA)—Some innovative teachers themselves speak less in the class, and give opportunity to their children to speak more. Here the science teacher acts as moderator (leading and moderating discussions) and a guide (helping slow learners). This is Child Centred Approach. In teaching science by Lecture Method or by Lecture-Demonstration Method, these innovative teachers involve their children in interaction [Teacher-Child Interaction, Child-Child interaction, Teacher-Material (Science apparatus or teaching aid) interaction, Child-Material interaction] and question-answer sessions that even their lecture and Lecture-demonstration become Child Centred.

Inquiry Approach, Problem Solving Approach, and Scientific Method are Child Centred Approaches.

Example

A teacher is teaching a concept "Air has weight" by scientific method. It involves "weighing" by a spring balance, which is a skill (process). The teacher teaches the skill (process) of weighing to the children by Teacher Centred Approach before he teaches the concept "air has weight".

Problem : Does air has weight? (This is TCA). Then children formulate their own.

Hypotheses : (i) Yes, (ii) No. (This is CCA) Then children (as already know the skill of weighing or reading a spring balance) test their hypotheses themselves.

Experiment : weighing an etopty football bladder, and the same football bladder of air. (This is CCA). Then they themselves draw.

Conclusion : that air has weight. The hypothesis "yes" is right, and hypothesis "no" is wrong. (This is CCA).

Here step-1 is Teacher Centred as teacher asks the question or poses a problem. Steps-2, 3, 4 are child centred. Therefore Scientific Method is 25% teacher centred and 75% Child Centred. Thus as a whole, Scientific Method is Child Centred Approach (CCA).

"Weight" is a Concept, and 'Weighing" is a skill. When skill of "Weighing" already taught by the teacher to the children by Teacher Centred Approach, the concept of "Weight" is to be taught by Child Centred Approach. (Do not tell to the child "air has weight", let him find out himself whether or not "air has weight" by the Child Centred Approach (CCA).

As "weight" is a concept and "weighing" is a skill; similarly "temperature" is a concept and "measuring temperature (reading of a thermometer)" is a skill; "photosynthesis" is a concept and "setting and doing the photosynthesis experiment" is a skill, and so on. When you will teach EVS (Science) you will see that almost in each lesson there are some Science Concepts and some Science Skills. So you will use both the approaches "TCA" and "CCA".

1. Teach skills (processes) by TCA and
2. Teach concepts by CCA.

Example

One day an electric bulb blew out in the class. "What happened?", asked the students. The teacher took out the bulb from the bulb holder, and showed it to the students. The students gathered around the teacher. He passed it around them, and said, "Look at it and try to develop hypotheses about what happened". "What is inside the bulb?", asked one of the students. "I do not know", said the teacher. "Is there air inside the bulb?", asked another student. "No", said the teacher. "Is there any other gas inside the bulb?", asked another student. "No", said the teacher. The students were puzzled, and they started looking at one another. Finally one student asked, "Is it vacuum inside the bulb?" "Yes", said the teacher. "Is it complete vacuum?", someone asked, "Almost" replied the teacher. "What is that little wire made of?" asked another student. "I do not know", said the teacher. "Is that little wire made of some metal?", asked some student. "Yes", the teacher said.

Such Yes-No Answer Questions continued between Teacher—Learners (Students) Interaction, till students identified the material of the wire inside the electric bulb, and the events that took place without teacher's ready made answers. Finally students began to formulate hypotheses about what happened. After the students formulated some hypotheses, they started searching through Reference Books (in the Library or at home) in order to verify them.

This is an example of Inquiry Approach of teaching science. Students are trained for inquiry. Inquiry begins with a puzzling event like "an electric bulb blew out in the class". Students inquired (What happened—a problem) when they were puzzled.

After the puzzling event is presented to the students, they ask the teacher some questions. The teacher should answer the questions in "Yes" or "No". The answer of each question may be a small hypothesis.

Inquiry Approach of teaching science may have the following Steps.

1. Encounter with the problem.
2. Formulation of hypotheses.
3. Datagathering—Experimentation and Verification.
4. Conclusion—Solution of the Problem.

Note : Inquiry Approach is a very effective technique of teaching science to fast learners in primary and upper primary levels, and even in higher classes.

There are various approaches/methods of teaching of science like—conceptual approach, process approach, integrated approach, child centered activity based teaching learning approach, problem solving approach, EVS approach, activity approach, scientific method, TCA, CCA and inquiry approach. Every method or approach has some merits and demerits. In conceptual approach stress is given in scientific theory and learning of scientific facts. Learning depends upon child's own experiences. The teacher makes sure that the students must have as much experiences as they could. In process approach observing, using numbers, measuring, inferring, classifying, communicating, predicting, formulating hypotheses, controlling variables, experimenting, interpreting data, using space-time relationship and defining operationally are science processes. The student should know how to make hypothetical statements and how to test hypotheses with experiments before reaching on any conclusion instead of memorising scientific facts and principles alone. In integrated approach both the concepts as well as processes are important. It has three aspects : (a) Nature of science, (b) Nature of learner, and (c) Nature of society. Thus not only the subject and learner are important but the society is also important. Child centred science teaching motivates the children for free thinking and to participate actively in finding the solution of a problem. This method increases the interaction between the teacher and the taught. In this method the curriculum is set, based on the needs of the students, their interests, attitudes and abilities. The child's development is evaluated in every field. Problem solving method may also be a scientific method. Students first of all identify some problems and after that with teacher's help and guidance the students themselves find out its solution by experimentation or critical thinking. Once a student gets competency over this method then he/she applies it to find out the solution of the problems related to his/her daily life. In this way this method is also useful for developing scientific attitude or scientific temper.

Questions

1. "Roots have various functions". How will you teach this concept by problem solving method?
2. What are main characteristics of the child-centred approach? How is it different from teacher centred approach? When will you use these approaches?
3. In teaching "reading of thermometer" to the students which approach of teaching science (child centred or teacher centred) will you use and why?
4. Presently used "reading a science book" method in Primary Schools is an example of which approach (child centred or teacher centred)?
5. Is science book for class V, the book of integrated science? Justify your answer.

6. (a) List 11 methods or approaches of teaching science discussed in this chapter.
   (b) Discuss with examples how will you use each method for teaching science at primary level.
   (c) Identify primary science topics and develop 30-40 minutes lesson plans for each method.
   (d) Discuss the merits and demerits of each method.
   (e) Discuss when will you use a particular method for teaching science at primary level.

6

Objective Teaching

Difference between Aims and Objectives—For carrying out any activity it is important to know its purpose. If the purpose is clear, the activity will be carried out effectively. If one knows what is to be achieved, the planning will be done accordingly and the work will be carried out properly. Thus when teaching EVS (Science) at primary (I-V) level, identification of aims and objectives is a very important task.

Whether Aims and Objectives are synonymous or they have different meanings?

Justification for teaching science suggests :

Aims for Science Teaching—Translation and Selection of Aims of Science teaching gives.

Objectives of Particular Science Course—By selecting these objectives and relating these to specific content and teaching methods, we obtain.

Objectives for Particular Science Lesson

General Objectives—Out of these three steps, No. 1 and No. 2 are Aims, or General Objectives of a Lesson Plan. They suggest general directions in which our science course may be steered. They may be achieved after completing the whole course and not just by teaching a science lesson. They are general targets with which we are concerned. They form the basis of the general place of science in a science course for given groups of pupils.

Examples

1. To develop in pupils the interest in learning science.
2. To help pupils to solve problems.
3. To inculcate creativity in pupils.
4. To help pupils to see science in relation to society.

Specific Objectives

Out of the three steps given above, Step No. 3 gives specific objectives of a particular lesson identified by you for your Lesson Plan. These specific objectives may be achieved after teaching a science lesson.

Examples

Topic: Thermometer

1. To enable the pupils to read the temperature from a thermometer.
2. To enable the pupils to draw the diagram of a thermometer.
3. To enable the pupils to describe the construction and working of the thermometer.

General Objectives of Primary Science Teaching

The General Objectives or Aims of science teaching at primary (I-V) level may be stated as follows :

1. The child should learn the method of inquiry in science and should begin to appreciate science and technology in everyday life.
2. The child should develop habits of cleanliness and healthful living and an understanding of the proper sanitation and hygiene of his neighbourhood.
3. The child should learn to cooperate with others and appreciate the utility of working together. Other desirable qualities of character and personality, such as initiative, leadership, honesty should be developed.
4. The child should be able to express himself freely in creative activities and should acquire habits of self-learning.

How long will it take to achieve such Aims or General Objectives—one lesson or whole course or even more?

NPE-1986 has the following two recommendations for Science Education:

1. Science Education will be strengthened so as to develop in the child well-defined abilities and values such as the spirit of inquiry, creativity, objectivity, the courage to question, and aesthetic sensibility.
2. Science Education Programmes will be designed to enable the learner to acquire problem solving and decision-making skills and to discover the relationship of science with health, agriculture, industry and other aspects of daily life. Every effort will be made to extend science education to the vast number of members who have remained outside the pale of formal education.

Can we put these two (1 and 2) in the above four (1, 2, 3, 4) Aims of Science Teaching at Primary Level. If yes, how and why?

Types of Objectives

Domains of Objectives

According to Bloom, educational objectives may be classified into three domains :

1. Cognitive Domain (remembering)
2. Affective Domain (feeling)
3. Psychomotor Domain (doing)

Examples

Topic : Food and Nutrition

Cognitive Objectives

To help the children to—

1. understand the need for adequate food and that proper nutrition is essential for physical and mental development, health and happiness,

2. become aware of the foods available in the locality and need to produce more food,
3. become aware of the ways in which food can be prepared and made attractive, tasty and nutritious in eating.

Effective Objectives

To help the children to—

1. take interest in selecting, and in liking to eat different groups of food,
2. feel the necessity of producing more food and take interest in kitchen gardening,
3. take interest in finding out what kinds of food are available in the locality,
4. become convinced of avoiding waste of food at all levels.

Psychomotor Objectives

To help the children to—

1. select and eat proper combination of food,
2. make a habit of washing hands before and after eating, and develop similar hygienic practices,
3. participate in food production at home and in school,
4. explain the kinds of food in the locality.

Types of Cognitive Objectives

Cognitive objectives are further classified into six categories knowledge, understanding (comprehension), application, analysis, synthesis and evaluation.

The first three cognitive objectives may be tried out at primary level (I-V).

1. Knowledge is the remembering of previously learned material.

   Examples : Knows common terms, specific facts, methods, basic concepts, principles and laws.
2. Understanding (Comprehension) is the ability to grasp the meaning of the material.

Examples : Understands facts and principles, interprets verbal material and charts.

3. Application is the ability to use learned material in new situations.

   Examples : Applies concepts and principles to new situations, applies laws to practical situations, makes charts, demonstrates correct usage of a method.

Types of Affective Objectives

Affective Objectives are further classified into five categories—receiving (attending), responding, valuing, organization and value complex.

Receiving (Attending) is to orient the learner to learn. This is the first step that he is willing to learn what is being given to him.

Examples

(i) Children are aware of scientific activities in the school.

(ii) Children are willing to take part in science activities.

(iii) Children attend science activities arranged by school.

Responding comes after the learner has given his attention.

Responding includes willingness to respond and getting satisfaction by responding.

Examples

(i) Children respond to questions asked by the teacher.

(ii) Children raise hands to answer questions every time a question is asked by the teacher.

(iii) Children feel happy after answering the questions correctly.

(iv) Children take pleasure in explaining scientific phenomenon to others.

Valuing causes self-motivation in the children and makes them committed to involve themselves in science activities.

Examples : Children have faith in experimentations and discussions.

Organization develops into children certain values which help them to organise themselves to do things on their own.

Examples : Children develop a plan for doing some science activities at school and at home as home work.

Value Complex enables the children to act constantly in accordance with the values they have developed.

Examples : Children develop a behaviour based on scientific attitude or scientific temper. They use scientific method in solving day to day problems and making some decisions. They develop scientific temper which they always use in their daily life.

Statement of Objectives

Behavioural Objective

Look at the objective given below :

Given a thermometer the child will measure the room temperature with 100% accuracy.

How is this objective differently written compared to the objective written above.

This objective has—

Condition—given a thermometer

Observable Behaviour—measure

Criterion—with 100% accuracy

An objective written in this way is called Behavioural Objective.

Behavioural Objective tells very clearly what the child is to do. It also tells what is the role of the teacher and what is the role of the child.

The teacher will give the child a thermometer and will ask him to measure the room temperature with 100% accuracy. (The teacher has already taught the skill of measuring the thermometer scale).

If the room temperature is 27°C and the child measures 27°C, the objective is achieved. If he measures 26.5°C or 27.5°C, the objective is not achieved as the Criterion of 100% accuracy is not achieved.

Generally in stating of objectives in behavioural terms, or writing behavioural objectives Condition and Criterion are not written, and only Observable Behaviour is written. Then the above Behavioural Objective may be written as 'the child will measure the room temperature.'

If we want to evaluate this objective, we will not ask the child—

(i) to draw the diagram of the thermometer,

(ii) to write the construction of the thermometer,

(iii) to write the working of the thermometer.

But we will ask the child to find the room temperature with the help of a thermometer.

Thus a behavioural objective tells very clearly :

(i) What the teacher is to do?

(ii) What the child is to do?

(iii) How the child is to be evaluated?

Writing Behavioural Objectives

When writing Behavioural Objectives for Observable Behaviour—

Do Not Use

Words open to many interpretations.

Like—know, understand, appreciate, enjoy, believe etc.

But Use

Words open to fewer interpretations.

Like—identify, write, recite, differentiate, solve, construct, list, compare, contrast etc.

Such words are called Key Words to be used in Behavioural Objectives for showing observable behaviour.

(A) When making Lesson Plains you write Specific Objectives. Write them in behavioural terms using such Key Words.

(B) When constructing Test Items, first select a Topic, then write a set of behavioural objectives using the above given key words, covering the whole topic. Then construct one or more test items for each objective.

When writing behavioural objectives decide :

(1) What will you test in Knowledge, Comprehension and Application?

(2) Which Key Words will you use for each from the following?

For Knowledge

Use—define, describe, identify, label, list, match, name, outline, reproduce, select, state etc.

For (Understanding) Comprehension

Use—convert, explain, extend, generalise, give example, infer, paraphrase, predict, rewrite, summarize etc.

For Application

Use—change, compute, demonstrate, discover, manipulate, modify, operate, predict, prepare, relate, show, solve, use.

Relating Objectives with Learning Outcomes

Objectives, Behavioural Objectives and Learning Objectives

We learned objectives of teaching and learning. Objectives may be general or specific. Objectives may be cognitive, affective or psychomotor. Cognitive Objectives may be of knowledge, understanding (comprehension) or application. Affective Objectives may be of receiving, responding, valuing, organization or value complex. Objectives may be stated in behavioural terms. When objectives are stated in behavioural terms, they are called Behavioural Objectives.

Objectives to be achieved after a lesson, after a course, after a term, after the school year when written in behavioural terms are called Learning Outcomes (LOs).

Learning Outcomes for EVS (Science)

The EVS (Science) syllabus for classes III, IV and V is divided into Units, and the syllabus of each unit is written in terms of learning outcomes. Look at the following pages how the syllabus of EVS (Science) for classes III, IV and V is written in terms of Learning Outcomes. Each unit is to be taught in such a way that all learning outcomes aree to be achieved. For each Learning Outcome test items are to be constructed and given to the children during periodic tests and examinations. The result of each child in these tests will tell you how far these learning outcomes have been achieved. This will enable you for remedial and enrichment teaching.

Learning Outcomes For Class-Evs (Science)

UNIT 1 : *Living Things*

In this Unit, the students will be able to—

1. classify things around them into natural and man-made, and living and non-living things,
2. identify differences between living and non-living things,
3. identify the differences and similarities between plants and animals,
4. identify the growth pattern of plants from seeds,
5. identify the different parts of a plant,
6. identify how animals adapt themselves to their food habits,
7. correlate the various body parts of animals with their movements.

UNIT 2 : *Our Body, Food and Health*

In this Unit, the students will be able to—

1. recognise and measure the growth of some parts of their body,
2. learn about the state of their sense organs like skin, eyes, ears, nose, tongue, and learn how to take care of them,

3. recognise the conditions of their teeth and learn how to take care of these,
4. classify the food-stuffs,
5. recognise good food habits.

UNIT 3 : *Materials and Their Properties*

In this Unit, the students will be able to—

1. classify materials on the basis of their common properties,
2. describe that materials occupy space and have weight,
3. recognise that materials can be changed from one state to another,
4. recognise that water destroys many materials and the amount of material dissolved is limited,
5. recognise that liquids other than water also dissolve some materials,
6. describe various conditions necessary for the dissolving of solids in liquids.
7. recognise the method of separating one substance from a given mixture.

UNIT 4 : *Weather and Seasons*

In this Unit, the students will be able to—

1. learn more about the changes in the weather in relation to the phenomenon of water cycle which involves the process of evaporation and condensation,
2. recognise and record weather changes, their implications in our daily life and the utility of weather forecasting,
3. distinguish between various conditions during different seasons,
4. identify the effect of change of season on plants, animals and on the life style of human beings.

UNIT 5 : *The Sky*

In this Unit, the students will be able to—

1. identify the objects seen in the sky during day and night.
2. learn the direction in which the SUN apparently rises and sets,
3. recognise that the MOON does not have light of its own,
4. learn about the stars in the sky.
5. learn how large the SUN, the MOON and stars are,
6. recognise and record the different phases of the MOON.

Learning Outcomes for Class-IV EVS (Science)

UNIT 1 : ***Living Things***

In this Unit, the students will be able to—

1. identify how plants hold themselves into the soil, with the help of roots,
2. understand that the plant gets water and minerals from the soil through the roots,
3. identify that the stem serves in the transportation of water from the roots to other parts of the plant,
4. understand that green leaves prepare food for the plant,
5. identify that most plants produce fruits and seeds,
6. understand that seeds of plants produce new plants,
7. recognise that seeds have to be dispersed away from the mother plant for healthy growth of successive generation,
8. identify the different ways in which plants are useful to us,
9. understand that animals need proper care and protection,
10. identify the ways in which animals are useful to us,
11. understand that plants too, like animals, need care and protection.

UNIT 2 : ***Human Body, Nutrition and Health***

In this Unit, the students will be able to—

1. identify the different internal organs like lungs, heart, stomach, liver of the human, and their functions,
2. classify various food-stuffs and understand their relationship in maintenance of proper health,
3. recognise different parts of digestive system and the simple process of digestion,
4. understand various ways and methods adopted in storing, cooking and serving so as to promote the preservation and conservation of food and its nutrients,
5. Understand how the food gets contaminated and how this can be prevented,
6. recognise impure water and how to purify the water to make it suitable for drinking,
7. recognise various unhygienic conditions that make breeding places of flies and mosquitoes and how to make the surroundings hygienic.

UNIT 3 : *Materials and their Properties*

In this Unit, the students will be able to—

1. classify objects according to specific attributes,
2. differentiate or compare objects and the materials that they are made up of,
3. classify materials according to their softness and hardness,
4. classify materials according to their heat conductivity,
5. classify materials on the basis of their capacity to dissolve in water/liquids,
6. observe and understand the composition of matter, that is made up of tiny particles,
7. understand that the composition of different materials determines their solubility in water,
8. identify the different methods by which solids can be separated from liquids,

9. recognise that some solids can be recovered from liquids by evaporation and crystallisation.

UNIT 4 : *Air, Water and Weather*

In this Unit, the students will be able to—

1. identify the importance of the sun for life on the earth, and how it determines the weather conditions,
2. distinguish between evaporation and condensation,
3. generalise the factors which affect the rate of evaporation of water,
4. understand the effect of cooling water vapours and the role of condensation of water vapours in causing changes in the weather,
5. identify the effects of certain weather conditions on the life of people and the crops.

UNIT 5 : *Soil and Crops*

In this Unit, the students will be able to—

1. identify the crops grown in their surroundings,
2. identify the crops grown in different seasons of the year,
3. identify that different crops require different amount of water and warmth,
4. identify the things needed for the healthy growth of crops,
5. recognise similarities and dissimilarities in the three kinds of soil.
6. recognise the difference between good and bad soil,
7. identify that different types of particles of soil, on kneading, unite differently,
8. identify clayey, loamy and sandy soil on the basis of retention and percolation power of water.
9. recognise that different types of soil allow different quantities of water to pass through them,

10. recognise that soils hold air in its inter-particle spaces,
11. recognise that different types of soil contain different quantity of air,
12. recognise that the soil is formed by breaking up of rocks,
13. recognise that stones formed in a locality are pieces broken from a big rock,
14. recognise that wind plays an important role in the weathering of rocks,
15. recognise that flowing water plays an important role in weathering of rocks,
16. recognise that wind carries soil from one place to the other,
17. identify the relationship between type of soil and the crop,
18. identify the ways by which soil is made fertile,
19. identify the relationship between adding of manure to the soil and the growth of a plant,
20. recognise the relationship between the amount of fertiliser given and the crop yield,
21. recognise the advantages of crop rotation,
22. identify the relationship between the improved variety of seeds and the yield of crops,
23. recognise the effect of timely irrigation on crop yield,
24. identify the ways of protecting crops against diseases,
25. identify the effective ways of storing food grains.

UNIT 6 : *Force, Work and Energy*

In this Unit, the students will be able to—

1. define force as a push or pull and state its effects on objects,
2. recognise that work is done by a force when it moves a body,

3. identify that animals and men exert force by their muscles,
4. identify that energy is needed to do work,
5. identify the different forms of energy (heat, mechanical and electrical).
6. understand that one form of energy can be converted into another,
7. appreciate the need to conserve energy.

UNIT 7 : *The Earth and the Sky*

In this Unit, the students will be able to—

1. identify the characteristics of planets,
2. identify the characteristics of a satellite,
3. distinguish between natural and artificial satellites,
4. know about the artificial satellites launched by India,
5. recall that the revolution of MOON around EARTH causes the various phases of the MOON,
6. see the relationship between the rotation of the EARTH and the occurrence of the day and night,
7. learn that the EARTH completes one rotation in 24 hours,
8. see the relationship between the revolution of the EARTH around the SUN and the changes in seasons.

Learning Outcomes for Class-V EVS (Science)

UNIT 1 : *Living Things*

In this Unit, the students will be able to—

1. differentiate between living and non-living things,
2. differentiate between animals and plants,
3. understand that plants and animals adapt themselves to their environment,
4. identify that all seeds of a plant do not necessarily grow with same vigour,

5. understand about the conditions for germination and growth.

UNIT 2 : ***Human Body, Nutrition and Health***

In this Unit, the students will be able to—

1. identify the different bones in the human body,
2. identify that bones give a definite shape to the body and also protect the delicate organs of the body,
3. identify the different kinds of joints and the movements made possible through them,
4. identify the muscles in the body and their major functions,
5. recognise the voluntary and involuntary muscles and their functions,
6. recognise the factors leading to proper development of muscles and importance of exercise in the development of muscles including the advantages of sitting in right postures,
7. establish relationship between the intake of food, the age and occupation of persons,
8. identify and classify different food items into energy-giving, body-building and protective food,
9. identify causes of deficiency diseases and common deficiency diseases with special emphasis on anaemic and eye defects,
10. identify that consumption of reasonable amount of food, protects from deficiency diseases,
11. identify common food practices of his/her locality and clarify their positive and negative aspects,
12. recognise the need for preservation and storage of food and proper methods for storing food and foodgrains,
13. identify different factors which contribute to spread of communicable diseases,
14. identify causes and prevention of insanitary conditions,

15. recognise the steps which can be followed to keep the environment clean.

UNIT 3 : *Soil Erosion and its Conservation*

In this Unit, the students will be able to—

1. recognise various factors that contribute to soil erosion,
2. recognise various ways in which soil is conserved.

UNIT 4 : *Air and its Usefulness*

In this Unit, the students will be able to—

1. state the properties of air,
2. state the names of gases present in the air and identify their uses,
3. distinguish between the fresh (unpolluted) and polluted air,
4. recognise the need for fresh air.

UNIT 5 : *Force, Work and Energy*

In this Unit, the students will be able to—

1. identify the effects of applying force on different objects,
2. state the different ways in which force is exerted and their role in doing work,
3. identify the different types of simple machines used in daily life to do work,
4. identify the reasons for conserving energy and to take steps for proper use of energy.

UNIT 6 : *The Earth and the Sky*

In this Unit, the students will be able to—

1. distinguish between transparent, translucent and opaque objects,
2. recognise that shadows are caused by obstruction of the light by opaque objects,

3. see relationship between shadow formation and size of the object,
4. see relationship between size of the shadow and distance of the opaque object from the source of light,
5. see relationship between shadow formation and occurrence of eclipses,
6. identify the causes of solar eclipse,
7. identify the causes of lunar eclipse,
8. distinguish between solar and lunar eclipses,
9. generalise that solar and lunar eclipses occur on the new-moon day and full-moon day, respectively.

UNIT 7 : *Natural Resources of the Earth*

In this Unit, the students will be able to—

1. identify and list down the various natural resources,
2. understand the significance of interdependence in nature,
3. identify the uses of natural resources,
4. appreciate the need to conserve natural resources,
5. identify renewable and non-renewable natural resources,
6. identify causes of pollution and list the ways in which pollution could be prevented.

Minimum Levels of Learning (MLLs)

Achieving well-defined standards of learning by children in schools is a powerful success indicator of the system that works. It is in this context that the NPE—1986 emphasised the need of laying down Minimum Levels of Learning (MLLs) for each stage of school education—primary (I-V) and upper primary (VI-VIII), so that teachers set themselves to perform their goals accordingly.

Minimum Levels of Learning (MLLs) at primary level are the Minimum Learning Outcomes (MLOs) which the children are to achieve when they pass the primary stage of education (Class V). The MLLs Based Curriculum equips all children (irrespective of caste, creed, location or sex) who complete primary education (I-V) with minimum/essential learning outcomes that will enable them to understand their environment more meaningfully and to function as socially useful and contributing adults. The MLLs Based Curriculum reduces substantially the load of information expected of a primary school child.

It is expected that MLLs should be achieved to 'mastery level' by all children. In operational terms, 80% or more of the children mastering at least 80% of the MLLs should be the performance target for the teacher.

There is the widely held perception that in a vast majority of government and municipal schools, children can barely read their own textbooks even after spending as many as five years (I-V) in school. Considering that, to a large number of them, opportunity for education is not likely to be available beyond the primary stage, and what they learn here must sustain them throughout their lives, it becomes imperative that the educational system makes sure that these precious school years of the children are not wasted. All children irrespective of the conditions they come from and condition of the schools they attend, reach a Minimum Level of Learning before they finish primary education that would eventually enable them to understand their world and prepare them to function in it as permanently literate, socially useful and contributing adults.

Taking all this into consideration MLLs in each subject—language, maths and EVS at primary level (I-V) are identified. Here we will discuss MLLs in EVS.

MLLs in Environmental Studies (EVS)

Major competencies for Classes I and II EVS (Science and Social Studies)

The five major competencies aimed at the cognitive, affective, and psychomotor domains of development with content elements associated with class I-II EVS (Science and Social Studies) are given below:

1. The pupil acquires awareness about one's well-being in the context of social and natural environment.
2. The pupil explores important aspects of one's socio-civic environment and comprehends their working.
3. The pupil knows about various people at work and appreciates the importance of the world of work.
4. The pupil understands and interprets the spatial and interactive relationship between man and his environment.
5. The pupil begins to see relationship between man's past and present and to hold the past in proper perspective.

These major competencies are further subdivided into specific sub-competencies for classes I and II, which are as follows :

MLLs of Class I EVS (Science and Social Studies)

Our body and its cleanliness

(i) Identifies the main parts of the body.

(ii) Understands the importance of keeping them clean.

(iii) Recognises the need of clothes and seasonal variation in them.

(iv) Practices personal cleanliness including toilet habits.

(v) Observes how animals and birds keep their bodies clean.

Our family and neighbours

(i) Identifies relationship of the different members of the family with himself and among themselves.

(ii) Shows courtesy to elders, peers etc. in the family and among the relatives and neighbours.

Parents and other members of family at work

(i) Observes various members of family at work in home.

(ii) Knows about occupations of parents and other family members for earning livelihood.

(iii) Shares information with peers about occupations of the parents.

Our Locality

(i) Identifies some important local land features, e.g., river, pond, ridge etc.

(ii) Recognises some common animals, birds and insects.

(iii) Estimates distances in the locality in terms of very near, near, far, beyond and before.

Local Festivals

(i) Knows simple facts about the traditions behind local fairs and festivals.

(ii) Shares experiences with peers about fairs visited and festivals celebrated.

MLLs of Class I EVS (Science and Social Studies)

Our food and shelter

(i) Understands the need of food and health.

(ii) Sees relationship in unclean food and diseases.

(iii) Appreciates why the house is an essential need.

(iv) Shares activities to keep the house and surroundings neat and tidy.

(v) Observes and compares various kinds of shelters including those of animals, birds and insects.

Our neighbourhood (locality)

(i) Identifies important public places such as the school, panchayat ghar etc. in the locality and knows their importance.

(ii) Realises the importance of going to the school, and attends it regularly and in time.

Occupations in the neighbourhood

(i) Observes and lists occupations carried on in the locality.

(ii) Finds out their usefulness.

(iii) Appreciates the variety in occupations and its need.

(iv) Realises the importance of work in life.

Our neighbourhood

(i) Uses sunrise and sunset to find out directions.

(ii) Relates the nature of weather with seasons, and seasons with human activities, plants, birds etc.

(iii) Gathers information about various uses of land features of locality by man.

(iv) Reads information from a given sketch map of the locality.

(v) Recognises some common trees, birds, crops etc. of the locality.

National Festivals and other celebrations

(i) Knows about the importance of national festivals.

(ii) Participates and understands the similarities and differences in celebrating national festivals and other celebrations.

(iii) Knows about the national flag.

(iv) Sings national anthem.

Major Competencies for Classes III, IV and V EVS (Science)

The four major competencies aimed at the cognitive, affective and psychomotor domains of development with content elements associated with classes III—V EVS Science are given below :

1. The pupil understands the factors contributing to the preservation of good health.
2. The pupil develops skill in gathering and classifying information about living things from one's environment and drawing simple inferences.
3. The pupil observes and examines some common characteristics of non-living things.
4. The pupil observes simple phenomena on the earth and in the sky and draws inferences.

These major competencies are further subdivided into specific sub-competencies for classes III, IV and V, which are as follows :

MLLs of Class III EVS (Science)

Functions and care of different parts of body

(i) Understands important functions of human body, such as digestion, respiration, blood circulation etc.

(ii) Knows how to take proper care of such parts of the body as eyes, hair and teeth.

Living things : their characteristics and classification

(i) Observes local surrounding and classifies things into

  (a) living and non-living,

  (b) natural and man-made.

(ii) Understands similarities and differences between animals and plants.

(iii) Identifies main parts of a plant.

(iv) Classifies common plants on the basis of size, life span and seasonality.

(v) Observes food habits of different animals and birds.

Common materials and their properties

(i) Identifies common materials on the basis of some easily observable properties, e.g., colour, texture and hardness.

(ii) Classifies given materials according to these properties.

The earth and the sun

(i) Observes earth-sun relation and consequences.

(ii) Describes the shape of the earth (evidence of photograph).

(iii) Relates occurrence of day and night to the rotation of the earth.

(iv) Observes differences in the duration of day-light over the year.

(v) Generalizes about the occurrence of seasons.

(vi) Observes consequences of the occurrence of seasons (some instances).

(vii) Observes importance of air in our life.

(viii) Explains the usefulness of air.

(ix) Knows how air gets polluted.

(x) Observes importance of water in our life.

(xi) Describes different uses of water.

(xii) Knows about different sources of water.

(xiii) Locates various sources of water in the locality.

(xiv) Finds out how water gets polluted.

MLLs of Class IV EVS (Science)

Nutrition, pollution and cleanliness

(i) Classifies foodstuff's according to nutritive functions and understands the need of balanced diet.

(ii) Knows how food and drinking water get contaminated.

(iii) Conducts simple experiments to purify drinking water.

(iv) Relates unhygienic conditions with the spread of diseases.

Living things : their usefulness to man

(i) Identifies some important ways of using plants and animals.

(ii) Identifies some harmful insects and weeds.

(iii) Examines the need of caring and protecting animals and plants, and describes simple ways of doing so.

(iv) Names the national bird, animal and flower.

(v) Takes part in tree plantation programmes of the locality and appreciates their importance.

Materials (matter) and their properties

(i) Knows the three states of matter—solid, liquid and gas.

(ii) Observes the three states of matter in respect of water.

(iii) Generalizes about inter-changeability of these states.

The earth and the sky

(i) Recognises and names heavenly bodies like sun, moon and stars etc.

(ii) Knows difference between sun, earth and moon (simple observable facts).

(iii) Recognises pole star and Great Bear (Saptarishi) and uses them for finding directions at night.

(iv) Observes phases of the moon.

(v) Observes weather phenomena.

(vi) Knows how air and weather are related (certain weather phenomena).

(vii) Knows about different forms of water affecting weather, e.g., humidity, fog, cloud, hail and snow.

(viii) Observes various weather phenomena and records them in pictographs.

(ix) Observes importance of soils in our life.

(x) Knows about usefulness of soils.

(xi) Classifies soils of the locality according to sizes of their particles and fertility.

(xii) Finds out how soil is kept fertile.

(xiii) Realizes the need of protecting soils from erosion.

MLLs of Class V EVS (Science)

Prevention of diseases and keeping fitness

(i) Knows about major sources of diseases.

(ii) Understands the usefulness of vaccination to prevent communicable diseases.

(iii) Suggests ways of collecting and disposing of garbage.

(iv) Applies simple first-aid skills.

(v) Reads thermometer to know body temperature.

(vi) Participates in child-to-child programme to save life of ailing infants, e.g., from diarrhoea.

Living things and environment

(i) Gives examples that animals and plants adapt themselves to environment.

(ii) Visualizes present and possible future harmful effects from diminishing forest cover, soil erosion and pollution.

(iii) Knows the present schemes (a few) to increase and improve forest cover, cleaning rivers, tanks and such others, e.g., Ganga.

Energy and work

(i) Knows important sources of energy used in daily life.

(ii) Understands how energy helps in doing work.

Man, science and environment

(i) Appreciates the importance of science in every day life.

(ii) Describes some outstanding achievements of science (discoveries and inventions).

(iii) Knows about dangers from the misuse of scientific knowledge e.g., in war.

(iv) Realizes the need of scientific ways of using environment and natural resources including conservation, e.g., soils, minerals, water and forests.

Competencies Based EVS (Science) Teaching

For each sub-competency effective and attractive procedures of teaching and learning should be followed. These sub-competencies are such that teaching techniques can be conveniently made activity based. The child should be given ample opportunities both individually and in groups, within the classroom and outside to observe, explore, analyse, interpret and appreciate the social and natural environment of which the child is an integral part. The text books and the teaching aids should be used for reinforcement of these processes.

Evaluation of Competencies Based EVS

Evaluation of learning outcomes should be integrated with the process of teaching and children's activities on a continuous basis. In classes I and II it may be largely observational and oral. Written tests may be gradually introduced from class III (and continued in classes IV and V) but should be supplemented by other techniques like observation, group participation, Learner-Learner interaction, Teacher-Learner interaction, Learner-material (learning material or teaching aids) interaction etc. The capacity of understanding and application of knowledge should be stressed in examinations rather than rote memorization.

General Objectives

Aims or goals are the general objectives, which cannot be achieved after a lesson. They can be achieved after completing the whole course, or even after that. Specific objectives can be achieved after completing a lesson.

Aims and objectives are not synonymous. They are different. There are different types of objectives—cognitive, effective and psychomotor. Cognitive objectives may be further classified into knowledge, understanding (comprehension) and application. Afffective objectives may also be further classified into receiving, responding, valuing, organisation and value complex.

If objectives are stated in behavioural terms, they can help the teacher in effective teaching and objective evaluation, and facilitate the children in meaningful learning. By behavioural objectives teachers know very clearly what to teach and what to evaluate, and children know what to learn. When stating objectives in behavioural terms certain key words are used to show the observable behaviour.

Objectives to be achieved after a lesson, after a course, after a term, after the school year when written in behavioural terms are called Learning Outcomes (LOs). In this chapter EVS (Science) syllabus for classes III, IV and V is divided into Units, and the syllabus of each Unit is written in terms of Learning Outcomes (LOs). This will give you a clear idea of Learning Outcomes (LOs) and of how they are written.

Minimum Levels of Learning (MLLs) at primay level are the Minimum Learning Outcomes (MLOs) which the children are to achieve when they pass the primary stage of education i.e., class V. MLLs in EVS (Science and Social Studies) for classes I and II, and in EVS (Science) for classes III, IV and V are given in this chapter. If you compare LOs and MLLs of classes III, IV and V EVS (Science) you will have an idea that MLLs are much less than LOs. Much work of MLLs based curriculum is being done these days throughout the country at formal as well as non-formal stage.

Questions

1. What is the difference between aims and objectives?
2. How can aims and objectives help teachers to teach EVS very effectively?
3. Select a topic from classes III-V EVS (Science), write down its general and specific objectives for a lesson plan.
4. What is the difference between cognitive, affective and psychomotor objectives? Explain with suitable examples.
5. Classify cognitive objectives into three categories. Give examples of each.
6. Classify affective objectives into five categories. Give examples of each.
7. Select a topic of your choice from classes III—V EVS (Science). Write ten behavioural objectives for this topic.
8. How can the behavioural objectives help the teacher, the child and the author?
9. Write 5 key words to be used in behavioural objectives for each of the following :
   - *(a)* Knowledge,
   - *(b)* Understanding (Comprehension),
   - *(c)* Application.
10. What do you mean by learning outcomes? Write 10 LOs for a topic from classes III—V EVS (Science).
11. What do you mean by MLLs?
12. How MLLs are different from LOs?
13. How MLLs are similar with LOs?
14. Do MLOs and MLLs mean the same? Why?
15. How is MLLs based EVS (Science) curriculum different from the existing EVS (Science) curriculum?

7

Children and Learning

Piaget's Work

The conclusions that Piaget had drawn from his many studies have led to a recognition of the difference in the way in which a child thinks at each stage of development—pre-operational, concrete operational and formal operational.

Pre-Operational Stage–At this stage a child begins to construct sentences. He learns to respond to the external world by means of symbols. He does not view his world as composed of 'constants'. Properties of objects, do not remain invariant for him. He does not have concept of conservation and is misused by perception. Preoperational children cannot understand science and mathematics concepts unless they do activities with concrete objects several times by their own hands.

Concrete Operational Stage–At this stage a child begins to structure basic ideas of conservation in the sense that certain properties of objects remain invariant. At this stage a child must have real objects upon which to operate—both physically and mentally. The child can organise data from objects which are present in his immediate environment but he cannot formulate generalizing hypotheses or mentally abstract all possible combinations of a given problem. Concrete operational children cannot understand Science and Mathematics concepts unless they do activities with concrete objects at least once by their own hands.

Formal Operational Stage–At this stage a child exhibits the ability to form hypotheses and deduce possible results from these hypotheses. He can think in terms of all possible combinations for a given problem and he can function at an abstract level without the necessity of preceiving the objects. Formal operational children can understand science and mathematics concepts even without doing activities with concrete objects by their own hands.

It implies from Piaget's work that at primary school level most of the children will be either at pre-operational or concrete operational stage and very few will be at formal operational stage. Therefore majority of primary school children will be unable to understand science and mathematics concepts and skills without working with concrete objects. Therefore, manipulating the objects, observing and performing experiments are very essential for primary school children in order to learn science.

Although a considerable amount of research had been carried out in United States, United Kingdom, and Switzerland, yet so far little investigation of the cognitive development of Indian primary school children was done in India. Therefore it was thought that research studies of this type might be useful specially at the time when primay science education was spreading so rapidly in Indian schools. The results of such studies might have significant implication for revising the existing primary science curricula, instructional materials and the teaching techniques.

Identifying the Research Problem : The research studies were to analyse what percentage of primary school children (class I-V) are at (i) pre-operational, (ii) concrete operational, and (iii) formal operational stage.

Conducting of the Research Studies–The studies were carried out in two phases.

Phase-I

Population : The sample from which these data were gathered was drawn from 9 Delhi Schools. These schools were selected from different localities of Delhi. The sample comprises of different type of schools.

A random sample of 50 students was taken from each school, 10 from each of the five classes (I—V). Thus 450 students (177 boys and 273 girls) were used in this study.

Selection of Schools : Education Officers of Municipal Corporation Delhi (MCD) and New Delhi Municipal Committee (NDMC) and Principals of the Government, Government-Aided and Public schools were invited to participate in this study. MCD was requested for 4 schools (Urban 2—1 Boys, 1 Girls; Rural 2—1 Boys, 1 Girls). NDMC was requested for 2 schools (1 Boys, 1 Girls). But only 9 schools could be obtained to participate in the study—MCD-2, NDMC-1, Government-2, Government Aided-3 and unaided public-1. None of these schools was from rural areas. Random sample of schools therefore, could not be obtained and selection of sample was on the willingness of the schools to participate.

Tools : The Piaget type tasks developed and used at Florida State University (USA) were slightly modified by the investigator and used in this study.

They are as follows :

(i) More-Less-Same Task

(ii) Number Task

(iii) Area Task

(iv) Weight Task

(v) Displacement Volume Task

Material for Tasks

The material used for these TASKS is very simple.

Tasks

These tasks were given to the children. 'E' is used for Experimenter and 'S' is used for the subject.

Equipment

6 squares of paper all of same colour and same type of paper—one 3 cm square, one 6 cm square, two 9 cm square, one 12 cm square and one 15 cm square [Fig.].

E places the 6 squares of paper on the table and says, "Here we have some pieces of paper. I am going to take one piece of paper." E takes one of the 9 cm squares, places it on his side of the table and says, "I am going to give you the other pieces of paper". E should put the other pieces near S.

(A) Then E should say, "Pick one of your pieces of paper that has more paper than my piece of paper" [Fig.].

(B) Next E should say, "Pick one of your pieces of paper that has less paper than my piece of paper" [Fig.].

(C) Next E should say, "Pick one of your pieces of paper that has the same amount of paper as my piece of paper" [Fig.].

Number Task

Equipment : 10 red circles of paper, 10 black circles of paper (all of the same size of 50 paisa coin) [Fig.].

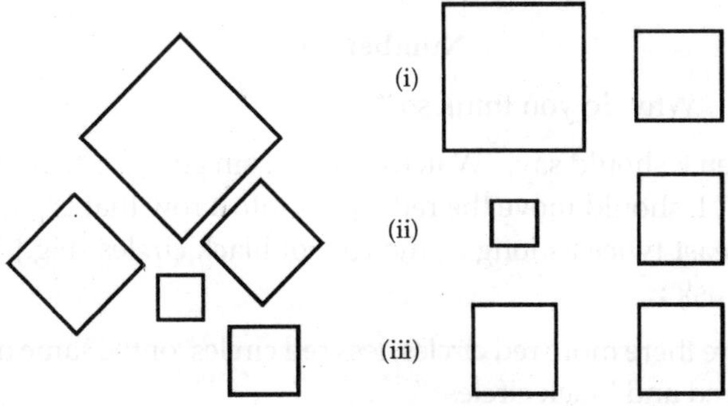

More Less–Same Task

E places and red circles on the table in front of S. The circles are placed in a straight line keeping about 2 cm space between each circle. Then E gives S 10 black circles and says, "I want you to make a row of black circles beside the row of red circles. Make your row so that there is one red circle for each black circle" [Fig.].

If S does not establish the one-to-one correspondence then E may say, "Are you sure that there is one black circle for each red circle?" If S still maintains that there is the same number of red and black circles, then E should terminate the task by saying, "let us try another game."

If S establishes the necessary equivalance, then E should say, 'Watch closely, I am going to move the red circles in a group" [Fig.]. E should not stack the circles one on top of another. Then E should ask:

A. "Are there more red circles, less red circles or the same number of red and black circles?"

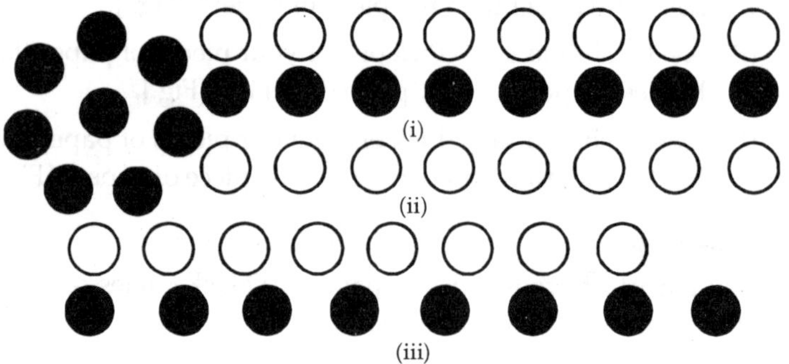

Number Task

(a) "Why do you think so?'

Then E should say, "Watch closely, I am going to move the red circles", E should move the red circles into a row that is parallel to and atleast twice as long as the row of black circles [Fig.] Then E should ask :

B. "Are there more red circles, less red circles, or the same number of red and black circles?"

(b) "Why do you think so?"

After S had responded E should say, "let's pretend that these (pointing the red circles) are chocolates wrapped in red paper and those (pointing the black circles) are the same kind of chocolates wrapped in black paper. Suppose I told you that you could have either the chocolates wrapped in red paper or the chocolates wrapped in black paper, which chocolates would you rather have?"

C. "Would you get more chocolates, less or same amount?"

"Why do you think so?"

Area Task

Equipment: 1 square piece of green paper of about 20 cm side, 4 squares of red paper of 2 cm side [Fig.].

E places the square piece of green paper on the table and says, "let's pretend this is a grass land." Then E places the four small red squares on the green square close to four comers [Fig.] and says, "Let's pretend these are houses, and there is a cow (showing the picture of a cow if available) who can eat this grass. Look at all the grass that the cow can eat."

E then says, "Now let's place the houses like this (four squares are put together touching each other at about the middle of the green paper)" [Fig.]. Then E should ask:

A. "Does the cow have more grass to eat, less grass to eat, or the same amount of grass to eat?' '

(a) "Why do you think so?"

E then arranges the red squares in a row with some distance apart at one side of the green paper [Fig.] and says, "let's place the houses like this". Then E should ask:

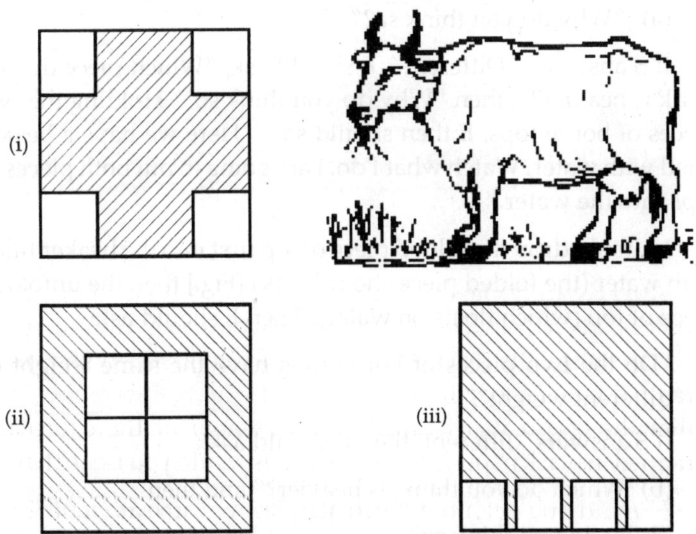

Fig. Area Task

B. "Does the cow have more grass to eat, less grass to eat, or the same amount of grass to eat?"

"Why do you think so?"

Weight Task

Equipment: 10 tops of milk bottles, one beaker or glass tumbler containing water [Fig.].

(If tops of milk bottles are not available something like this made by aluminium foil or tin foil may be used).

E places 4 tops of milk bottles on the table. [Fig.] E then asks, "Here we have some tops of milk bottles. Pick up the 2 pieces that have the same weight." E should take those two tops and remove the other two from the table [Fig.].E then says, "Watch closely, I am going to fold one of these pieces." E should proceed to fold one piece of top as many times as possible. [Fig.] Then E should ask:

A. "Look at the two pieces of the tops. Do these pieces of tops have the same weight or different weight?"

If S answers "same" then E should ask :

(a) "Why do you think so?"

If S answers, "Different", E should ask, "Which piece do you think is heavier?", then "Why do you think so?" Holding the two pieces of bottle tops, E then should say, "Here we have a beaker filled with water. Watch what I do. I am going to put both pieces of tops into the water."

E should drop the folded piece of top first into the beaker filled with water (the folded piece should sink) [Fig.] then the unfolded piece of top (which floats on water). Then E should ask:

B. "Do the two pieces of bottle tops have the same weight or different weight?"

If S answers 'different' then E should ask :

(b) Which do you think, is heavier?" and then :

"Why do you think so?"

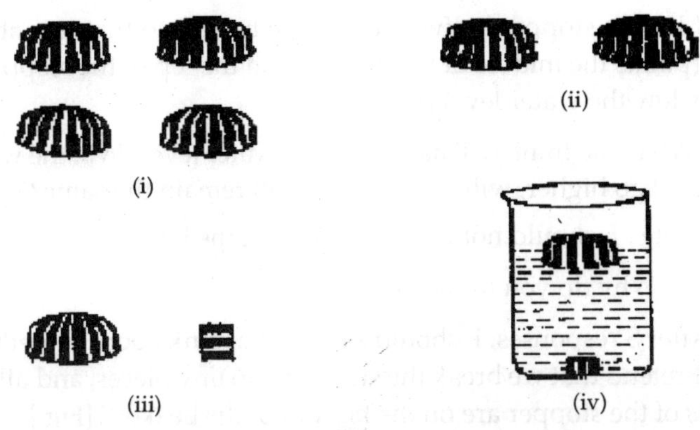

Weight Task

Displacement Volume Task

Equipment: One beaker or glass tumbler 2/3 full of water, one rubber stopper with hole, one piece of thread, one rubber band [Fig.].

E shows a beaker or glass tumbler about 2/3 full of water, and then asks, "Do you know what I mean by water level? Can you point to the water level on this beaker?" If S does not understand the term "Water Level", then E may show "top of the water." Then E should say, "I will hold the beaker while you put his rubber band on the beaker at the water level. Place the rubber band so that it is even with the water level. After S does this (E may help if necessary) E should say, ' 'Here I have a rubber stopper tied with a thread. If I lower the stopper into the beaker, the stopper sinks to the bottom of the beaker" [Fig.].

Then E should say, "What you think will happen to the water level in the beaker? Will the water level go higher, will go lower or will remain same?" After the response E asks, "Why do you think so?" (Responses to these questions are not to be recorded and scored).

After response, E then lowers the stopper so that it is on the bottom of the beaker [Fig.] and asks, "What happened to the water level." After the response (not recorded) E says, "Now pretend that I lift the stopper halfway up in the beaker so that it is about here (points the middle of the beaker) and the top of the stopper is still below the water level [Fig.].

A. "What you think will happen to the water level? Will the water level go higher, will go lower, or will remain the same?"

(Note : E should not lift the stopper in the beaker).

(a) "Why do you think so?"

After S responses, E should say, "Let's think about something else. Pretend that we break the stopper into tiny pieces, and all the pieces of the stopper are on the bottom of the beaker" [Fig.].

Then E should ask :

B. "What will happen to the water level? Will the water level be higher, lower or will it remain same?"

(b) "Why do you think so?"

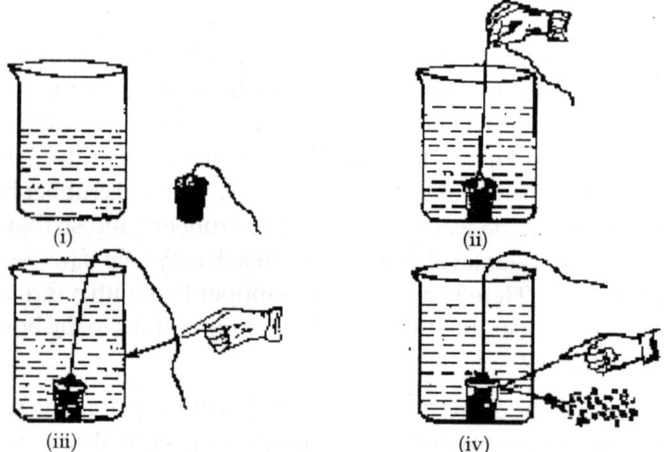

Displacement Volume Task

Putting the Child in a Cognitive Stage

(i) ***Pre-operational :*** If a child is a non-conserver for all the tasks.

(ii) ***Concrete operational :*** If a child is conserver for some tasks and non-conserver for others.

(iii) ***Formal operational*** : If a child is conserver for all the tasks.

Scoring the Tasks

Categories	*Criteria*
1. Conserver	Selects all correct choices and gives an acceptable reason for each choice..
2. Transitional	S selects atleast one correct choice with an acceptable reason.
3. Non-conserver	S selects all incorrect choices.

Recording of Responses

The responses were recorded on Interview Response Sheets, the SAMPLE of which is given below :

Interview Response Sheet

Date ....

Child's Name .... Class .... Age ....

Task No. 1 : More-Less-Same

(A) Child chooses larger piece of paper (Yes/No)

(B) Child chooses smaller piece of paper (Yes/No)

(C) Child chooses same size of paper (Yes/No)

Category 1 2 3

TASK No. 2	Number
(A)	
(a)	
(B)	
(b)	
(c)	
(c) Category 1 2 3	

TASK No. 3	Area

(A)

(a)

(B)

(b) Category 1 2 3

TASK NO. 4	Weight

(A)

(a)

(B)

(b) Category 1 2 3

TASK NO. 5	Displacement Volume

(A)

(a)

(B)

(b) Category 1 2 3

Comments (Tick one)

Child is (i) Pre-operational

(ii) Concrete operational

(iii) Formal operational

(Interviewer's Signature) Name :

* Responses were recorded on such Interview Response Sheets and scored (a) to put the child in one of 3 categories—(1) Conserver, (2) Transitional, or (3) Non Conserver for each Task and finally (b) to put the child in one of the 3 Cognitive stages—(i) Pre-operational, (ii) Concrete operational, or (iii) Formal operational.

Experimental Procedure

(a) Two teachers from each of the 9 selected schools were invited in a 6-day training workshop. Not all the schools sent 2 teachers. Three of them sent only one teacher each and six of them sent two teachers per school. Thus 15 teachers participated in the study. These teachers were imparted 30 hours training by the investigator, for interviewing the children, recording their responses on the tasks on a prescribed Interview Response Sheet. They were also trained in analysing the data to decide the category of the child whether he/she is at pre-operational, concrete operational or formal operational stage.

(b) These teachers then took a random sample of 50 students (10 from each of the five classes I—V) from their respective schools and interviewed them during January-February 1976. They recorded the children's responses on the Interview Response Sheets and categorised them in respective cognitive stages—pre-operational, concrete operational and formal operational.

All the experimental schools were visited by the investigator during the period when the teachers were interviewing the children. It was found that the uniform work was going on in all the experimental schools. Interviews of some of the children were taped and photographs were taken. 35 mm coloured slides were also made.

(c) The experimental school teachers again gathered in a 6-day workshop (February 1976) to analyse the data which they collected from their respective schools. They listened to audio-taped interviews, recorded the responses of the children on the Interview Response Sheets and categorised each child in one of the three cognitive stages—pre-operational, concrete operational or formal operational. Their analysis was discussed till all the participating teachers agreed to place a particular child in the same cognitive stage.

Then each of the teachers rechecked the Interview Response Sheets of their students, and made the necessary corrections if any in putting the children in respective cognitive stages. Then double and final checks were made by the teachers on the Interview Response Sheets filed by him, till they were quite certain that they put their children in the right cognitive stages.

Percentages of the children at each cognitive stage were calculated for each school. The results of each school were added up and percentages of the children at the three cognitive stages (in each of the classes I—V) were calculated and recorded.

Similar analysis was made for the four tasks (Number, Area, Weight, Displacement Volume) given to the children, and percentages of the children, conservers to these tasks in each of the classes (I—V) were determined and recorded.

Cognitive comparison of boys and girls and cognitive comparison of children in different type of schools were also made.

Phase-II

Population and Selection of Schools

In the second phase (1976-77) the study was replicated with similar method. This time a bigger sample of 15 schools was taken including 5 schools from rural areas. The sample consisted of 756 children—boys-365, girls = 391 [class I = 152, class II—148, class III—152, class IV—152 and class V—152] (Tables) from 15 Delhi schools—MCD = 8, NDMC = 2, Government = 1, Government-Aided = 2, Public = 2 [urban boys = 3, urban girls = 5, urban coeducational = 2, rural boys = 3 and rural girls = 2].

Tools and Experimental Procedure

The same Piaget-type tasks were used. 29 teachers, one or two from each experimental school were similarly trained (like PHASE—I) in a 6-day workshop (December 1976) to interview the children for these tasks as well as to record and analyse data. They took a random sample of about 50 children, about 10. from each of the five classes I.

- — V in their respective schools, and interviewed them during January
- — February 1977. These teachers from experimental schools were again invited in a 6-day workshop during February 1977 to analyse the data, which they collected and same technique was used as in PHASE-I to place the children in right categories of cognitive stages.

The results of each school were added up and percentages of the children at the three cognitive stages (in each of the classes I—V) were calculated and recorded.

Similar analysis was made for the four tasks (Number, Area, Weight and Displacement Volume) given to the children, and percentages of the children conservers to these tasks in each of the classes I—V were determined and recorded.

Cognitive comparison of boys and girls, cognitive comparison of urban and rural children and cognitive comparison of children in different types of schools were also made.

Finally the results of Phases I and II were averaged.

Findings and Implications : The findings of the studies are as follows :

(1) In primary classes only 4.4% children are formal operational and the remaining 95.6% are either pre-operational (45.8%) or concrete operational (49.8%). This shows that only 4.4% of primary school children can understand science concepts and skills without working with concrete objects and for the remaining 95.6% children working with concrete objects is absolutely necessary otherwise they will not be able to learn science and will memorize without understanding.

(2) In classes I and II, it was found that no child was formal operational and a majority of children was at pre-operational stage. (class I = 76.3%, class II = 61.7%). These children are unable to understand science concepts and skills even if they work with concrete objects, till they reach concrete operational stage. Therefore they will have to have continuous experience of manipulating the concrete objects. This again shows that these children will have to do experiments and repeat them again and again in order to learn science [On the basis of these findings class I—II science syllabus was revised and activities were developed].

(3) In classes III, IV and V a majority of children is at concrete operational stage (class III—54.1%, class IV—63.7%, class

V—69.2%), and hence these children need concrete objects to learn science and without experiments they are unable to learn science concepts and skills.

(4) It was found that certain concepts are difficult to understand at a certain age (class) level e.g., a majority of classes I—II children (I = 78.5% as only 21.5% are conservers, II = 62.5% as only 33.7% are conservers) is unable to understand the concept of Number, though the concept is taught in classes I and II, and children memorize without understanding, as they memorize tables.

Similarly a majority of classes I—IV children is unable to understand the concept of area, weight and displacement—volume. Therefore these concepts should not be taught in these classes, and it is suggested that such a study should be replicated for more concepts to be collected from the existing primary science texts; and if it is found that some of these concepts are not compatible with the cognitive level of children, they should be deleted from that class and shifted to next higher classes where children could understand them.

(5) If we compare the results of phase-I (1975-76) with those of phase-II (1976-77), we find that they are very similar. In phase-II 4.3% of the primary school children were found as formal operational against 4.4% in phase I, the remaining 96.7% were pre-operational or concrete operational. In classes I—II in both the phases none of the children was formal operational. Most of them were pre-operational and the rest concrete operational. In phase—I (1975-76) the percentage of formal operational children was 4.4 in class III and 3.3 in class IV which was not logical, but in phase—II these percentages were 2.0 for class III and 6.5 for class IV, which are quite logical.

(6) When cognitive comparison of boys and girls was made, it was found that there was not much difference between the cognitive development of boys and girls, though percentage of formal operational boys (5.1%) was slightly higher than that of girls (3.6%).

(7) When cognitive comparison of urban and rural children was made, it was found that percentage of formal operational urban children (5.1%) was slightly higher than that of rural children (1.9%).

(8) When cognitive comparison of children in different types of schools was made, it was found that there was not much difference between the cognitive development of children in different types of schools, as percentages of formal operational children in different types of schools are very close (public = 4.5%, MCD = 4.1%, NDMC = 6.0%, Govt-Aided = 3.1%, Govt. = 4.0%).

These studies reveal that experiments are very essential for primary school children and without experiments these children will not be able to understand any science concept or skill and will memorize without understanding. It implies therefore that existing teaching techniques to teach science to primary school children should be revised. 'Reading a science text book' or 'listening to the teacher' will not work. Children should be involved in doing experiments by their own hands. The traditional teaching practices 'book reading' or 'teacher telling' should be discouraged. Activities should be developed in which concrete objects are involved, and they should be introduced in the existing primary science texts in place of those which do not involve concrete objects.

Conclusions : The purpose of these studies was to find out what percentage of primary school children (class I—V) are at (a) pre-operational, (b) concrete operational and (c) formal operational stage. The studies were done on 1206 children from 24 Delhi school of different localities (Tables). About 300 hours were spent on interviewing the children. It was found that majority of the primary school children is either pre-operational or concrete operational and a very small percentage is at formal operational stage (Table). Therefore working with concrete objects or doing experiments is a very important part of primary science education programme. The sample obtained might be considered to be somewhat representative of the school population within Delhi. Similar results for children could be expected in other schools of Delhi and elsewhere in the country.

Recommendations : The following recommendations are based on these studies for the purpose of providing information to teachers who teach science to primary school children, and to science educators who develop instructional material—text books, teacher guides, equipment etc. and design teaching techniques.

1. Discourage traditional teaching techniques like 'book reading' or 'teacher telling'.
2. Involve children in activities with concrete objects and doing experiments by their own hands.
3. Encourage children to find out science facts by doing experiments and not memorise.
4. Delete the science concepts and skills from the existing science texts which are not compatible with the cognitive level of children.
5. Delete the activities from the existing primary science texts which do not involve concrete objects.
6. Use environment and local resources which is full of real and concrete objects when teaching science to primary school children.

Impact of Research Studies

Class I-II Science Programme : NCERT developed a new primary science programme "Science is doing" which was introduced in 40 Delhi schools in 1970 as a pilot project under UNICEF assisted Science Education Programme (SEP), and then this programme was used in all the 1800 primary schools in Delhi. The programme consisted of class III—V Science Text Books and Teacher Guides. But for classes I and II it had only the prescribed syllabus. Therefore it was felt necessary that there should be at least something in the hands of the teachers teaching science to classes I—II children. This project was carried out in three phases with the help of primary school teachers, teacher educators, and science supervisors ofMCD, NDMC, TTI, CIE, and Directorate of Education, Delhi.

PHASE-I—Revision of Science Syllabus : On the basis of the findings of "Research Studies on the Cognitive Development of

Delhi Primary School Children" and feedback from 106 Primary schools, necessary changes were made in the NCERT ciass I—II science syllabus and revised syllabus (so developed) was approved by the curriculum committee of Delhi Administration.

PHASE-II—Development of Activities : In a series of workshops 72 activities for class I and 78 activities for class II were developed on the revised syllabus, taking into consideration the findings of the Research Studies on Cognitive Development of Delhi Primary School Children. These activities could be performed with cheap materials either available in the Primary Science Kit or to be obtained from the environment.

PHASE-III—Class I—II Science Teachers' Guides : In the final phase Experimental Editions of class I—II science Teachers' Guides were prepared.

These Teachers' Guides were tried out in 42 Delhi schools. They were revised after getting feedback from experimental schools. Then they were distributed to all the 1800 primary schools in Delhi free of cost for the use of teachers teaching science to classes I—II.

Revision of Existing Teaching Techniques : Even after the introduction of 'Science is Doing' in Delhi schools teaching practices like 'reading a book', and 'teacher telling' were very common, though 'discussion-demonstration method' was also being used by some enthusiastic teachers. Even by the teacher educators, lecture-demonstration method was being used in teacher training programmes.

But teachers teach the way they are taught. If we lecture them that they should involve the children in doing experiments, they will never do, unless we also involve the teachers in doing experiments by their own hands in teacher training programmes.

On the basis of the findings of the "Research Studies on the Cognitive Development of Delhi Primary School Children", a 'Teacher Training Package for class III, IV and V Science', was developed. This package was developed by the Science Supervisors and teacher educators of MCD, NDMC, TTI, CIE and Directorate of Education, Delhi under the supervision of Siddiqi who conducted these studies.

About 1000 teachers were being trained to teach science to class III-V every year for several years with the help of the Teacher Training Package at 13 science centres (MCD =11, NDMC = 1, Science Branch, Directorate of Education Delhi-1). Science Branch also organised orientation programmes for teacher educators and resource persons. This new technique of teacher training had quite an impact on classroom teaching, our primary school children started doing activities by their own hands in small groups.

Crash Programme for Orientation of Delhi Primary School Teachers for Teaching Science with the help of Primary Science Kit: Just after the completion of first phase (December 1975—February 1976) of the 'Research Studies on the Cognitive Development of Delhi Primary School Children', it was felt that Delhi Primary School teachers should immediately be oriented to involve primary school children with concrete objects when teaching science. For this a crash programme was organised (May 11-15, 1976). 4742 primary school teachers were oriented in this programme to involve small children with concrete objects.

Revision of Primary Science Curriculum : 'Science is Doing' programme was started in 1990 in 40 Delhi schools as a pilot project was used in all the 1800 primary schools in Delhi. On the basis of the recommendation based on the 'Research Studies on the Cognitive Development of Delhi Primary School Children', 'Science is Doing' syllabus for classes I—V was revised. Environment which is full of real and concrete objects was taken into consideration when the revised science syllabus was formed, and the Instructional Materials were developed based on the revised Environmental Studies (EVS) Syllabus. The new curriculum is now called EVS Programme. This programme is developed at NCERT. It has the following materials :

(1) EVS class I—II (Science and Social Studies) Syllabus.

(2) EVS (Science) text books for classes III, IV and V.

These materials were tried out by the Science Branch, Directorate of Education, Delhi, in 50 Delhi schools. They were revised before implementation according to the feedback received from the experimental schools, taking into consideration the findings of the 'Research Studies on the Cognitive Development of Delhi Primary School Children'.

Handbooks of Activities Using Environment and Local Resources : According to the findings of the "Research Studies on the Cognitive Development of Delhi Primary School Children", majority of primary school children need concrete objects in order to learn science concepts and skills. Our environment is full of real and concrete objects, which the children can use to learn science. Based on the findings of these research studies and their implications a package of "Handbooks of Activities Using Environment and Local Resources" was developed at Science Branch, Directorate of Education, Delhi for the use of primary school teachers teaching science and social studies to classes I and II and science to classes III, IV and V. This programme was funded by UNICEF and consisted of an environmental kit and a package of seven booklets—

1. Classes I—II (Science & Social Studies) and Classes III-V (Science) Syllabus,
2. Environmental Kit Guide, (for the Environmental Kit developed)
3. Class I EVS (Science and Social Studies) Activities,

   Class II EVS (Science and Social Studies) Activities,

   Class III EVS (Science) Activities,

   Class IV EVS (Science) Activities, and

   Class V EVS (Science) Activities.

This was a bank of activities for the use of teachers. For one minor idea several activities were developed to be fit in different environments. This programme was developed with the help of primary school teachers, MCD and NDMC Science Supervisors, and teacher educators of CIE, NCERT and Directorate of Education, Delhi. This package was tried out in 56 Delhi schools—Rural, Urban, Boys, Girls, Co-educational, MCD, NDMC, Govt, Govt. Aided and Unaided Public schools. It was revised after getting feedback from experimental schools, before implementation, and the revised version was also translated from Hindi to English for the use of teacher's teaching EVS in English medium schools. The English version of the Handbook was also found very useful for those who were interested and engaged in developing such materials in other states of the country.

DIETs and Teaching-learning in Science

Why DIETs?

India has now more than 425 District Institutes of Education and Training (DIETs). The primary objective of the DIETs is to improve quality of pre-service and in-service education at elementary level.

Teaching-learning of Science in Delhi DIETs

In pre-service as well as in in-service teacher training programmes, Delhi DIETs train the teachers

(a) to identify the pre-operational, concrete operational and formal operational children in primary classes, and

(b) to use teaching strategies according to their cognitive levels.

In this way children learn better. They understand and do not memorise without understanding. They enjoy learning when they understand.

Identifying Cognitive Levels of Children by Delhi DIETs Trainees (1989-92)

ETE (Elementary Teacher Education) First year students during practice teaching in MCD Primary Schools in the years 1989-90, 1990-91, 1991-92 also identified what percentage of primary school children class I-V are at (a) pre-operational (b) concrete operational and (c) formal operational stage. The major findings of the studies were as follows:

During 1989-90

1. In primary classes only 9.9% children are formal operational and the remaining 90.1% are either pre-operational (38.6%) or concrete operational (51.5%). This shows that only 9.9% of primary school children can understand

science concepts and skills without working with concrete objects and for the remaining 90.1% of children working with concrete objects is a must, otherwise they will just memorise science.

2. In classes I and II it was found that none of the children was formal operational and a majority of children was at pre-operational stage (class I-86.6%) while in class II the majority was concrete operational (62.3%). In class I thus they will have to have continuous experience of manipulating concrete objects. Thus learning science through activities is essential for all classes.
3. In classes III, IV and V a majority of children are concrete operational viz., 49.2%, 70.8% and 62.2% which implies that without experimenting they are unable to learn science concepts and skills.

During 1990-91

Similarly for the data collected in 1990-91, it is found that in class I (65%) are pre-operational while in class II (78.3%) are concrete operational. In classes III (75.6%), IV (64.1%) and V (56.6%) most of the children are at concrete operational stage. While from Classes (I-V) 7.1% children are formal operational, 61.9% concrete operational and 31.0% are at pre-operational stage.

During 1991-92

The data collected in the year 1991-92 also shows similar trend. In class I (57.2%) children are pre-operational while in class II most are concrete operational (80%). While in classes III, IV and V majority of them are at concrete operational stage viz., 63.6%, 74.5% and 57.9% respectively. While from classes I-V 12.2% are formal operational, 63.7% concrete operational, 24.1% pre-operational.

The data from the practice teaching schools for all the three years showed similar trends which can be attributed to the care taken by the pupil teachers in teaching the students.

Comparative Study of Committee Development of Children in Urban and Rural Areas of Delhi by Delhi DIETs' Trainees (1994).

Percentage of Children in Different Cognitive Stages (I-V)

Class (Age) *Cognitive Stage*	*Year*	*I* *(6-7 yrs)*	*II* *(7-8 yrs)*	*III* *(8-9 yrs)*	*IV* *(9-10 yrs)*	*V* *(10-11 yrs)*	*I-V* *(6-11 yrs)*
Pre-operational	89-90	86.6%	37.7%	41.8%	25.2%	11.3%	38.6%
	90-91	65.0%	21.7%	16.7%	18.3%	23.3%	31.0%
	91-92	57.2%	11.4%	18.5%	9.0%	24.3%	24.1%
Concrete Operational	89-90	13.4%	62.3%	49.2%	70.8%	62.2%	51.5%
	90-91	35.0%	78.3%	75.6%	64.1%	56.6%	61.9%
	91-92	42.8%	80.0%	63.6%	74.5%	57.9%	63.7%
Formal Operational	89-90	0.0%	0.0%	9.0%	4.0%	26.5%	9.9%
	90-91	0.0%	0.0%	7.7%	17.6%	20.1%	7.1%
	91-92	0.0%	8.6%	17.9%	16.5%	17.8%	12.2%
No. of children interviewed	89-90	15	90	67	72	114	358
	90-91	20	60	68	67	30	245
	91-92	35	35	195	165	202	632
	Total	**70**	**185**	**330**	**304**	**346**	**1235**

Based on the data collected by ETE Ist year students during practice teaching in MCD Primary Schools under the guidance of their Foundation Lecturers, Mrs. Pratibha Sharma and Naresh Gupta.

In 1994, a comparative study of cognitive development of children in urban and rural areas of Delhi was undertaken. The sample size was 1000. The major findings are as follows:

1. In classes I-V in urban areas the no. of children in pre-operational stage are 45%; 52% in concrete operational stage and 3% in formal operational stage.
2. In rural area classes I-V the children in pre-operational, concrete operational and formal operational are 27%, 66% and 7% respectively.
3. It has been found that the number of children in concrete operational and formal operational stage are more in urban area than the rural area.

Percentage of Children in Different Cognitive Stages (I-V) Rural-Urban (1994)

Cognitive Stages	*Rural (400)*	*Urban (600)*
Pre-operational	45%	27%
Concrete Operational	52%	66%
Formal Operational	3%	7%

It also has the same trend as found by Siddiqi in his research studies discussed above.

Recommendations

The major recommendation based on the above findings indicate that:

1. The existing teaching teachniques should be replaced by Learner-Centred Method to enable the pupils to be actively engaged in activities and learning by doing.
2. Textbooks developed on activity based method should be introduced in the school curriculum to help the pupils to perform activities under the supervision of their teachers.

3. During the pre-service training the pupil teachers should be practically made aware of these methods to bring about a attitudinal change in them. This concept should be ingrained into the teaching methodologies whereby the teacher educators should present themselves as an ideal.
4. Use of kits available in the school, community resources and use of environment and local resources should be made of to make the teaching-learning process more effective.
5. Emphasis should be laid on the competency based teaching in schools and use of locally available material.
6. DIETs, trainees should identify the pre-operational, concrete operational and formal operational children in primary classes during their practice teaching, and should use teaching strategies according to their cognitive levels when teaching science. This process should also be practiced by regular primary school teachers so that children should understand and enjoy learning science.

Results and Implications

This research indicates that for cognitive development of children the books should be activity based and teaching should be Child Centred. Pre-service Teachers of Delhi DIETs classify their Primary School Children (I-V) into three categories.

(*a*) Pre-operational

(*b*) Concrete Operational

(*c*) Formal Operational

When they go to schools for practice teaching, they teach them according to their cognitive level. Hopefully, they will continue this practice when they become regular primary school teachers. Such work if done in other DIETs of the country, it will have very useful impact on the quality of education at primary level.

SEP

UNICEF, Assisted Science Education Programme (SEP) was started in the Union Territory of Delhi in July 1970 SEP brought "Science is Doing' programme for primary classes. This programme was used in Delhi primary schools till 1978. After this Environmental Studies, EVS started, and now this is being used in all Delhi primary schools. This change is very much related with the findings of the studies undertaken in 1975-76 and 1976-77 and are discussed.

Several primary level science texts are available in the market, they are mostly content oriented. Though 'Learning By Doing' is accepted as the best way of learning science, yet reading a textbook or listening to the teacher when he reads the book, are still in use in our primary science classes. It appears that curriculum planners, text-book writers, apparatus designers and teachers have generally gone about their work without taking into consideration the cognitive stages (pre-operational, concrete operational and formal operational) of primary school children for whom the materials which they produce, are intended.

NEP, 1986 document has two recommendations for Science Education.

Science education will be strengthened so as to develop in the child well defined abilities, and values such as the spirit of inquiry, creativity, objectivity and the courage to ask questions.

Science education programme will be designed to enable the learner to acquire problem solving and decision making skills and to discover the relationship of science with health, agriculture, industry and other aspects of daily life.

If we really want to implement these recommendations we will be very choosy in selecting "What?" and "How?" "What we teach?" and "How we teach?" must be compatiable with the cognitive level of children. The research studies discussed in this chapter will provide guidelines for those who are really interested in this type of work.

Questions

1. Name three cognitive stages of primary school children as identified by Piaget. Describe the characteristics of the child at each stage.

2. (a) How will you find out whether a child is conserver, transitional or non-conserver for the following tasks?

   (i) Number Task

   (ii) Area Task

   (iii) Weight Task

   (iv) Displacement Volume Task

   (b) How will you put a child in a cognitive stage?

   (i) Number Task

   (i) Pre-operational

   (ii) Concrete Operational

   (iii) Formal Operational

   (c) How should we teach science to children of each cognitive stage?

3. Answer the following questions.

   (i) What is the percentage of formal operational children in classes I and II? How should we teach science to these children?

   (ii) What is the percentage of pre-operational, concrete operational and formal operational children in primary classes I-V? How should we teach science to these children?

4. Answer the following questions?

   (i) What is the percentage of conservers in primary classes I, II, III, IV, V (I-V) ? for the following concepts :

   (a) Number

   (b) Area

   (c) Weight

   (d) Displacement Volume

(ii) In which classes do we start teaching these concepts, and in which class should we teach? Why so?

5. (a) Summarise the Findings, Implications, Recommendations and Conclusions of the Research studies discussed in this chapter.

(b) What was the impact of these studies on Primary Science Education ?

(c) How Delhi DIETs used the findings of these studies in teaching science at primary level ?

6. Answer the following questions.

(i) What is the percentage of pre-operational, concrete operational and formal operational children in classes I, II, III, IV and V? How should we teach science to these children?

(ii) What is the percentage of pre-operational, concrete operational and formal operational children in primary classes I-V? How should we teach science to these children?

7. Answer the following questions.

(i) What is the percentage of pre-operational, concrete operational and formal operational children at primary level in rural and urban areas?

(ii) Why is this difference?

(iii) How should we teach rural primary school children?

(iv) How should we teach urban primary school children?

8. (a) Describe the recommendations, results and implications of the "Studies on Cognitive Development of Primary School Children" conducted by Delhi DIETs trainees during 1989 90, 1990-91, 1991-92 and 1994.

(b) What will be the impact of such studies on pre-service and in-service education imparted by DIETs?

8

The Resources

At primary level most of the children cannot understand what we teach them in EVS or Science, unless they do some activities by their own hands using concrete objects. If they are not given this opportunity they will memorise without understanding.

We do not want this. So involve your students in doing.

At primary level when teaching EVS, there is lot of scope for doing activities. For doing activities there is a provision of Primary Science Kit, and a Mini Tool Kit. The materials present in the Primary Science Kit can be used by your students for doing activities. Tools present in the Primary Science Kit and the Mini Tool Kit may be used to improvise some low cost or no cost teaching aids for doing some activities. Outdoor physical facilities and Community Resources can also be used for effective teaching of EVS and Science.

Primary Science Kit

Under the Operation Black Board (OB) a number of essential facilities have been listed, one of which is the Primary Science Kit. The NCERT has been engaged upon the development of a Primary Science Kit since 1969. After having developed a prototype, the NCERT sent the Primary Science Kit to all the states and UTs in 1970s. A number of states and UTs manufactured Primary Science Kits on the design of the NCERT Prototype.

The Primary Science Kit developed in 1970s has undergone several revisions and modifications. This has been necessary because of changes in the curriculum—from "Science is Doing" to "EVS". The latest 1986 Model of the Primary Science Kit has altogether 81 items.

I.	Low Cost Equipment	46 items
II.	Hand Tools	8 items
III.	Consumables	19 items
IV.	Chemicals	8 items

The kit basically is a demonstration kit. The lid of the box is chalkboard. It costs Rs. 300.00.

When you are teaching EVS by EVS Approach, you can eliminate many out of 81 items, which you can procure from the local resources—your home, children homes, school etc. Identify those items, eliminate them, procure them from the local resources, and do all the activities of EVS (Science)

Low Cost Equipment

For Measuring Experiments

1. Half Metre Scale
2. Polyethylene or Glass Beaker (100 ml.) S. Funnel
3. Funnel
4. Rectangular Hollow Vessels (equal volume)
5. Measuring Cylinder (100 ml.)
6. Hollow Cubic Decimetre (l0 cmx l0 cmx 10 cm) vessel
7. Cubic Centimetre (1 cm x 1 cm x 1 cm) block
8. Syringe—Transport Plastic Parts
9. Spring Balance (1 kg)
10. Weight (1 kg)
11. Top Pan Spring Balance (2 kg)

For Mechanics Experiments

12. Water Wheel
13. Pulley

14. Model of Water Pump
15. Wind Vane

For Optics Experiments

16. Hand Lens (Magnifying Glass)

For Heating Experiments

17. Test Tube (150 mm x 25 mm)
18. Test Tube (15 mm x 125 mm)
19. Kerosene Burner
20. Tripod Stand with Wire Gauge
21. Thermometer (10°C—110°C)
22. Clinical Thermometer

For Magnetic Experiments

23. Pair of Bar Magnets
24. Compass Needle

For Electricity Experiments

25. Electric Circuit Board with Battery, Bulb, Switch and Electric Motor Stand
26. Electric D.C. Motor with Pulley

For Miscellaneous Experiments

(To be Procured from Environment—School, home)

27. Football Pump
28. Torch (2 cells)
29. Small and Big Balls
30. Aluminium Katori
31. Aluminium Tubes
32. Plane Mirror in Plastic Frame
33. Sieve
34. Wedge
35. Sheet Board having 8 cm x 8 cm Square Hole

(To Be Procured from School, Home and Market)

36. Super Enammelled Copper Wire (24 SWG)
37. Marbles
38. Glass Jar (Jam Bottle)
39. Glass Rod
40. Comb (Plastic)
41. Plastic Tubing
42. Tumblers
43. Polythelene Bags
44. M.S. Wire
45. Same Volume Solid Cylinders (Aluminium, Steel, Wood)
46. Tailor's Measuring Tape

Hand Tools (8 Items)

1. Triangular File
2. Claw Hammer
3. Hand Drill (with Screw Drills)
4. Knife
5. Pliers
6. Hack Saw
7. Tin Cutter
8. Screw Driver

Consumables (19 Items)

(to be purchased when needed)

1. rubber stoppers
2. test tubes
3. rock samples
4. blades for hacksaw frame
5. blotting paper
6. card board

7. cotton thread
8. cellophane sheet
9. iron nails
10. drawing pins
11. plasticine
12. rubber balloons
13. rubber bands
14. sand paper
15. sealing wax
16. straws
17. steel wire
18. gum
19. vaseline

Chemicals (8 Items)

(To be purchased when necessary)

1. Calcium Superphosphate (fertilizer)
2. Copper Sulphate Crystals
3. Glycerine
4. Common Salt
5. Potassium Permanganate
6. Sugar
7. Washing Soda
8. Urea (Ammonium Sulphate)

Primary Science Kit Manual comes along with the Kit, which has all the details.

There are uses of all the 46 items of low cost equipments. Illustrated diagrams of most of the items are also given.

Use all this material plus a lot of material from your environment to do all the activities.

Mini Tool Kit

Mini Tool Kit is one of those items which are short listed as the essential facilities at the primary stage under Operation Black Board (OB). Hand tools for children of the Primary School have been specially designed by NCERT in 1988, keeping in view their physical and mental ability. The kit costs Rs. 125.00 and has small and light tools which primary school child can use very easily. The Kit has (22 items):

1. Vice
2. Half Round Rasp
3. Multi-tool Body
4. Carpenter Saw
5. Carpentry Chisel
6. Screw Driver
7. Triangular File
8. Collet and Flat Drills
9. Junior Hacksaw
10. Cutting Blades
11. Hammer with Handle
12. The cutter-cum-pliers
13. Bicycle Wrench
14. Steel Ruler
15. Divider
16. Centre Punch
17. Pair of Magnets
18. Soldering Iron
19. Connecting wire with Crocodile clips
20. Cell Holder
21. PolyfabBag
22. Container Box

The tools of this kit may very easily be used by small children to make different things like :

1. Blade Holder
2. Pulley
3. Circuit Board
4. Insect Bottle
5. Tripod stand
6. Bulb Holder
7. Sun Dial
8. Flat Spring Balance
9. Table for Birds
10. Aquarium
11. Test-Tube Holder
12. Kerosene Burner
13. Laboratory stand
14. Wind Vane
15. Bow and Arrow Balance etc.

Mini Tool Kit Manual comes along with the Kit, which has all details.

Improving Equipment, Low Cost Learning Devices and Outdoor Physical Facilities

"Our education has got to be revolutionised. The brain must be educated through the hand. If I am a poet, I would write poetry on the possibilities of five fingers. Those who do not train hands, and go through the ordinary suit of education, lack music in their life".

— ***Mahatma Gandhi***

This shows how important are our hands, hands by which we can do experiments when learning science. For experiments we need some apparatus. We learned about the Primary Science Kit. We can do a number of experiments with the apparatus present in the kit when teaching science at primary level. Look at the list of equipment in the kit. Which of the items can you procure in your environment—school, house, neighbourhood for the day you need them for doing some experiments? Which of the items can you improvise? You can delete such equipment which you can procure from your environment or improvise.

For improvisation you need :

(i) Waste material,

(ii) Fitting and fixing material, and

(iii) Some ordinary workshop tools.

Workshop tools are already provided in the Primary Science Kit. You can use these tools to improvise apparatus.

You have also learnt about Mini Tool Kit. It has a set of small, handy and multipurpose workshop tools. The Kit Manual also gives guidelines in how to improvise some apparatus. Improvise that apparatus. If you need some apparatus which you think you can improvise when doing experiments at primary level, improvise it. The tools of the Mini Tool Kit will help you a lot. You can also collect some material from the environment and use it for improvisation. Improvised equipment is an example of low cost learning devices.

Your environment is full of resources which as such you can use for learning science.

Examples

(i) Bicycle is a wonderful teaching aid in learning science. You can use it to teach friction, forces, simple machines work, energy, pressure, good and bad conductors, vibrations in the bicycle bell etc. To learn so much science, you do not have to buy anything. You can use your own bicycle for learning all this science.

(ii) Kitchen is a wonderful place for learning science. You can learn a lot of science in your own kitchen like—boiling and freezing point, evaporation and boiling, condensation, solidification, solid-liquid-gas, good and bad conductors, fuels, flame, thermos flask, pressure cooker, water pressure, balanced diet, fats and carbohydrates, cooking and preservation of food, cooking and storage utensils, green vegetables, electric heater, cooking gas, stove etc.

These are outdoor physical facilities for learning science as well as no cost (not even low cost) learning devices.

Think of some other improvised apparatus and make it. Also think of some other low cost or no cost learning devices, and outdoor physical facilities for learning science at primary level, and use them. You will love to learn science on your own with such materials.

Community Resources

At primary level we teach EVS. In classes I-II EVS, it is an integrated package of social studies and science. In classes III-V EVS is taught as separate subjects, EVS (Social studies) and EVS (Social science). Community Resources are very valuable to teach EVS at this stage.

When we teach EVS, we use some materials of the Environment, which consists of family, house, school, neighbourhood, earth, sky and body. These materials as well as some people we can get from the community. Both these materials and people from the community can help us a lot to teach EVS.

Our family lives in the house. The house is built on a piece of land (earth). Many people come to our house like postman, plumber, electrician, doctor, carpenter, mason, telephone mechanic and so on. They come from neighbourhood. They are part of community. They are community resources. We go to neighbourhood and use different means of transport. We go to the market, railway station, bus terminal, airport, cinema halls, circus, fairs etc. We meet different type of people, and different type of materials at these places. These are also some community resources to learn EVS.

On earth we have rivers, roads, bridges, oceans, deserts, forests, mountains, different type of animals, plants and trees. In the rivers we see boats. In the ocean we see ships. In the sky we see aeroplanes. With all these some people are involved. These materials and people are some valuable community resources for learning EVS.

Look at your body. Some of us are tall. Some of us are short. Some of us are slim. Some of us are fat. Some of us have dark complexion. Some of us have fair complexion. We belong to different religions, states and countries but all of us have similar body parts. All of us have same body temperature 37°C. All of us are part of community. This also can help us a lot in learning EVS.

We can collect some materials from the environment, and we can use these materials as such or improvise a few things with the help of tools available in the Primary Science Kit and the Mini Tool Kit. This will also help us a lot in learning EVS. Wherever needed we can consult the concerned people of the community.

So our community is full of people, materials and places.

These are our community resources. When teaching EVS" think what of these resources you need. Procure these resources. Use them in various activities. Identify your role, and the role of your students, when using these resources for effective teaching of EVS.

Effective Manner

Teaching of science can be done in a proper and effective manner by means of various activities. For this various kinds of equipments are needed. Thus to perform these activities systematically and smoothly at primary level the primary science kit is furnished with 81 items (tools and equipment). Some equipment/apparatus can be improvised by the students and teachers according to their needs with the help of tools available in 'primary science kit' and 'mini tool kit'. We can have certain equipments, tools and resources from our community also. Experts in special fields, our houses, schools, neighbourhood etc. can be used as community resources. Apart from these earth and sky, can be useful community resources in teaching of science.

Questions

1. Make a list of any ten items present in the science kit, and write their uses.
2. Give some examples of low cost apparatus which can be improvised with the help of
   (a) mini tool kit and
   (b) hand tools of Primary Science Kit.
3. Of what topic of class II our neighbouring school garden may be used when teaching science?
4. How community resources be utilized in teaching of science?

9

EVS Course

Environmental Studies

Environmental Studies (EVS) is an important area of study at primary stage. Earlier, subjects like General Knowledge, Nature Study, General Science, Social Studies etc. were taught. Why has EVS replaced these subjects, what is the meaning of EVS and what is its significance? These are some questions which are discussed hereafter.

Teaching of language and numerical skills have always been the major concern of primary education. Emphasis has been on developing the three 'R's which meant reading, writing and arithmatic. Subsequently, however, it was considered necessary to impart some useful knowledge to the students. Subjects like General Knowledge and Nature Study became important. Later on, in place of these, more systematic subjects like General Science and Social Studies were introduced in primary schools. Teaching of these subjects, however was more information oriented and not very relevant to the child's need and requirements. The problem was discussed by the Kothari Commission which recommended teaching of Environmental Studies. Its contents were to be drawn from social sciences and natural sciences. After a decade, the Ishwar Bhai Patel Committee (1977) examined the concept of Environmental Studies and recommended that health education should also be included under Environmental Studies.

The main considerations for introducing EVS in primary education was a growing concern for environment, its conservation and improvement. By and large those who had this concern for environment appreciated the fact that man is a part of the natural environment but he is also the most powerful modifier. It is he who not only perceives and understands the laws of nature, but also manipulates them in his self-interest. It is he who sets the social and cultural environments.

Man tries to modify and bring about changes in natural and social environments. In doing so he sometimes indiscriminately destroys it, thereby creating imbalances and crisis.

Taking all this into consideration, it was thought necessary to give the child an awareness and understanding of the environment right from the early stages of education so that he may feel concerned about it. Environmental studies was introduced with this broad objective in mind. Thus environmental studies is the study of environment. Its main components are nature, man and society and the interaction between these components. The main objective of EVS is to help the child and to make him/her aware of the environment and feel concerned about it. To do so, the child systematically observes and explores the environment, asks questions related to various phenomena and events, records observations, collects data, analyses, classifies and compares it and draws inferences. Thus the child develops study skills that are useful for further learning and are also helpful in day-to-day living. The child also develops attitudes regarding conservation and preservation of environment and the ability to decide as to what is useful and good in the environment and develops the ability to take judicious decisions for affecting modifications and changes in the environment.

At the early stage of primary education the children should be provided opportunities to experience and interact with the immediate environment but gradually as they grow their mental horizons should be widened and they may be helped to understand the wider environment of which they and their own immediate environment is a part.

By its nature, EVS is flexible. The environment may vary from place to place, thus the content too would vary. However, there are some basic facets of environment which are universal. The content of a particular environment may be the source for developing some basic concepts (weather, family, economic interdependence amongst community members etc.) and competencies (scientific approach, civil behaviour, sanitary habits etc.) which may be universally.

EVS deals with the social and scientific aspects of the environment. These include social customs, traditions and other activities taking place around the children. It also deals with the psychological aspects of human activities. Such a study may draw its content from subjects like history, geography, sociology, social studies and sciences etc. but it does not cover the syllabus in the true forms where principles, generalisations in EVS are studied in an incidental manner as much as they are the part of the child's environment—near and remote, both in terms of time and space. Thus EVS has a close relationship with social studies and sciences but itself is not social studies and science in a strict sense.

Abilities to be Developed

It is expected that at the end of the study of the EVS Course, the following broad objectives (abilities) will be achieved :

The pupil teacher—

- understands the meaning and nature of EVS and its importance at the primary stage,
- understands the issues involved in constructing the curriculum in EVS,
- appreciates the significance of EVS in the primary education curriculum,
- develops interest and motivation in learning more about EVS from standard books and journals,
- develops skills to collect materials from different sources regarding the issues related to the environment.

The above statement of objectives is very broad and provides a basic framework. To impart meaningful educational experiences to the children, through environmental studies, it may be necessary to specify the objectives of EVS.

Specific Objectives

The learner—

- acquires knowledge about the objects, events, phenomena, processes taking place in the environment,
- develops an understanding of the cause effect relationship of events and phenomenon taking place in nature and society,
- observes keenly the things and processes around him,
- collects evidence and data and records them,
- analyses data, evidences, classifies and compares them in a given order,
- draws inferences and generalisations,
- develops attitudes and values such as objectivity, open-mindedness, perseverance, concern for maintenance and improvement of environment,
- develops the spirit of enquiry, inquisitiveness and scientific temper regarding natural and social phenomena,
- develops skills like performing experiments, reading and making tables and handling various kinds of tools etc.

The above instructional objectives do guide teachers and other functionaries to take some specific steps. However, for further clarification which is helpful in developing teaching-learning programmes it will be necessary to identify instructional objectives of each unit of teaching and specifying each objective in terms of observable pupil behaviour or performance e.g., identifies, draws lists, describes names, defines, gives examples etc.

Content and its Organisation

Every subject area has a particular content area of its organisation of curriculum. What are the characteristics of organisation of curriculum in environmental studies and what issues are involved in it?

In the national curriculum framework, for classes I and II environmental studies is taught as a composite area of study. From class III onwards, the courses follow a systematic pattern and it has been suggested that we should use examples and resources taken from the local environment while transacting the curriculum.

The chief characteristic of the syllabus in EVS is that science and social studies are integrated in classes I and II. The approach has been adopted because the child in the early stages interacts with the environment in its totality. The other characteristic of the curriculum for classes I and II is that it takes into account the immediate environment of the child. Units like "Our Family, Our House, Our School, Our Neighbourhood, Our Earth, Our Sky, and Our Body" have been identified and sequentially arranged. The teaching-learning programmes in these areas will expose the child to the things and happenings taking place in the child's immediate environment.

Therefore, selection of content for classes I and II would be based on the situations and resources available in the local environment. Thus a formal and rigid syllabus cannot be prescribed at this stage. Whatever themes (topics) have been identified in the national syllabus, are suggestive. The teacher is free to select the content from the local environment. He/she, however, has to see that minimum learning outcomes and the core components are attained by the students.

For the convenience of the teachers, the suggestive syllabus of EVS (Science and Social Studies) for Class I and II is as follows:

Class I and II (Science and Social Studies) Syllabus

Our Family: Small and large family; Mother's work; Father's work; Children's work; Plants give us fruit; Plants give us vegetables; Plants give us pulses and cereals; Animals give us food; Utensils and fuels; Recreation; Festivals; Pet animals; Domestic animals.

Our House: We need house, Animals need house; Types of houses; House and its cleaning; Our clothes; Kinds of clothes.

Our School: School building; School staff; Things in school; Things around School; Health habits; Good manners.

Our Neighbourhood: Things around us; Market; Sunday market; Places of Worship; People who help us; Others who help us; Distance and directions; Time; Transport Safety rules.

Our Earth: Water; Sources of Water; Things on the earth; Soil; Plants—herbs; Shrubs; Trees, Climbers, Water plants, leaves and animals; Water animals; Things around the earth; Man changes shape of the earth; What do we have inside the earth?

Our Sky: Day and night; Day sky; Night sky; Different phase of the moon; Weather keeps on changing; Rainy day; Cold day; Hot day.

Our Body: Our body and its parts; Our sense organs.

Class I (Science and Social Studies) Syllabus

Our Family–Small family; Big family; Food; Nutritious Food, Good eating habits; Clothes; Festivals—Holi, Id-ul-fiter, Guruparva; Christmas, Onam and Pongal etc.

Our House–Story of shelter; Materials used in houses.

Our School–School activities; Care of school property.

Our Neighbourhood–Places; Sanitation; National Festivals—Independence Day, Republic Day, Gandhi Jayanti; Safety rules; Plants—Herbs, Shrubs, Trees, Creepers, Climbers, Twiners; Water plants; Animals :— Four-footed animals, Flesh eating animals, Crawling animals, Birds and Insects.

Our Earth–Earth's surface; Water; Drinking Water; forests.

Our Sky–Directions; Day and Night sky.

Our Body–Body parts; Healthy habits; Sleep and rest; Exercise and play; Correct posture.

Classes III-V Syllabus

The curriculum in Syllabus is divided into two parts from class III onwards. Part I is termed as social studies and part II as science. Both the subjects, however, are under the umbrella of EVS. It means that whatever will be selected as part of the EVS syllabus will have directly or indirectly an environmental content and orientation.

Teaching-learning programmes in these subjects will also have an EVS approach.

While selecting the content for social studies, the emphasis is on the interaction of man With his social environment. This, therefore, includes history, social institutions, cultural ethos, traditions, the economy etc. Thus, the life of man in the neighbourhood, in the district, state and country, and in the world becomes the main focus of study. Nature influences the patterns of life of a person and he/she has always made efforts to control and use nature to live a comfortable life. This has been a determining factor for selection of content for social studies. The concept, ideas and activities suggested in the curriculum are expected to be helpful in understanding this broad generalisation.

The syllabus in EVS part II viz. Science has been developed to create among children an awareness, understanding and concern for natural and physical environment. While selecting the content for the syllabus in science, broad areas of the child interaction with the natural and physical environment have been taken into account. A thematic approach for selection of content has been adopted and themes like living things; body, food and health; materials and their properties; force, work and energy operating in the environment; weather and its influence; soil and its relationship with crops; earth and sky etc. have been identified. The content for these units has been arranged spirally from classes III to V developing from simple to complex and also from near to remote.

Attempts have been made to interweave the core-components in the syllabus of social studies and science. Wherever it was possible, these have been incorporated in a natural way.

It is further reiterated that the content included in the national syllabus is suggestive. It will be adapted according to local situations. However, it must be seen that the minimum learning outcomes and the core components are included in all the syllabus.

It may further be pointed out that actual environmental orientation will be reflected in transaction of curriculum. The teaching-learning programmes should exploit the environment and its resources through well-thought out activities which may lead to develop the desired competencies and understanding related to selected themes and topics. If this is not done, there is danger of teaching of the subjects of social studies and science in isolation from environment defeating the very purpose of including EVS in the curriculum.

Class III Syllabus

1. Things Around us
2. Plants and Animals Around us
3. Animals and their Way of Life
4. Our Body
5. Our Food
6. Care of the Teeth
7. Cleanliness of Surroundings
8. Materials Around us
9. Solids, Liquids and Gases
10. Water, a Wonderful Liquid
11. Weather
12. The Seasons
13. The Sky

Class IV Syllabus

1. Functions of different Parts of a Plant
2. Uses of Plants and Animals
3. Care and Protection of Plants and Animals
4. Our Body and its Functions
5. Food and Food Sanitation
6. Safe Water
7. Sanitation and Diseases
8. Materials and their Properties
9. Weather and its Influence on Life
10. Soil and Crops

11. Work, Force and Energy
12. The Sky and the Earth

Class V Syllabus

1. Growth and Response to Stimuli in Living Things
2. Respiration and Reproduction in Living Things
3. How Living Things adapt themselves
4. From seeds to seedlings
5. The Bone Cage : Our Body and its Movements
6. Deficiency Diseases
7. Communicable Diseases
8. Community Sanitation
9. Soil Conservation
10. Air : Its Uses and Pollution
11. Forces : Work and Energy
12. Simple Machines
13. Shadows and Eclipses
14. Accidents can be Avoided
15. Man, Science and Environment

Minimum Levels of Learning

A reference to MLLs is necessary here. In the Curriculum and Syllabus developed by NCERT "Minimum Levels of Learning at Primary stage (1991)" and in the "Report of Committee set up by MHRD-1991", the MLLs have been stated as Minimum Learning Outcomes (MLOs) and also as competencies. Thus, the instructional objectives of every unit of a class have been stated in terms of MLOs.

For instance, in science for the Unit on 'Living Things' for class IV the following could be Minimum Learning Outcomes (MLOs) :

The learners—

- identify and list the ways in which human beings use plants and plant products,

- identify and list the ways in which animal products are used by human beings,
- identify the ways in which plants and animals are cared for and protected,
- cite examples of steps taken for protection of plants and animals in the country,
- name important wildlife sanctuaries and locate them on the map of India,
- identify and state the functions of different parts of a plant,
- recognise that dispersal of seeds is necessary for growth of new plants,
- list different ways by which seeds are dispersed,
- see relationship between characteristic structure of seeds and modes of their dispersal.

In a Unit there could be more than one lesson. Thus, there is a need for laying down MLO of each lesson.

For instance, in science in the unit of 'Living Things' for class IV, there may be a lesson of 'Uses of Plants'. MLOs for this lesson could be as under :

The learners—

- identify the plants which are used by human beings,
- classify the plants human beings use for themselves and the ones they use as animal fodder,
- list the plants which human beings use directly as their food,
- list the plant products which are used by human beings,
- name the plants which are sources of medicures,
- list the names of plants which give fibre for clothing,
- give the reasons why the decayed parts of plants become manure,
- collect leaves of plants which are medicinal, which are used as food and which produce items of food.

Sometimes lessons are also organised in the form of an activity. For instance, for class II 'A visit to the school garden' could be an activity. Teachers, however, have to identify what MLOs he/she will have in his/her mind when children will be undertaking this activity. It is necessary to have the MLOs to make the activity purposeful. Some of the MLOs for the above activity could be as under :

The learners—

- observe the plants in the school garden,
- name the plants in the school garden,
- identify the types of plants as trees, herbs, shrubs, or creepers,
- compare the size of plants,
- identify the parts of a tree and name them,
- collect the leaves of the plants,
- compare the shape of the leaves of different plants,
- draw inference that leaves of different plants have different shapes,
- arrange leaves of plants according to their size,
- draw inference that the size of leaves does not depend on size of plant,
- prepare an album containing different kinds of leaves.

It is emphasised that describing instructional objectives or MLOs at each level is a very useful exercise. It helps teachers to develop their teaching-learning strategies. The specific objectives in terms of child behaviour also help in evaluating the achievement of children.

Core Components

According to NPE-1986 and POA for its implementation of MHRD, NCERT brought out exampler packages on Core Curricular Areas which are as follows :

EVS (Social Studies)

1. History of India's freedom movement.
2. Constitutional obligations.
3. Content essential to nurture national identity.
4. India's common cultural heritage.
5. Equalitarianism, democracy and secularism.
6. Equality of sexes.
7. Removal of social barriers.

EVS (Science)

8. Protection of the environment
9. Observance of the small family norm
10. Inculcation of scientific temper

The EVS course at primary level (I-V) should cover these core components, according to the need and comprehension of the children.

Study of Natural Phenomena

The nature and scope of Environmental Studies (EVS) has been discussed in detail. The meaning and objectives of EVS have been spelled out in very clear terms. Environmental Studies (EVS) deals with the study of natural phenomena which takes place in the environment of the child. It also deals with social aspect of environment. EVS has been divided into two parts. Part I—Social Studies, and Part II—Science. Both are incorporated in EVS. The concept of Minimum Levels of Learning and Core Components have also been discussed giving examples from Environmental Studies Programme.

Questions

1. Describe the significance of EVS in primary education curriculum.
2. Explain the nature of social studies and science in the content of environmental studies syllabus in your state.

3. Classify the concept of EVS as an area of study and as an approach to study.
4. Felxibility of curriculum is said to be one of the main characteristics of EVS curriculum. Select one topic each from social studies and science syllabus from the national syllabus and adopt it according to your local situation.
5. In what manner is laying down of instructional objectives (MLOs) of a lesson useful? Discuss the answer by giving concrete examples of instructional objectives of a lesson.
6. What are Core Components of EVS Course at primary level? Identify the details of each component to be taken at this level.

10

Enrichment Course

Content and Organisation

What we teach in Science is 'Content'. Now the question arises, 'What is Science ?' Science is a way of describing and explaining some aspects of the world around us. To the extent that a lot of human effort has already been expended in developing such explanations, our students do not have to 'start with scratch'. A large and ever-increasing body of scientific knowledge already exists, and evidently part of the task as teacher is to pass some of it to the students. But this is only part of the job, for Science is also a package of processes by which we can increase our knowledge of the external world. Teaching Science implies involving our students in investigation, so that they become 'Scientists for the day'. There are facts, theories, concepts and also a way of working which together constitute 'the subject Science'. Thus Science is not just content. Science is content plus processes.

One of the things you will be doing as a science teacher is familiarising your students with theories, helping them to develop concepts and appreciate the structure which connects them.

Content to be taught at Upper Primary level (VI-VIII) or at any level should be carefully selected. It is a hard task. Scientific knowledge keeps on increasing. It doubles every decade. Our students are to keep pace with increasing scientific knowledge. We should teach them what they really need at this level. If it is more to be completed in a classroom in the allotted time, we should develop such techniques so that students could learn a part of content on their own outside the classroom.

'What we teach (Content)' should be compatible with—

(i) cognitive level of students,

(ii) identified objectives, and

(iii) existing classroom conditions.

The 'Content' presented to the student should be such that he could understand it, and not just memorise. Learning is understanding, and not memorising. In every class there is some content in Science, which most of the students, memorise without understanding. Such content should not be included at that level, but shifted to a level where students can really understand it.

Syllabus given by the education departments or school education boards are usually outlines. Therefore different authors go to different depths for the same content when writing the textbooks. If our Science Syllabi are well-defined in the form of 'objectives written in behavioural terms' the authors will know exactly what they are to write, students will know what they are to learn and teachers will know what they are to teach.

Discussion

Physicists, Chemists and Biologists are specialists in Physics, Chemistry and Biology respectively. Our students at Upper Primary Level (VI-VIII) are not specialists. For them each of Physics, Chemistry and Biology is Science. So when teaching Science at this level, we should not compartmentalise Science into Physics, Chemistry and Biology, as it was the case since mid-sixties, and we used to teach NCERT developed Disciplined Science Courses (Physics, Chemistry and Biology) in classes VI, VII and VIII. We should teach Science at this level as a package of Integrated Science Course.

Many of the processes we see in nature are not classifiable as Chemistry only, or only Physics, or purely Biological. For example, when the polar bear hibernates in the Arctic winter, its action is biological. During this fact, we should be thankful for the stored fat and its properties. For the physical property of the fat 'fat is a bad conductor of heat' aids the bear in keeping warm, for the chemical property of fat 'it lowers oxygen content' makes it energy-rich fuel, better than carbohydrates, and for the biology of being able to take and store the fat in its tissues. This shows how Physics, Chemistry and Biology are integrated. With this philosophy in mind 'an Integrated Science Syllabus' was framed for Upper Primary classes (VI-VIII), and based on this syllabus Integrated Science Textbooks, 'SCIENCE' were written for classes VI, VII and VIII by NCERT, which are being used in our schools these days.

NPE—1986 has laid greater emphasis on teaching of Science at all levels, and so at Upper Primary level. According to its recommendations, "Science education is to be strengthened so as to develop in the child well-defined abilities and values such as the spirit of inquiry, creativity, objectivity and the courage to ask questions. Science education programmes are to be designed to enable the learner to acquire problem-solving and decision-making skills". These recommendations were taken into consideration when NCERT framed Integrated Science Syllabus and wrote Integrated Science Textbooks for classes VI, VII and VIII.

You as a teacher trainee of Second year will teach Science to classes VI—VIII during your practice teaching. So alongwith learning methodology of teaching Science at this level you should also enrich yourself in Science content. Go through the science syllabus and the Science textbooks of classes VI—VIII. Analyse them. For your convenience VI—VIII Integrated Science Syllabus is divided into 8 units, and is given as under :

Unit-1	:	Science in Everyday Life
Unit-2	:	The Measurement
Unit-3	:	The Universe
Unit-4	:	Motion, Force and Machines
Unit-5	:	Work and Energy-energy, heat; sound; light; light and optical instruments; static electricity; electric current; conservation of natural resources; alternative sources of energy; magnetism.

Unit-6	:	Matter, Its Structure and Properties—nature and composition of substances; acids, bases and salts; carbon and its compounds; metals and non-metals; man-made materials.
Unit-7	:	Air and Water
Unit-8	:	Living World—the living world; structure and function of living body; balance in nature; organisation of the living body; life processes; food, health and diseases; soils; agricultural practices and implements; the microbial world; adaptation and organic evolution; useful plants and animals.

Select any Sub-unit. Write behavioural objectives, covering the whole syllabus of the sub-unit. Go through the Science textbook for that sub-unit, and see whether all the behavioural objectives are covered in the book for that sub-unit.

Science Content

Unit 1. Science in Everyday Life

Role of Science in solving many basic problems in our everyday life and misuse of Science.

Unit 2. The Measurement

Use of various devices in measuring length, area, volume; measurement of mass; need for accurate measurements in daily life; measurement of temperature, various types of thermometers, measurement of time.

Unit 3. The Universe

Numerous stars and planets in the universe; classification of heavenly bodies, galaxy, shapes and sizes of the heavenly bodies and idea of their distance from the earth; artificial satellites; various uses of artificial satellites; meteors and meteorites.

Unit 4. Motion, Force and Machines

Different types of motion—linear, random, rotatory, circular, periodic, oscillatory; speed, force; change in speed, direction and shape by applying force; various types of forces; magnetic force, electrostatic force, frictional force; advantages and disadvantages of friction. Different kinds of simple machines—lever, inclined plane, pulley and wheel; complex machines—a combination of simple machines; maintenance and care of machines.

Force, its magnitude and direction; pressure; atmospheric pressure; thrust; buoyancy; Pascal's law; Archimedes' Principle; floatation of bodies.

Unit 5. Work and Energy

Energy

Energy, relationship between work and energy; renewable and non-renewable sources of energy; electric energy from coal; solar energy, wind energy, energy from water, energy from biomass; mechanical energy; potential and kinetic energies; transformation of energy.

Heat

Temperature and its measurement; heat and its measurement; units of heat; melting and boiling points; expansion of solids, liquids and gases, properties of substances used in constructing thermometers; transfer of heat by conduction, convection and radiation; thermal properties of substances.

Sound

Various types of sound; modes of production of sound; formation of echo, noise and its hazards; human ear.

Light

Formation of shadow; solar and lunar eclipses, laws of reflection; image formation in plane and spherical mirrors.

Light and Optical Instrument

Refraction of light and its applications in daily life; convex lenses; formation of images in lenses; microscope; telescope; binoculars.

Static Electricity

Charging of bodies; like and unlike charges; attraction and repulsion of charges; flow of charges: electroscope; conductors and insulators.

Electric Current

Source of electric current; dry cells; generator; storage battery. A.C. and D.C. transformation of electricity; conductors and insulators; electric circuits; effects of electric current; hazards of electricity.

Conservation of Natural Resources

Matter or material from earth; energy from Sun; energy directly or indirectly from the Sun; proper distribution of resources; various types of natural resources, renewable and non-renewable, depletion of resources and their causes, conservation of natural resources for human survival; conservation efforts at individual/ community/ governmental/international level necessary.

Alternative Sources of Energy

Source of energy; Fossil fuels; hydro-energy; bio-energy, wind energy as renewable sources of energy; energy needs; development of energy; judicious use of energy.

Magnetism

Magnet and its properties, repulsion of like poles and attraction of unlike poles; electromagnets; Earth as a magnet.

Unit 6. Matter, Its Structure and Properties

Nature and Composition of Substances

Different states of matter, molecules constituting particles and matter; forces between molecules; gap between molecules—diffusion, plasticity; elements, compounds and mixtures; preparation of oxygen; molecules; atom; symbol of elements; significance of symbols; chemical formulae of elements and compounds; significance of chemical formula; representation of chemical reaction by an equation.

Acids, Bases and Salts

Oxides; formation of metallic (basic) and non-metallic (acidic) oxides; acids; bases; some common physical and chemical properties of acids and bases; preparation of hydrogen; neutralization; formation of salt; various uses of acids; bases and salts in domestic and industrial areas.

Carbon and Its Compounds

Uses of carbon compounds; forms of carbon; hydrocarbons; fuels; petroleum and its products; domestic cooking gas; coal and its products; combustion; fire extinguishing.

Metals and Non-metals

Rocks and minerals; ores; extraction of metals from ores; characteristics of metals; alloys and their uses.

Man-made Materials

Various types of materials and their application; synthetic fibres; plastics and its uses in daily life; glass and its formation; ceramics; soaps and detergents; fertilizers; pesticides.

Unit 7. Air and Water

Air

Composition of air; oxygen—a supporter of combustion and life; necessity of air for substances of life; various uses of air to human beings.

Various constituents of air; oxygen an important constituent of air, air pollution; acid rain; uses of various constituents of air.

Water

Importance of water for living beings; sources of water; purification of water for drinking; some special physical properties of water; different forms of water; change of one form into another; water cycle in nature; uses of water in day-to-day life; need of conservation of water.

Composition of water; electrolysis of water; electrical attraction of water; some chemical properties of water dissolution of various minerals and salts in sea-water; hard and soft water; removal of hardness; water pollution.

Unit 8. Living World

The Living World

Variety in shape, food habits, habitats, structure and mode of living; individuals with close similarities in form with above characteristics, species, naming species, classification of living and non-living; characteristics of living forms; classification of plants into flowering or non-flowering or the nature of roots, stems and leaves, life span, animals, classification—presence or absence of backbone and other characteristics.

Structure and Function of Living Body

Organization of the living body to perform different functions; loss of part affects functioning; parts of plant-root and shoot systems; roots, stems, leaves, flowers, fruits and seeds have definite functions; modification of plant parts.

Animal organ systems for different functions; digestive system; respiratory system; nervous system; excretory system; locomotion and reproduction.

Balance in Nature

Living and non-living components of environment; interdependence; food and energy relations; balance in nature; indiscriminate human interferences are often harmful.

Organisation of the Living Body

Definite organization of living bodies for functioning; Levels of organization, unicellular and multicellular organisms; cell structures and functions; differences between the plant and animal cells; cells arise from pre-existing cells; plant tissues and their function; conduction, mechanical support; animal tissues and their function; epithelia, connective, muscular and nervous.

Life Processes

Basic life processes; photosynthesis by green plants; nutrition in non-green plants; animal nutrition: the alimentation process; respiration-organs, common cellular processes; aerobic and aerobic respiration; transport of materials in animals (mention of blood transfusion) and plants; excretion—organs and modes of removal of wastes; coordination—nervous and hormonal; movements, continuity of life; vegetative, asexual and sexual reproduction; growth and development in plants and animals.

Food, Health and Diseases

Basic constituents, their main functions including water and roughage; balanced diet in relation to age and work; judicious choice of food; avoidance of fats: malnutrition; deficiency diseases: food preservation; contamination/spoilage; healthy living depends oil hygiene: sanitation and habits; diseases; disorders; role and spread of disease causing micro-organism; personal hygiene and environmental sanitation; non-communicable diseases; smoking, alcohol and drug addiction as health hazards.

Soils

Composition of soils : gravel, clay, organic matter; humus and living organisms in top soil, soil formed by weathering; soil as important natural resource; soil erosion and conservation; soil pollution.

Agricultural Practices and Implements

Management of plants and animals : usefulness, general methods; improved agricultural practices for increased food production; basic practices; sequencing; variation from crop to crop; practices common to gardening, agricultural implements and their uses and care; qualitative and quantitative improvement of crop yields; necessity and methods, improved practices and varieties; judicious use of soil, fertilizers and pesticides; animal management; need for keeping animals; general needs and maintenance of domestic animals with special reference to cattle, sheep, poultry, bee and fish rearing.

The Microbial World

Micro-organisms have diverse forms; fungi, protozoa, bacteria, viruses and certain algae; causes of disease in man and animal bacteria (cholera, typhoid): virus (cold, measles, polio, chicken pox), protozoa in fungi (malaria, dysentery, etc.) : animal diseases (anthrax and foot and mouth), plant diseases (rust, bacterial wilt, leaf curl, mosaic) : modes of transmission of diseases; vectors; control of microbial disease; proper storage and preservation to prevent microbial damage to clothing, timber and food.

Adaptation and Organic Evolution

Meaning of adaptation; adaptation of aquatic, terrestrial and volant organisms; origin of life from simple substances; origin of complex forms from simpler forms; evidence of evolution, external and internal structures, fossils, organic evolution through the process of natural selection.

Useful Plants and Animals

Harmful and useful plants of economic importance—wild and cultivated; useful animals; animal products from wild and domesticated animals (ivory, lac, horn, lime, pearls, leather, honey, etc.).

Science, a Subject

There are facts, theories, concepts and also a way of working which together constitute 'the subject Science'. Thus Science is not just content. Science is content plus processes. 'What we teach in Science i.e. content' should be compatible with cognitive level of children, identified objectives, and existing classroom conditions.

Science syllabus given by the education departments or education boards are usually outlines, that is why it does not mean the same for authors, teachers, students and paper-setters. If our science syllabus is well defined in the form of 'objectives written in behavioural terms,' the authors will know exactly what they are to write, teachers will know what they are to teach, students will know what they are to learn and paper-setters will know what questions they are to set. Thus such a syllabus will mean the same for all of them.

Physicists, Chemists and Biologists are specialists in Physics, Chemistry and Biology. Our students at Upper Primary level are not specialists. For them each of Physics, Chemistry and Biology is Science. That is why NCERT switched over from disciplined Science (Physics, Chemistry and Biology) of mid-sixties to Integrated Science at Upper Primary level.

NPE—1986 has laid greater emphasis on teaching of Science at all levels, and so at Upper Primary level. According to its recommendations, "Science education is to be strengthened so as to develop in the child well-defined abilities and values such as the spirit of inquiry, creativity, objectivity and the courage to ask questions. Science education programmes are to be designed to enable the learner to acquire problem solving and decision making skills." These recommendations were taken into consideration when NCERT formed Integrated Science syllabus and wrote Integrated Science textbooks for classes VI-VIII.

If you analyse VI-VIII Integrated Science syllabus, it could be divided into several units-Science in everyday life; energy; matter, its structure and properties; air and water; living world. All this content can be translated into objectives in behavioural terms.

Questions

1. 'What we teach in science (content)' should be compatible with three things. List them ?
2. How should be the science syllabus written so that it means the same for the authors, teachers, students and paper-setters ?
3. Why did the NCERT switch over from disciplined science to Integrated Science at Upper Primary level ?
4. State two NPE—1986's recommendations for science education. Are they being taken into consideration at Upper Primary level ?
5. Divide Integrated Science syllabus for classes VI—VIII into eight units, and write down only their headings.
6. Select any topic of your choice from any unit of VI—VIII Science, and write down the objectives in behavioural terms covering the whole topic.

11

Dynamic Experiments

Science education forms an integral part of our school curriculum upto the secondary level in the process of 'Universalisation of Education'. The National Policy on Education—1986 (NPE—1986) has laid considerable emphasis on strengthening the science education in the school education system. The current situation of teaching of school science content is as Environmental Studies at the primary level (classes I—V). Integrated approach of teaching science is followed at the upper primary stage (classes VI—VIII) and secondary stage (classes IX—X) by integrating all disciplines of Science in a natural fashion. The NPE—1986 envisages extension through every effort of Science education not only to those who are in the formal school system but also to those who have remained outside the system under non-formal and adult education programmes. The qualitative improvement in science education depends on many vital components. The teacher is considered as a crucial factor in the teaching-learning process, developing positive attitudes in the learners for better achievement and the formulation and implementation of science education programmes. The teachers have to discard their traditional methods and usual practice in relying entirely on textbook. The teaching has to be integrated with environment based on real life situations using local experiences, expertise and resources. The classroom territory has to be expanded over the whole environment so that the activities become supplementary to classroom teaching. If such an approach is systematically implemented with mobilisation of needed resources, it is very much likely that there may be an improvement in our science education at the elementary stage, especially the upper primary of school education. Several attempts are being made to improve science teaching in our country, both at the formal as well as non-formal sectors of school education. Some of the innovative experiences in science education at the upper primary level include Nehru Science Exhibition, Science Museums and Mobile Science Units, Hoshangabad-Ekalavya Experience, Kerala Sastra Sahitya Parishad, Vikram Sarabhai Community Science Centre, EVS Project (UNESCO), Urban Marginal Project (UNESCO) etc. In such innovative experiences and science activities, the learning is fitted to the abilities and interests of learners as there exists an opportunity for individuals initiative, independent or collective study and creativity. A large number of such activities are organised in India. A few of the major activities are listed and described briefly here.

Nehru Science Exhibition

November 14 is the birth anniversary of Pandit Jawaharlal Nehru, our first Prime Minister. Children call him Chacha Nehru, as he used to love children very much. We celebrate Children's Day on November 14. On this occasion a National Science Exhibition is also organised by the NCERT. This exhibition is called Nehru Science Exhibition. To start with, this exhibition used to be organised at Teen Murti, New Delhi where Pandit Nehru used to live, when he was our Prime Minister. Now this exhibition is organised in different states. Children from all over the country, from all states and UTs participate in this exhibition with the selected exhibits. Science exhibitions (fairs) are organised at three levels—District, State and National. National level exhibition is NEHRU SCIENCE EXHIBITION.

Every year NCERT announces a main theme and sub-themes for Nehru Science Exhibition. Children make their exhibits on these sub-themes.

Example

Main Theme : Science in our Environment. *Sub-Themes:*

(i) Agriculture, Horticulture, Farming and Animal Husbandry

(ii) Conservation of the Environment

(iii) Health

(iv) Energy Conservation and needs

(v) Astronomy

(vi) Town and Village Planning

(vii) Machines in the Service of Rural Areas

(viii) Teaching Aids for Science and Mathematics

(ix) Innovations.

This information along with the last date of submitting the entry forms along with the dates of exhibition reaches every school of the country, from NCERT to states and UTs and from states and UTs to all schools. On receiving this information children start working on their projects static or working models, or investigatory science projects under the guidance and supervision of their science teachers. If a school has a Science Club, it becomes quite active after receiving this information under the supervision and guidance of the Science Club sponsor, the Science Teacher.

Very often in Nehru Science Exhibition we see some static and working models, or some noble experiments demonstrated by the students with the help of charts and graphs. These are projects but not Investigatory Science Projects. Students should be encouraged and motivated to work on some investigatory science projects, and bring them to Nehru Science Exhibition, as their exhibits.

A project may be any purposeful activity. It may be a model—static or working, or experiment. Here are examples of some good science projects displayed in Nehru Science Exhibitions :

(a) Improved bullock cart

(b) Solar cooker-cum-solar power generator

(c) Computer controlled car

(d) A simple device to prove Newton's third law of motion

(e) Working model of the solar system

(f) Determination of the time of a falling body

(g) A device for conversion of waste mechanical energy to electrical energy

(h) Sewage treatment and reuse of water

(i) Extraction of oil from rice bran

(j) Very cheap symbiotic rhizobium substituted for expensive nitrogenous fertilizers

(k) Cheap record player

(l) Digital clock

(m) Kitchen flask

(n) Milk plant in Chandigarh

(o) Multipurpose charkha

(p) Food feeding machine for physically handicapped

(q) Low cost tricycle for physically handicapped children

(r) Magic door

(s) Artificial sunset, and so on.

A project which involves investigation, discovery and finding out something which was not known to the student before, is an investigatory project. An investigation is much more than the repetition of standard experiment. Here the student is to decide what experiments are necessary and how he is going to carry them out. He may have to design his own apparatus, if that is not available in the laboratory. He has to search for the appropriate principles, laws, formulae, apparatus and data, and originate a solution to a problem. The student has to behave like a scientist.

You should also encourage your students to work on investigatory science projects under your guidance and send it to Nehru Science Exhibition through District and State Science Exhibitions and Fairs.

Science Museums and Mobile Science Units

You must have seen some science museums. They are very effective and interesting sources of learning science. What experiences do you get from a science museum ?

Objectives of Science Museum

Main objectives in establishing science museums are :

(i) To help young science learners in understanding concepts of science by play-way method.

(ii) To provide a glimpse of past as well as an insight into the future.

(iii) To help schools in their class activities by providing them with a number of equipments and specimens which are otherwise difficult for a single school to procure.

(iv) To arrange extension activities such as field trips, lectures, film shows and exhibitions for the students as well as public.

Science Museums

During the last decade or so, a couple of science museums have been set up in the country including one at Delhi, the Natural History Museum. Recently in Delhi's Pragati Maidan, National Science Centre (National Council of Science Museums) has been set up. It has several units. 'FUN GAMES' and 'ENERGY' units are very interesting for students at upper primary level. Delhi also has two Primary Science Museums :

(i) Municipal Corporation Children Resource Centre (MCCRC) at R.K. Puram, Sector VI.

(ii) New Delhi Municipal Committee (NDMC) Science Centre at Lakshmibai Nagar.

(iii) National Museum of Natural History, Mandi House, New Delhi

1. It has MOBILE SCIENCE UNIT which can come to your school with exhibits you need from all it has.
2. It has four galleries consisting of
   - our solar system
   - plants for life
   - animals with and without backbones
   - reptiles
   - birds
   - mammals

- — deserts
- — rain forests
- — energy for life
- — leaf the biggest factory on earth
- — wild life conservation
- — problems of air and water pollution
- — energy conservation
- — cell, the basic unit of life.

3. It has Work Sheets for visiting galleries
   - — grouping animals
   - — classification of animals
   - — skin of animals
   - — How do animals protect themselves ?
   - — food chain
   - — Why do animals become endangered?
4. It has MODELLING UNIT consisting of Discovery Room and Bio. Sc. Computer Lab.
5. It has TEXIDERMY UNIT (Stuffed animals)
6. It has SCIENCE LAB. (Preserved specimens)
7. It has NATURE STUDY PROJECT KIT consisting of water net, leaves presser and magnifying glass.
8. It has Nature Facts Sheets for Children—deodar, birds' nests etc.
9. You can also do PROJECTS here LIKE
   - — bees around us,
   - — know the birds around us,
   - — mammals,
   - — nature study activities in woods,
   - — plants and insects,
   - — pond life activities,
   - — activities with small animals in soil,

- — observation of life activities,
- — seeds,
- — conservation of nature
- — collect-classify-catalogue etc.

10. It has SCHOOL LOAN KITS
    - (i) solar system
    - (ii) honey bee
    - (iii) silk worm
    - (iv) food chain
    - (v) plants and their uses
    - (vi) insects
    - (vii) butterflies and moths
    - (viii) koel
    - (ix) owl
    - (x) snakes
    - (xi) skins Loan period is one week.

Loan kits will be delivered to your school and picked up from your school by museum vans.

There are good science museums in various parts of the country—Mumbai, Bangalore, Calcutta. All these science museums are doing very good job, carrying out various innovative activities, exhibition in science for the improvement of science education. Let us discuss some more science museums a little bit in detail.

Nehru Science Centre

The Nehru Science Centre (NSC) is established in Mumbai by the National Council of Science Museums. The most important and attractive part of the NSC is a 'Science Park' for children. With green surroundings, the Children's Science Park has exhibits on time, motion, energy, power and work.. Also, there are models of railway engines, tram cars, aeroplanes, steam lorries, a wind-mill and a sun-dial. There are birds, animals and fish to acquaint children with nature. While children enjoy the Science Park the most, it also helps them to understand 'what' 'why' and 'how' of the querries, questions and problems haunting their minds.

Nehru Science Centre, Mumbai is basically multi-disciplinary in character. Collection of antique exhibits of historic value, presentation of the same through permanent and temporary exhibitions on selected themes, extension activities offering multiple avenues of learning, enjoyment and training to the student community as well as the public, taking science to rural areas through mobile science exhibitions, aiming towards interacting mode of presentation of themes are some of the ways in which the NSC operates. The Science Centre also offers a gallery on 'light and sight'. It presents different principles involved in the process of 'seeing and the vision'. A survey is made of vision, its defects, its importance, its complexities and varieties. Nehru Science Centre also organises extension activities such as science extension in rural areas, film shows, science seminars for schools, film loan service, amateur weather station, amateur radio classes for children, sky observation programme, astronomical camps, popular science lectures, special science film festivals, aeronautic modelling programmes and training camps for underprivileged children.

Visvesvaraya Industrial and Technological Museums

The Visvesvaraya Industrial and Technological Museum is established in Bombay. It organises various activities and programmes such as motive power gallery (science museum), teacher training, hobby centre, students' science seminars, science quiz, science fair, temporary exhibition, science demonstration lectures, mobile science exhibitions, film shows, popular science lectures etc. The museum has also a regional science centre at Gulbarga.

If you have a science museum at the place where you teach, plan a visit to that museum. If your students go to some places, where there are science museums, ask them to visit them with their parents or if you arrange a field trip to any place, where there is a science museum, take your students there, and see how much science they learn-the science which is not there even in their science books.

Mobile Science Units

Some science museums have mobile science units, museums on wheel. They are usually sent to the places, where there are no science museums. They are not as big as a science museum. They do not have as many science exhibits as a science museum has. But even this is a very effective source of learning science for students at upper primary level.

Natural History Museum, New Delhi, National Science Centre, New Delhi and Nehru Science Centre, Bombay have Mobile Science Units. You try to find out whether there is some science museum, not very far from the place you are teaching, and whether that science museum has the facility of mobile science unit. You can ask such museums to send that unit to your school. If you are 105 successful to bring it, your students may visit the science museum even in their school, and can learn a lot of science.

An Experience

Hoshangabad Science Teaching Project (HSTP) started in 1973 in sixteen Government Rural Middle Schools of district Hoshangabad in Madhya Pradesh for teaching science through environment based discovery approach. This programme was started by Kishore Bharati an NGO, in collaboration with Friends Rural Centre, Rasulia another NGO with the support of the Department of Education, Government of Madhya Pradesh. A large number of teachers and scientists from various institutions and organisations such as the All India Science Teachers Association, Physics Study Group; Bombay Municipal Corporation; Gandhi Vidyapeeth, Vedehi, Surat District; Lok Bharti, in Gujarat; The Space Application Centre, Ahmedabad; Universities of Delhi, Rajasthan and Indore; The Tata Institute of Fundamental Research, Bombay; Indian Institute of Technology, Kanpur; NCERT, DAV College of Education, Abohar (Punjab) etc. participated in the development of curriculam, workbooks, science kit, other materials and training of teachers.

In 1978 this programme of science teaching was extended to all the 206 middle schools of District Hoshangabad.

Objectives

1. Implementation of introducing innovations as envisaged in Ekalavya Experiences within the given framework of the Government school system.
2. Encouraging science teaching through discovery approach in Indian schools.
3. Providing science education experiences through environment.
4. Developing ability among students for applying scientific method in different situations.
5. Developing scientific attitude among the students.

Curriculum

Keeping in view the objectives of this Ekalavya experiences the curriculum of science teaching has been based on process approach rather than product approach. The process approach of learning science provides numerous opportunities to children to explore scientific phenomena of their local environment. Most of the curricular contents have been taken from their environment. Advanced scientific concepts, such as abstract chemical symbols, theoretical concepts of atomic and molecular structure, and human anatomy etc., have not been included in the curriculum because these concepts are beyond the students, direct interaction with the environment.

The selection of curricular content is dependent upon : (a) relatedness to environment, (b) relatedness to the needs, interests and mental level of the students and (c) possibility of the application of discovery approach.

Through the above mentioned procedure the curricular contents for classes sixth, seventh and eighth have been developed. Some of the examples of the curricular contents for various classes are given below :

Class VI	:	Kuchh Khel Khilwar
		Samuh Banana Sikho
		Hamari Phaslen aur Samuhikaran Vidyut

		Ganak Ke Khel Jeev Jagat me Vividhata Mitti, Pathar aur Chattane
Class VII	:	Ek Majedar Khel Jar aur Patti Keeron Ki Duniya Phaslon Ke Dushman Apni Haddi Pahachano Aakash Ki Or Taraju Ka Sidhant
Class VIII	:	Jantuon Ka Jivan Chakkar Phool aur Phal Paudho me Prajanan Vargikaran Ke Niyam Jantuon Ka Vargikaran Gasen

Work Book and Science Kit Materials

In this programme, the workbook is introduced in place of text-books, which is process based. Principles of science are discovered through experiments. Science Kit is very conducive for discovery approach to science teaching.

Teaching Method

Discovery Approach, EVS Approach, Process Approach and Scientific Method are the main teaching methods followed in this programme. Students learn science through inquiry approach especially by experimentation, discussion and field trips. The whole class is divided into sub-groups of four students each known as a Toli. This Toli pattern is also followed in their teacher training programmes. Students were free to identify problems, formutate hypotheses, perform experiments in their respective tolies, collect and analyse data and draw conclusions on the basis of the guidelines given in the workbooks.

Examination

In the Ekalavaya Experience, the examination is not based on memory or recall etc. Independent observation, data collec-tion, data analysis and drawing conclusions have been given due weightage. It also seeks to test the extent of a pupil's readiness to innovate through physical experimentation.

The examination is conducted to test three basic elements of science teaching namely, scientific skills, scientific attitudes and understanding of scientific concepts and principles. Books, workbooks, class records were allowed in the examination. There was no time limit in written and practical examinations.

Misconceptions Like

"Flies are born spontaneously from cattle dung",

"Butterflies suck out all the goodness of flowers, and so flowers die as a result",

"Sun makes your shadow which disappears at Noon"

are removed in this science teaching.

EKLAVYA another NGO set up in 1982-83 did similar work in other SUBJECTS—Social studies programme for Middle Schools, integrated programme for LANGUAGE. Maths, EVS, for primary schools.

INNOVATIVE Hoshangabad Science Teaching Project (HSTP)

(i) Born in 1973,

(ii) Young in 1978.

Now it is not so well taken. WHY?

If a school programme is successful at MICRO Level, should it be expanded to MACRO Level?

Who will do this—Govt., DIETS or some other NGOs? Should it be expanded to the whole state of MP or CLOSED? What's about Kunji Writers, Publishers and some teachers who want TUTIONS and NO HARD WORK? What do they say about this project? Discuss these issues.

Kerala Shastra Sahitya Parishad

The Kerala Shastra Sahitya Parishad (KSSP) is a voluntary organisation. It was established in 1963. KSSP has around 10,000 members comprising scientists, doctors, engineers, social scientists, teachers, students, workers, peasants and technicians. It has 600 units all over Kerala.

Objectives

1. To popularise science amongst society.
2. To generate science literacy amongst people.
3. To increase community involvement for developing scientific temper in the society.
4. To develop appropriate rural technology in the field of energy.
5. To organise health camps, classes and audio-visual campaigns on a wide scale.

Activities

The society has ten major areas of activities— (A) Publications, (B) Non-formal Education, (C) Formal Education, (D) Environmental Bridge, (E) Research and Development Wing, (F) Rural Science Forums, (G) Health Brigade, (H) Art and Science, (I) Balvadis, (J) Women's Group.

The details of these activities are as follows :

Publications : KSSP prints a variety of scientific periodi-cals and books meant for popularisation of science and generation of science literacy amongst the people. These include :

(i) Eureka—monthly magazine for primary classes.
(ii) Sastrakeralam—monthly magazine for high school children.
(iii) Sastragathy—monthly magazine for adults.
(iv) Parishad Vartha—monthly bulletin for members.

Non-formal Education : These activities cover a wide spectrum, the main ones being 'Science Campaign' and 'Science Centre'.

Formal Education : KSSP promotes a number of activities aimed at improving science clubs, talent tests and promotion of awareness about the education system amongst the public. The talent tests are :

(i) Eureka Talent Tests—at elementary level.

(ii) Sastrakeralam Quiz—at high school level.

(iii) Sastragathi Talent Tests—at college level.

Environmental Bridge : KSSP was involved in Silent Valley Campaign, Social Forestry Programmes and campaigns against industrial pollution.

Research and Development Wing : Its responsibility is to develop appropriate rural technology in the field of energy, environment etc. A high efficiency Chulha (Stove), developed by them has been widely propagated.

Rural Science Forums : KSSP has initiated these forums to prompt villagers to think on their own about their problems and solutions.

Health Brigade : KSSP organises health camps, classes and audio-visual campaigns on a wide scale.

Art and Science : It organises Sastra Kala Jatha and Bharat Kala Jatha.

Balvadis : They are working for very young children.

Women's Group : The organisation yet works for welfare and education of women.

Vikram Sarabhai Community Science Centre

For improving the quality of science learning in non-formal system of education, Vikram A. Sarabhai Community Centre was established in Ahmedabad in 1963. The Centre is one of the pioneer organisations in the country providing a variety of out-of-school activities in science for students, teachers and community. It has a team of highly skilled staff which act as a nucleus and catalyst for various programmes undertaken by the Centre.

The Centre conducts research and innovative programmes for improving education and community life. These programmes include studies on science and mathematics, environmental studies, integrated science and science learning improvement programmes through enquiry approach, mathematics laboratory, teacher orientation, designing and development of teaching and learning material packages.

The Centre also organises programmes for rural as well as urban community. These programmes are related to the problems of pollution, health, security, population, communication, settlement and values. The Centre is basically a community centre where people come with their children and learn science where interested teachers and scientists experiment new ideas in teaching and learning. The Centre organises science seminars, film shows, popular lectures, exhibitions, sky-gazing through a telescope, etc. The Centre has a library, laboratories, science museum, workshop, science playground, mass media and A.V. facilities for the community. The Centre provides facilities in rocketry and electronics hobbies to children. In science playground, the children get a glimpse of science through play toys, colour filter towards musical pipes, sand pits, water pond and evolution pillar.

The centre has also started some small extension centres to the rural areas. A mobile van equipped with a laboratory and A.V. materials tours different villages. Science club activities are organised in rural areas based on emphasis on the environmental awareness.

Any other Local Experiment

Studies on the Cognitive Development of Primary School Children. In Delhi, Directorate of Education, Siddiqi (Founder Principal, DIET, Rajinder Nagar, N. Delhi, and one of the authors of this book) conducted these studies during 1975-77 on 1206 students studying in 24 primary schools in Delhi (MCD=10, NDMC=3, Govt.=3, Aided=5, Public=3). Children from 24 schools (about 50 from each school, and about 10 from each class I—V in each school) served the purpose of sample for this study.

Piaget's Work : The conclusion that Piaget has drawn from his many studies has led to a recognition of the difference in the way in which a child thinks at each stage of development—pre-operational, concrete operational and formal operational.

Pre-operational stage (from about 2 years to 6 or 7 years of age): At this stage a child begins to construct sentences. He/she learns to respond to the external world by means of symbols. He/she does not view his/her world as composed of 'constants' properties of objects, do not remain invariant for him/her. He/she does not have concept of conservation. A pre-operational child cannot understand science concepts unless he uses concrete objects and does the same activity several times.

Concrete operational stage (from 6 or 7 years of age to 11 or 12 years of age) : At this stage a child begins to form basic ideas of conservation with the sense that certain properties of objects remain invariant. At this stage a child must have real objects upon which to operate, both physically and mentally. The child can organise data from objects which are present in his immediate environment but he cannot formulate generalising hypotheses or mentally abstract all possible combinations of a given problem. A concrete operational child understands science concepts when he works with concrete objects.

Formal operational stage (from II to 12 years of age) : At this stage a child exhibits the ability to form hypotheses and deduce possible results from these hypotheses. He/she can think in terms of all possible combinations for a given problem and he can function at an abstract level without the necessity of perceiving the objects. A formal operational child can understand science concepts without unsing concerete objects.

The Piaget type tasks developed and used at Florida State University, U.S.A. were slightly modified and used (by the investigator, Siddiqi) in these studies, and it was found that in Delhi (and so in India) at primary level, percentages are as follows :

Pre-operational = 45 8 °/s Concrete operational = 49.8% Formal operational = 4.4%

Recommendations from the Study

The following recommendations are based on these studies for the purpose of providing guidelines to teachers who teach science to primary school children and to science educators who develop instructional material—textbooks, teachers' guides, audio-visual aids etc., and design teaching techniques :

(i) Discourage traditional teaching techniques like book reading and teacher telling.

(ii) Encourage children to find out facts of science by doing experiments and not by memorising.

(iii) Involve children in activities with concrete objects and doing experiments with their own hands.

(iv) Delete the science concepts and activities from the existing science texts which are not compatible with the cognitive level of children.

(v) Introduce only those concepts which are compatible with the cognitive level of children of a particular class and in which use of concrete objects in his immediate environment may be possible.

(vi) Use local resources and environment which is full of real and concrete objects when teaching science to primary school children.

(vii) The above recommendations are the findings of one study which may not necessarily be applicable in all situations.

Academic Games in Science Teaching

To motivate the students especially at an elementary stage it is required that the teacher takes them out of the classroom atmosphere and involves them in activities which seem, to them at least, to be a non-school activity.

Generally, most of the students play a number of games such as science charade and password and other guessing games.

Dr. Kaira, a Prof. in NCERT has developed some games and have found them very successful. The following games can be introduced successfully in a science class especially at the upper primary stage :

Science Charade

The most regular form of this assessment is the acted charade in which the meaning of separate syllables of the word is acted out (by one student) and the audience (other students in class) being left to guess each syllable separately and, finally, the meaning of the dramatized recombination. Like ordinary charades, science charade is a game in which the students try to guess the right elements, compounds or substances acted out by a designd actor student from the class. Although this student actor is not allowed to speak, the student audience is permitted to query him/her. For exaniple :

1. How many words are there in the substance ? (The student actor reveals the number by holding up the appropriate number of fingers).
2. How many letters are there in the substance ? (Again the number is indicated by raising the correct number of fingers).
3. Is it an element or a compound ? (The student actor points to the periodic table to indicate an element).
4. Is it a solid ?

   (The student actor, points to the bench).
5. Is it a liquid ? (He/she indicates the water tap).
6. Is it a gas ? (He/she waves his/her hand in the air). The designated actor may indicate properties of elements and compounds under study by demonstration. Meanwhile the class is writing the guessed elements and their properties with their uses in their notebooks without referring to previous elements. This activity converts memorization as a fun activity.

Science Password

Equipment

1. "A" card containing one-half of a clue of a scientific concept/principle/definition.
2. "B" card containing the complementing half of the scientific concept/principle/definition.
3. Two holders to contain the cards.
4. A scoring dial containing number one to ten and a movable pointer.

Organization

The class is divided into two teams "A" and "B" and arranged in pairs with an opposing partner. (In this way each student participates).

Objective of the Game

To guess the correct "password" from any scientific concept/ principle/definition or clue presented by an opponent pair (The 'A' and 'B' members of the opponent pair alternately "give" and "receive" clue words, contained in a holder to prevent the opposing partner from viewing the correct response).

Procedure

1. The indicating "A" player places the pointer of the scoring dial at 10, he/she then gives a clue word to his/ her partner.
2. If the "B" player fails to make the correct "password" response after this clue, the pointer of the dial is moved to 9 and the turn goes to the opposing "A" and "B" partners.
3. When a player finally guesses the correct password, he/ she scores the point value on the dial indicated by the pointer. For example, if two clue words have been released without a successful "password" response, the point value for the correctly guessed third clue word is 8.
4. If after clues, however (5 given by each player) the password still has not been responsed no "B" player scores for that word. Some examples of password in a science class (chemistry).

Card "A"	*Card "B"*
Ion	Electrically changed particles
Temperature	Represents degree of hotness or coldness
Formula	Represents a molecule of a compound.

To summarize there may be other games such as "snakes and ladders" which may be utilized in a science class indicating "SCIENCE IS FUN."

Environmental Studies Project

These days most of the schools in the country are using NCERT developed Environmental Studies (EVS) Programme at primary stage Before that NCERT developed "science is doing" programme was being used.

With a view to study the existing Science Education Programmes in India, a Planning Mission from UNESCO visited several stages and UTs in 1964 and made some recommendations for improve-ment in teaching of science in Indian schools, in order to expedite the implementation of the scheme. It was decided by the Ministry of Education, Govt. of India to launch a pilot project from the beginning of the next academic year (1965-66). The pilot project covered primary classes (I—V) and middle classes (VI—VIII), and was funded by UNICEF. This project was named UNICEF Assisted Science Education Programme (SEP).

Science is doing

Under this project NCERT developed a National Primary Science Programme, "SCIENCE IS DOING", which was at tryout stage in July 1970. This Programme was a package of :

(a) Class III—V Syllabus and Text Books

(b) Class III—V Teachers' Guides

(c) Class I—II Syllabus

(d) Primary Science Kit and Kit Guide

(e) Two 16 mm films for Teacher Training :

(i) Science is Doing, and

(ii) Primary Science Kit.

In spite of such a good primary science Programme, when the Planning Mission went to the classrooms, they found that science was not doing, it was either reading, telling or in very few cases it was demonstrating.

Environmental Studies

The National Policy on Education 'Kothari Commission Report' (1964-66), implemented in 1975, adopted by the Government of India, recommended that Science should form an integral part of general science for the first ten years of schooling. NCERT examined the question of what type of science courses should be introduced at various levels. One of the major recommendations of the NCERT was that the child should learn the method of inquiry in science right from early days of his schooling. Therefore, the NCERT further recommended that in classes I and II science should be taught as Environmental Studies (EVS) in an integrated form which should include both the social and physical environment i.e. Social Science as well as General Science. Later on in classes III, IV and V two subjects, viz, EVS (Social Science) and P^VS (General Science) should be taught separately. Hence it was proposed that the materials already available in the local environment should be used for teaching science, e.g. bicycle, bullock cart, water pump etc., available in the village environment could be used in explaining many important concepts in Science. Natural environment and its materials should be used as a laboratory for science teaching.

Objectives of EVS : On the basis of Kothari Commission Report NCERT laid down certain objectives for teaching science through environment. They are stated as follows :

1. The main objective is to enable children to observe their environment and to enrich their experience, thereby developing skills in the processes of science, such as observing, communicating, measuring, hypothesising and experimenting to test the hypotheses etc.
2. Besides developing skills in some processes of science, the children, through EVS (Science), if given knowledge of scientific facts and principles, have a better understanding of the phenomenon taking place in the environment around them.
3. The understanding of the environment through application of scientific method, will help children to develop scientific attitude or temper in life, which may comprise

such components as rational outlook, open-mindedness, a positive inclination for democratic, secular stand, socialistic outlook to situations in life, opposition to the prejudices based on sex, caste, religion, language or region.

4. Children will be helped to develop their creative faculties—their imagination and independent thinking for locating problems, suggesting solutions and trying out their ideas.

Revision of Primary Science Curriculum

Based on the Kothari Commission Report (1964-66) implimented in 1975 and the objectives of EVS 'Science is Doing' syllabus for classes I—V was revised. Environment which is full of concrete objects was taken into consideration when the revised science syllabus was framed, and the instructional materials were developed based on the revised Environmental Studies (EVS) syllabus.

The new curriculum, "EVS Programme" developed by NCERT has the following materials :

(i) EVS class I-II (Science and Social Studies) syllabus.

(ii) EVS (Science) syllabus, textbooks and teachers' guides for classes III, IV and V.

(iii) Primary Science Kit

(iv) Mini Tool Kit. This programme may be adopted or adapted by the states and LJTs depending upon tlieir own environment and local resources.

Handbooks of Activities Using Environment and Local Resources

UNICEF also funded several States and Union Territories for developing 'Handbooks of Activities Using Environment and Local Resources' for the use of primary school teachers teaching science, so that they could use NCERT developed EVS textbooks more effectively when teaching science with environmental approach.

Science Branch, Directorate of Education, Delhi also took this project. According to the findings of the Siddiqi's Research studies on the "Cognitive Development of Primary School Children (1975-77)" majority of primary school children (95.6 percent) are either pre-operational or concrete operational and they need concrete objects to learn science concepts and skills. Our environment is full of real and concrete objects, which the children can use to learn science. Based on the findings of these research studies and their implications a "Handbook of Activities Using Environment and Local Resources" was developed by Science

Branch, Directorate of Education, Delhi for the use of primary school teachers teaching science and social studies to classes I and II and science to classes III, IV and V. This UNICEF assisted programme consists of an Environmental kit and a package of seven booklets:

(i) Class I Activities;
(ii) Class II Activities;
(iii) Class III Activities;
(iv) Class IV Activities;
(v) Class V Activities;
(vi) Environmental Kit Guide;
(vii) Class I-II (science and social studies) and classes III-V (science) syllabus.

This is the bank of activities for use of teachers. For one minor idea several activities have been developed to be fit in different environments. This programme was tried out and revised according to the feedback received from experimental schools. Its English version also available which might be useful for those who are interested or engaged in developing such materials in other States and Union Territories of the country as well as in other countries.

Urban Marginal Projects (UNESCO, NCERT, DESM)

Department of Education in Science and Mathematics (DESM) of NCERT took a project 'Environmental Education—A pilot Project on Problems of Urban Marginal Areas in collaboration with Science Branch, Directorate of Education, Delhi (1983). The project was funded by UNESCO.

Need of this Project

The emergence and growth of urban marginal populations, located on the outskirts of towns and cities have been so rapid that their situation has recently been regarded as a cause of concern. The so called "urban poverty belts" are mainly a consequence of the emigration of millions of rural dwellers to town and cities. This material is available with Science Branch, Directorate of Education, Delhi.

Because living conditions in rural areas have been depressed and have become less and less attractive. In consequence, the migrants have been obliged to accept precarious living conditions characterised by such factors as little or no sanitation, drinking water, transportation, unemployment, low levels of education, environmental pollution and landscape deterioration.

In coping with urban marginality, at least in the short term, there is growing conviction that real improvement of the situation should be achieved through specific measures adopted to the needs, problems and characteristics of such population. Education has been an important part to play in contributing of the environmental improvement of these communities in the field of housing, nutrition, health, sanitation and recreation.

Objectives of the Project

1. To contribute to the application of modern scientific and technological achievements to the comprehension and solution of specific environmental problems and to the development of values and attitudes favouring harmonious relationship between people and their environment.
2. To contribute to renovation of educational principles and practices vis-a-vis the environment, that is, development of new interdisciplinary and problem-solving approaches of the challenges of the environment.

Methodology

DESM (NCERT) undertook all the work in connection with planning, development of material and working in the field. This involved :

1. Selection and survey of areas in Delhi.
   — Katwaria Sarai, Khirkee, Chandrawal, Bhooli Bhatiary.
2. Development of questionnaire.
3. Translation of questionnaire from English to Hindi.
4. Selection of monitors (32-38 from each of the 4 areas).
5. Administration of questionnaire.
6. Preparation of coloured slides and black and white photo album.
7. Holding a workshop to write modules.
8. Editing and rewriting of modules.
9. Translation of modules from English to Hindi.
10. Duplication of educational materials both in Hindi and English.
11. Orientation programme for monitors.
12. Use of educational material in the field.

Materials Developed and Used in the Project

Water is essential for Life

1. Need of water for life.
2. Sources of water.
3. How water becomes contaminated ?
4. Harmful effects of contaminated water.
5. How to prevent contamination of water and to avoid water related diseases ?
6. How to make water safe for drinking ?
7. Activity sheet on purification of water.

Diarrhoea

1. How do people get diarrhoea ?
2. Symptoms of diarrhoea.
3. How can it be prevented ?
4. What should be done in case of diarrhoea ?

Waste Disposal

1. Septic tank.
2. Soak pit.
3. "Rog Se Bachav".
4. Malaria.
5. Who is responsible ?
6. Living beings and clean house.

Air Pollution

1. Refined chulha.
2. Solar cooker.
3. Smoke.
4. Fuels
5. Kitchen.

16 mm Films used in the Project

1. "Kachra Mat Phainko".
2. "Vriksha Hamare Mitra".
3. Environmental sanitation.
4. Planning for better living.
5. Spread of diseases-Cholera.
6. Water, friend or enemy.
7. Importance of water.
8. How diseases travel.
9. Cholera.
10. Typhoid ("Anokhi Kahani").

Findings

From the data collected through various visits, interviews with the people and the questionnaire (by the monitors), it was found that:

1. Mostly the members of the family were educated upto secondary level, but there were some people who had their education upto college level.

2. The monthly income of some of the families was quite high, but majority of the people were poor.
3. They had got LPG in their homes, but only a few of them preferred to make use of it. They used cow dung cake, coal etc. as fuel.
4. Most of the houses had electric and tap connections. People preferred to draw water from the well wherever they were there. Some of them washed their clothes on the well and bathe their cattle near the water sources.
5. The houses were built in an old fashion.
6. In some areas the number of rooms in a house was quite high in comparison to the number of members of the family. But mostly the houses were one room tenements.
7. Most of the houses lacked lavatories. Even residents of houses with lavatories preferred to go in the open for defecation. The number of lavatories was less than the number of users.
8. These areas had a smoky atmosphere in the evenings, especially in winters.
9. In Katwaria Sarai and Khirkee there was not much problem of noise pollution, but it did exist in the other two areas.
10. All the areas except Bhooli Bhatiary, had a community lavatory, but it was not being used by most of the people.
11. All the four areas did not have any proper way of disposal of waste.

Use of Educational Materials in the Field

The monitors went to their respective areas with educational materials. They tried to implement the ideas in the people living there. Many residents of the areas were keen to know more about the Environmental Education Project. They performed the activities listed in the activity sheets using the local resources. The materials developed were supplemented with film shows to motivative the people.

Monitoring and Evaluation

Various feedback meetings were held to take note of the impact of the project in the areas. It was observed that people who took interest in such type of activities tried also to bring behavioural change in them. But habit formation was found to be very different, especially in adults, though it was easier to change the habits of the younger generation. The project implementation in the field was of too short a duration to have any visible impact, therefore, it could not be inferred with certainty that there was any significant behavioural change among the people.

Innovative Experiences

There are thousands of innovative experiences in science education. If you know some of them, they might help you in better science teachings. Some examples of such innovative experiences are-Nehru Science Exhibition, Science museums and Sahitya Parishad, Vikram Sarabhai Community Science Centre, Studies on the Cognitive Development of Primary School Children and Handbooks of activities using Environment and Local Resources, Environmental Studies Project, Urban Marginal Studies Project (UNESCO) etc. You can add some more in this list. Study them and see how far they are helpful for better science teaching.

You must have visited Nehru Science Exhibition which is organised around 14th November, the Children's Day, the birth anniversary of Chacha Nehru. In this investigatory projects from all over the country made by school students are displayed. A project is any purposeful activity. It may be a model (static or working), or experiment. A project which involves investigation, discovery and finding out something which was not known to the student before, is an investigatory science project.

You must have seen some science museums. They are very effective and interesting sources of learning science. Some science museums have mobile science units, museums on wheel. They are usually sent to the places where there are no science museums. They are not so big as a science museum. They do not have as many science exhibits as a science museum has. But even this is a very effective source of learning science for students at upper primary level.

Ekalavya is a group of innovative university and school teachers of science and social studies. It has developed some curriculum material in science and social studies in Hoshangabad, Madhya Pradesh for the use of upper primary school children. That is why it is called Hoshangabad project. This curriculum material is full of very interesting activities, and it is being used in some Madhya Pradesh schools for several years.

The Kerala Shastra Sahitya Parishad (KSSP) is a voluntary organisation of scientists, doctors, engineers, social scientists, teachers, students, peasants and technicians. It was established in 1963. It has number of science activities based on some identified objectives.

Vikram Sarabhai Community Science Centre is situated in Ahmedabad, Gujarat. It has science and computer labs, workshops, a number of science publications and a lot of simple, handy and attractive science equipment. You and your students can learn a lot of science if you are there and engage yourself even for few days.

In Delhi Directorate of Education, Siddiqi (Founder Principal District Institute of Education and Training, Rajinder Nagar, New Delhi) conducted studies on the Cognitive Development of Primary School Children during 1975-77, 1206 Primary School Children were interviewed on Piagets' type tasks. On an average 15 minutes took to interview a child, thus 300 hours were spent for interviewing 1206 children. It was found that only 4.4% children were at formal operational stage, who could perhaps understand science concepts without using concrete objects. The remaining 95.6% children were either at concrete operational stage (who could not understand science concepts without using concrete objects) or pre-operational stage (who could not understand science concepts, unless they do activities by their own hands again and again using concrete objects). This shows that you have to teach science to children in the same class with different methods according to their cognitive stages. Based on the findings of these studies, Delhi Directorate of Education, with the help of some innovative teachers and teacher educators developed 'Handbooks of Activities Using Environment and Local Resources' for classes I—V. They were tried out in Delhi schools, and according to the feedback received, they were revised. Afterwards they were published by Delhi Bureau of Textbooks (DBTB) and are being used by MCD and NDMC primary school children.

In 1970 NCERT developed 'Science is Doing' programme for primary school children. The programme included textbooks. teachers' guides, primary science kit and a kit guide. The kit had all the materials to do all the activities given in the textbooks and listed in the kit guide. Then in 1980s NCERT switched over to Environmental Studies (EVS) from 'Science is Doing'. The primary science kit was revised. Now the EVS activities can be performed with the help of the materials of the revised primary science kit along with the materials existing in the environment. Now NCERT developed EVS programme is being used in primary classes throughout the country.

Department of Education in Science and Mathematics (DESM) of NCERT took a project 'Environmental Education—A Pilot Project on Problems of Urban Marginal Areas' in collaboration with Science Branch, Directorate of Education, Delhi (1963). The project was funded by UNESCO. Four urban marginal areas in Delhi were selected and surveyed. Some materials (water is essential for life, diarrhoea, waste disposal, air pollution) were developed and used in these areas. This contributed to the environmental improvement of these areas in the field of housing, nutrition, health, sanitation and recreation.

Questions

1. List eight innovative experiences.
2. What is the difference between a 'science project', and 'an investigatory science project' ? Cite some concrete examples.
3. What is the difference between a 'science museum' and a 'mobile science unit' ? How will you use them in science teaching ?
4. What are the cognitive stages of primary school children? How will you teach children in the same class but in differ-ent cognitive stages ?

5. What is the difference between 'Science is Doing' and 'Environmental studies' projects at primary level ?
6. (i) When is the 'Nehru Science Exhibition' organised?
   (ii) Name science museums you have seen.
   (iii) In which city and state Ekalavya Experience Project was started ?
   (iv) What do you mean by 'KSSP' ? When was it established?
   (v) Name the city and state where "Vikram Sarabhai Community Science Centre' is situated ?
   (vi) Who conducted the studies on the cognitive development of primary school children in Delhi, and developed 'Handbooks of Activities Using Environment and Local Resources ?

12

Evaluation Process

Construction of Test Items

If a teacher wishes to have an adequate basis for judging the quality of his instruction, he should use tests that accurately and representatively reflect his objectives. How can he assure this accuracy? Unless he has access to prepared items, he must get into the business of writing tests himself. Tests that the teacher produced have the advantage of being right on the instructions format that is essentially equivalent to the teachers' instructional goals. The performance of students therefore, can be used to make valid judgements regarding the performance of the teacher, generally in terms of the previously established class minimal level of students' performance.

Tests designed exclusively to measure the objectives taught are called criterion-referenced tests. Their purpose unlike that of norm-referenced (standardized) tests is not to make differentiations among achievement levels of various students but to measure accurately how well each student has attained stated objectives. Norm-referenced tests are relative measures.

Criterion-referenced tests are usually employed at the conclusion of an instructional sequence. Testing is usually product based knowledge, understanding and application (Based on Bloom's Taxonomy of Educational Objectives).

Knowledge, Understanding and Application

Knowledge. It includes the recall of specifics and universals. The recall of methods and procedures, or the recall of a pattern structure, or setting. For measurement purposes, the recall situation involves little more than bringing to mind the appropriate material. The mental ability involved in this operation is just memory and not any higher ability.

Examples

Objective type (Multiple Choice)

Put a tick mark (ü) on the statement which is most appropriate. Food stuff which is a rich source of energy is named :

1. Vegetable	☐	2. Cereals	☐
3. Pulses	☐	4. Fruits	☐

Short Answered

Mention two uses of bacteria.

Long Answered

Why cycling is less strenuous on a smooth road as compared to a rough road ?

Understanding–It is based on knowledge. Knowledge is necessary but not sufficient for understanding, because the latter requires the ability to translate, to interpret, or to extrapolate. One example of understanding may be taken from Science, where one is required to translate verbal material into a symbolic statement and vice-versa. Statement that if we add dilute hydrochloric acid on marble pieces, carbon dioxide gas is given out, if translated in formula we write :

$$CaCO_3 + 2HCl = CaCl_2 + H_2O + CO_2$$

Examples

Multiple Choice

Put a tick (✓) mark on the statement which is most appropriate. Gas which helps in extinguishing fire is called :

(1) Hydrogen ☐

(2) Nitrogen ☐

(3) Oxygen ☐

(4) Carbon dioxide ☐

(5) Chlorine ☐

Short Answered

How moving water can be used as a source of energy ?

Application It requires something more than knowledge and understanding. Application is a step ahead of this level. It implies the ability to apply an abstraction e.g. formula, principle, law etc., to an unfamiliar or novel situation. In fact, this is one of those abilities or skills, which are of great functional importance in every day life. The test of useful or meaningful learning is that it can be applied in relevant situation other than the one in which it has been acquired.

Short Answered

1. Why does it take longer time to make tea or cook food in hill stations ?
2. A lighted candle is fixed on a small metal plate and is kept in a trough half filled with water, and then a glass is inverted over the lighted candle, keeping the mouth of the beaker under water. After some time the candle gets extinguished and the level of water inside the glass increases. Why the water level inside the glass increases?

Process Skill Items

It has already been stated that process skill in science can be divided into 13 areas—observing, classifying, using numbers, measuring, using space-time relationships. Communicating, predicting, inferring, defining operationally, formulating hypotheses, interpreting data, controlling veriables, and experimenting.

Example

Children are taken for outing in the tour. Students may be grouped in small batches and advised to see and make a note of things in their copy book. Objective of the outing is to get children acquainted with the phenomenon or Force, Work and Energy, in their surroundings.

Before they are taken for outing, lesson on force, work and energy, has already been taught in the school.

Teachers ask them to observe the things around them. They will observe many things, may be some tools in a workshop, bullock cart, cycle, bus, cars, scooters, etc. being plied on the smooth or rough roads. They might come across some labourers loading or unloading heavy articles from a truck or they might see flour mill or tools of a carpenter or of a tailor master.

On the basis of observation a list of all the things observed is prepared. Groups compare their notes. Teacher now asks them to classify the things, where force has been used, work is being done, and the energy which helps in the working.

In the school, different groups will communicate [Learner—Learner Interation (LLI)] with each other on the basis of their observations or may be, they might make some sort of communication with the carpenters or the owner of tailoring shop. They can also be asked to make models of the tools they observed. Experimentation starts which follows interpretation and prediction.

Following Questions can be asked by the Teacher

1. Name four situations where force is used to move objects.
2. Why on a rough road the speed of cyclist was slow as compared to a smooth road ?
3. What was the source of energy in moving a cart, cycle, car or train ?
4. What are the alternative sources of energy ?
5. Give two examples where friction is used.
6. Why cannot we walk comfortably on ice ?
7. Why do we slip if our feet fall on banana scale lying on a road ?
8. Give two examples where work is done, even when force is applied.

9. Can air be used as alternative source of energy? Give examples.
10. How a flour mill works ?

Interests and Attitudes

Interests and attitudes are non-scholastic areas.

Interests

Observation is made by the teacher and rating scales can be prepared on the following topics pertaining to science :

Scientific Areas

1. Reads science literature.
2. Prepares charts and models.
3. Improvises science apparatus.
4. Takes part in science activities like debates, chart making, science clubs, contributing articles to magazines on scientific topic.
5. Collects material pertaining to science, insects, flowers, leaves, seeds, fruits, small scientific toys, museum specimen etc.
6. Maintains herbarium or acquarium.
7. Has interest in visiting places of scientific interest.
8. Meets people working in the field of science and discusses with them.
9. Appreciates inventions and discoveries.
10. Makes scientific models and participates in science quizes etc.

Attitudes

1. Listens to the teacher attentively in the class.
2. Puts problems and solutions before teaching.
3. Is curious to learn more and at times uses the library.
4. Participates in science clubs, fairs, exhibition etc.
5. Contributes to the scientific activities.

6. Helps the teacher in finding solutions in scientific field.
7. Cooperates with school mates.
8. Prevents others from disturbing the functioning of science fairs, science clubs, exhibitions, and museums.
9. Is considerate with his class mates.
10. Contributes to science activities.

Exercise: For evaluating Intersts and Attitudes you can observe your students. Discuss how will you do this Evaluation?

Citizen Referenced Tests

Criterian referenced tests are the tests designed to measure the identified objectives. They measure how well each student has attained stated objectives. These tests are usually used at the conclusion of an instructional sequence. They test knowledge, understanding and application. Norm referenced tests make differentiations among achievement levels or various students. They are relative measures.

For each knowledge, understanding and application you can construct different types of tests-multiple choice, very short answered, short answered, long answered (essay type), true and false, matching etc. It will be very useful if you identify a topic, and its content, and write objectives in behavioural terms before constructing test items. Then for each objective construct one or more test items.

Observing, classifying, measuring, communicating, experimenting, inferring, interpreting and predicting are some examples of science processes when students are doing some science activities. You can test whether your students have learned science processes, by looking at them, listening to their discussion, interacting with them and asking them to do something.

Interests and attitudes are non-scholastic areas. Written tests perhaps will not be able to test whether your students are interested in science or have scientific attitude. For this you are to identify some activities for scientific interest and some activities for scientific attitude, say ten each. Then observe which activities they really do. If they do all the activities, grade them as A; if they do more than half the activities, grade them as B; if they do about half the activities, grade them as C; if they do less than half the activities, grade them as D; if they do none of the activities, grade them as E. This is only suggestive. This will tell you where your students stand in scientific interest and scientific attitude.

Questions

1. What is the difference between 'criterian-referenced tests' and 'norm-referenced tests' ?
2. Select a topic of your choice from upper primary science course and construct the test items as directed below :
   (i) *Knowledge* : one multiple choice, one short answered and one long answered.
   (ii) *Understanding* : three questions as above.
   (iii) *Application* : three questions as above.

   Note. For each question first write a behavioural objective.
3. How will you test that the students have learned science processes ? Cite some concrete examples.
4. Write ten activities being done by your students for observing with which you can say whether they are/are not interested in science.
5. Write ten activities being done by your students for observing them with which you can say whether they have/do not have scientific attitude.
6. Select a topic of your choice for (a) Class VI, (b) Class VII, and (c) class VIII. Write 10 behavioural objectives for each topic. For each behavioural objective, construct multiple choice test items—3 of knowledge, 4 of understanding and 3 of application.

13

Behavioural Objectives

Writing Objectives in Behavioural Terms

1. A statement of instructional objective is a collection of words or symbols describing one of your instructional intents.
2. An objective will communicate your intent to the degree you have described what the learner will be doing when demon-strating his achievement and how you will know when he is doing it.
3. To describe the terminal behavior (what the learner will be doing):
   (a) Identify and name the overall behaviour act.
   (b) Define the important conditions under which the behaviour is to occur given or restrictions or both).
   (c) Define the criterion of acceptable performance.
4. Write a separate statement for each objective; the more statements you have the better chance you have of making clear your intent.
5. If you give each learner a copy of your objectives, you may not have to do much else.

Example : Given a thermometer (condition): the student will read the temperature—(Behaviour) with 100% accuracy (Criterion)

When writing behavioural objectives condition and criterion may be eliminated but not the Behaviour.

Behavioural Terms for Stating Specific Objectives

When stating objectives in behavioural terms, some keywords (called behavioural terms) are used. In the cognitive domain there are six categories of objectives—knowledge, understudying (comprehension), application, analysis, synthesis and evaluation. The teachers should practise in writing behavioural objectives in all these categories. For convenience behavioural terms for each category are given below :

Knowledge—define, describe, identify, label, list, match, name, outline, reproduce, select, state.

Understanding (comprehension)—convert, explain, extend, generalize, give example, infer, paraphrase, predict, rewrite, summarize.

Application—change, compute, demonstrate, discover, manipulate, modify, operate, predicate, prepare, relate, show, solve, use.

Analysis—break down diagrams, differentiate, discriminate, distinguish identify, illustrate, infer, outline, point out, relate, select, separate, subdivide.

Synthesis—categorize, combine, compile, compose, create, devise, design, explain, generate, modify, organize, plan, rearrange, revise, rewrite, summarise, tell, write.

Evaluation—appraise, compare, conclude, contrast, describe, discriminate, explain, justify, interpret, relate, summarize, support.

Test Items and Behavioural Objectives

When objectives are clearly defined and stated in behavioural terms, it is easy to develop test items for evaluation. Teachers should practise in constructing test items for identified objectives stated in behvioural terms. Some sample test items developed on some behavioural objectives are as follows :

An Atom

Behavioural Objectives	*Test Items*
1. The students will identify the definition of atom with 100 per cent accuracy.	1. The smallest unit of element is a/an (a) electron (b) atom (c) molecule (d) proton
2. Given a list of material objects such as proton, positron, electron and neutron the students will	2. The atom consists of all the following EXCEPT (a) electron (b) proton (c) positron (d) nucleus
3. The students will write, how weight of electron, neutron and proton are related (weight of neutron is approximately equal to the weight of proton and weight of electron is negligible compared to the weight of proton and neutron) by memory with 100 per cent.	3. The weight of a neutron approximately equal to the weight of (a) electron (b) proton (c) twice the proton (d) none of them 4. Weight of an electron is (a) equal to the weight of neutron (b) equal to the weight of proton (c) negligibly small (d) more than the weight of proton or neutron.
4. The students will write the charges of electron, proton and neutron (negative, positive, neutral) by memory with 100 per cent accuracy.	5. The charge of a proton is (a) positive (b) negative (c) neutral (d) sometimes negative and sometimes positive 6. A negatively charged atomic particle is (a) proton (b) electron (c) neutron (d) nucleus 7. The neutral particle of an atom is (a) electron (b) proton (c) neutron (d) nucleus

Contd.

Behavioural Objectives	*Test Items*
5. Given a diagram of atomic model the students will label the parts (shells) and nucleus with 100 per cent accuracy.	8. 'A' represents (a) shell (b) nucleus (c) both a and b (d) none of them. 9. 'B' represents (a) shell (b) nucleus (c) both a and b (d) none of them.
6. Given the number of protons and electrons in an atom the students will write the charge of that atom with 100 per cent accuracy.	10. If an atom has 17 protons in its nucleus and 17 electrons in the shells the charge of the atom is (a) positive (b) negative (c) neutral (d) none of them
7. The students will write the position of protons, neutrons, and electrons in the atom by memory with 100 per cent accuracy.	11. The nucleus of an atom has (a) protons only (b) neutrons only (c) both neutrons and protons. (d) electrons only. 12. Which of the particles are found outside the nucleus in an atom? (a) neutron (b) electron (c) proton (d) none of them.
8. Given the number of protons and neutrons, the students will write the atomic weight of the element.	13. An element has 11 protons, 11 electrons and 12 neutrons. The atomic weight of the element is (a) 11 (b) 12 (c) 22 (d) 23
9. Given the number of electrons or protons in an atom, the students will write the atomic number of the element.	14. An element has 8 electrons, 8 protons and 8 neutrons. The atomic number of the element is (a) 8 (b) 16 (c) 24 (d) 36

Contd.

Behavioural Objectives	*Test Items*
10. Given the number of particular shell (1st, 2nd last, next to last) the students will write the maximum number of electrons in that shell with 100 per cent accuracy.	15. An atom has 8 electrons. The number of electrons in its 2nd shell will be (a) 2 (b) 6 (c) 8 (d) 18
11. Given the atomic number and atomic weight of an element the students will write the number of electrons in various shells and the number of protons and neutrons in the nucleus with 100 per cent accuracy.	16. The atomic number of an element is 17 and its atomic weight is 35. All of the following statements are correct EXCEPT (a) the nucleus will have 17 protons and 18 neutrons (b) the nucleus will have 18 protons and 17 neutrons (c) the first shell will have 2 electrons (d) the third shell will have 7 electrons.

Answers

1. (b)	7. (c)	13. (d)
2. (c)	8. (b)	14. (a)
3. (b)	9. (a)	15. (b)
4. (c)	10. (c)	16. (b)
5. (a)	11. (c)	
6. (b)	12. (b)	

Behavioural Objectives and Learning Outcomes

Objectives written in behavioural terms to be achieved by students of a particular class level are called Learning Outcomes.

Cognitive Domain

Knowledge

The student acquires KNOWLEDGE of terms, facts, concepts, definitions, fundamental laws, principles and processes in the field of Science.

Learning Outcomes

The Student

1. recalls, terms, facts, concepts, principles and processes related to Science.
2. recognises various terms, facts, concepts and principles of Science.

Understanding (Comprehension)

The student develops Understanding of terms, facts, concepts, fundamental laws, principles and processes in the field of Science. Learning Outcomes

The Student

1. translates verbal statements into symbolic equation and vice-versa.
2. gives illustrations of principles of Science.
3. sees relationship between cause and effect of Scientific phenomena.
4. compares various methods, concepts, principles, etc.
5. detects errors in given statements, circuit, arrangements, etc. and rectifies the same.
6. classifies as per criteria, the objects, etc.
7. gives explanation or scientific phenomena, principles, concepts etc.
8. reads and interprets graph.
9. solves numerical problems involving Scientific concepts etc.
10. recognises the significance and limitations of scientific principles.

Applications

The student applies his knowledge and understanding of Science to unfamiliar situations.

Learning Outcomes

The Student

1. analyses the unfamiliar situations, statements, observations, evidence, etc.
2. formulates hypotheses based on data, observations etc.
3. devices new experiments for verifications of the hypotheses and for known laws and principles etc.
4. establishes relationship between cause and effect, the known and unknown.
5. selects the principles relevant to a phenomenon.
6. gives reasons to explain unfamiliar scientific phenomena.
7. draws inferences and conclusions from the given data or observed phenomena.
8. makes predictions on the basis of data, evidence etc.
9. judges the relevance, adequacy and consistency in statement, data, evidences etc.

Psychomotor Domain

Skills

The student develops :

(a) observation skills

(b) manipulation skills

(c) drawing skills

(d) Reporting skills.

Learning Outcomes

Observation Skills

The student

1. reads instruments accurately.
2. lakes observations in a systematic and sequential manner.
3. takes the number of observations necessary.
4. reads graphs accurately.

Manipulation Skills

The Student

1. selects appropriate apparatus, tools etc.
2. checks the tools, apparatus, equipments, regarding its working.
3. knows the limitation of the apparatus etc.
4. sets the apparatus in a proper way.
5. performs the experiments with reasonable accuracy, neatness.
6. makes correct substitution of formula (if any).
7. calculates the result accurately.
8. interprets data and draws conclusion.

Drawing Skills

The Student

1. draws neat, proportionate and correct diagrams.
2. labels the diagram correctly.
3. draws graph, selecting proper scale.

Reporting Skills

The Student

1. presents the observations in an appropriate manner/ sequence.
2. presents the calculations/results in proper sequence/ manner/units.
3. calculates (and compares) the percentage error etc. using appropriate symbols and formulae.
4. explains orally the procedures, precautions and limitation of the equipments, apparatus and experiments.

Appreciation

The student Appreciates the contribution of Science to human happiness.

Learning Outcomes

The Student

1. follows and adjusts to the impact of science on society and individual.
2. derives pleasure in understanding the scientific advances.
3. feels that more inventions and discoveries are possible.
4. shows respect and admiration for great scientists.
5. manifests a spirit of scientific enquiry.

Interests

The student develops interest in the world of physical science.

Learning Outcomes

The Student

1. puts questions in scientific discussions frequently.
2. reads scientific literature and biographies of prominent scientists with a satisfaction.
3. takes up scientific hobbies in his spare time.
4. takes parts in science talks and debates willingly.
5. visits places of scientific interest on his own.
6. organises and actively participates in science club activities.
7. contributes articles on topics of scientific interest frequently.
8. enjoys observing natural and man-made surroundings.

Attitudes. The student develops scientific Attitude through the study of science.

Learning Outcomes

The Student

1. respects the Science teacher.
2. records and interprets his observations honestly.

3. bases his judgements on verified facts and not on opinion.
4. is willing to consider new ideas and discoveries.
5. is prepared to reconsider his own judgement.
6. develops independent thinking.
7. pursues his activities with precision and consistency undaunted by failures.
8. shows spirit of team work, self-help and self-reliance.
9. realises the danger in the misuse of scientific knowledge.

14

The Analysis

Evaluation procedures are based on the objectives of teaching the subject. Therefore, any evaluation tool or technique which is not related to the goals of teaching the subject is meaningless and will not result in getting valid evidence. A well-conceived evaluation programme will reveal upto what extent a particular objective has been achieved. This can be secured by defining objectives in terms of learning outcomes or the behavioural changes intended to be brought in the students. For all this we need to analyse the evaluation data, so that we can find out which of expected behavioural changes have not been brought in the students. Poor results in relation to a particular objective indicate that it is highly pitched and is beyond the level of students achievement. Conversely, an exceptionally high score by all students with respect to an objective shows that the objective is below the standard of the students and hence may be discarded or modified.

In this way teachers can (through proper analysis of the test results) know whether the objectives prescribed are suitable or not for a particular level of students or class.

Scholastic and non-scholastic areas are being continuously tested. Tests are analysed and interpreted before drawing up conclusions and finally for entering the findings in the progress report.

The data can be analysed differently:

— subject wise,
— learning outcome wise,
— topic wise,
— response wise.

Subject Wise Analysis

Subjects	*A*	*B*	*C*	*D*	*E*	*F*	*G*	*H*	*I*
Science	40	8	42	50	37	46	38	45	46
Maths	60	25	100	80	50	57	46	68	65
Language	58	20	60	75	40	28	35	66	36

— The class as a whole is weak in science but their general performance is very good in mathematics and fairly well in language.
— Though student C has scored 100 marks in maths, but on an average student D is better than C.
— Student B has shown very bad results. He needs remedial teaching and diagnosis.
— Tests in science may be high pitched as compared to other subjects.

Learning Outcome Wise Analysis
(Objective Understanding)

Specifications Students	*Trans-lates*	*Cites Examples*	*Compares*	*Classifies*
A	60	68	18	15
B	70	65	15	18
C	75	80	17	22
D	80	72	22	18
E	78	52	14	9

— Achievement on understanding objective is not satisfactory.

— Students are good in their ability to translate and cite examples.

— Attainment with relationship to compare and classify is very poor and needs special attention.

— Teaching process needs improvement.

Topic Wise Analysis
Class VI (Science)

Topic / *Students*	*Communicable Diseases (100)*	*Force, Work Energy (100)*	*Shadows Eclipses (100)*
A	61	12	50
B	55	8	40
C	80	10	60
D	52	7	57
E	75	15	61
F	60	9	42

— Students have better understanding of topic 'Communicable Diseases'.

— Force, Work and Energy topic has not been well understood by students. Teacher has to be more attentive.

— Shadows and Eclipses topic is well treated.

Response Wise Analysis
(Multiple choice questions)

Item No.	*A*	*B*	*C*	*D*	*O*	*Total*
1.	15	10	*50	14	11	100
2.	05	*86	00	06	03	100
3.	12	*07	12	30	39	100
4.	*04	12	00	09	75	100
5.	05	05	02	*88	00	100

— Figures indicate percentage of students who attempted that alternative.

— *indicates the correct answer.

— ABCD are the choices given in the item.

— O means the item omitted.

Analysis

— Item No. 1 was attempted almost by all the students except 11%. 50% gave correct answer. From difficulty level the question is good, as the distractors are homogeneous.

— Item No. 2 is very easy as 86% gave correct answer. Distractor C did not work as none marked this as correct.

— Item No. 3 is difficult as only 7% gave correct answer.

— For item No. 4 only 4% gave correct answer and 75% omitted. It may be that the question is misleading and needs investigation.

— For item No. 5, 88% gave correct answer, none omitted it. It is an easy item. It seems that almost none of the distractors is functional.

So there is need for the analysis and its scope is quite wide.

Feedback to Students

Diagnosis by Formative Assessment

On the basis of formative assessment where the different kinds of achievement tests are given at regular intervals, we can know the weak and strong points about the person who has been tested and suggestions can be made. Good examples are :

1. If a student scores 45 marks in Science, teacher will consider the child as mediocre. But if the teacher goes into details and finds that the maximum score in the class in Science is 55 and minimum is 10, and in the previous test the student has scored 35 marks, opinion of the teacher changes and the student is considered to be a good one who is making progress.

2. If a student's score in Science is 80 and in maths it is only 40, it means he is excellent in Science but poor in Maths. If the teacher compares the scores with the scores of the class and finds that the highest score in Maths achieved is 50 and lowest 6, then the opinion changes and the student is considered to be one of the best students.

Diagnostic Test Charts

Teacher has to prepare two charts which may be called diagnostic test charts.

Student Error Chart: The teacher has to put a mark right (^/) or wrong (x) against each item. He has also to state the actual error in the following form :

Student Error Charts

Name of the Student .... Class..............................

Subject .... Test Title ....

Item No.	*Right or Wrong*	*Actual error if wrong*
1.		
2.		
3.		
4.		
5.		

Student Item Chart. After having scored all the answer books or answer scripts, the teacher prepares a "Student Item Chart" in the following form :

Student Item Chart

Class......................... Subject.................... Test title..................................

S.No. .... Name of the students...

Name of the students are to be entered in the chart in order of merit, the student getting the highest score being put at the top. Against each student's name the right and wrong answers are to be indicated by two separate marks, say (✓) and (X) respectively. A look at this chart will clearly reveal groups of students giving wrong answers to specific items. The next step for the teacher to take would be to go back into the 'student error chart' of each student to get an idea as to what specific mistake the student has committed. Equipped with the information the teacher gets feedback and can go in for remedial action which can be one or both of the following.

Remediation

1. Personal consultation with the teacher—the teacher will know if the mistake committed is due to carelessness or misunderstanding. Student can be given a chance for correcting the mistake.

   In some cases the causes of the mistake may be maladjustment or some emotional problems. This can be remedied by personal counselling. Sometimes the case can also be referred to psychological clinics.

2. Remedial exercises and other strategies—the teacher can help students by giving remedial exercises in the form of oral drill, written exercises, library reading, mutual help in group under teacher's supervision, supervised self-learning through programmed material, audio-visual aids, demonstrating experiments or allowing students to do scientific activities under his supervision.

So formative assessment provides useful feedback to students by locating their errors and difficulties. This gives an information to the student about the ideas he still needs to learn or review.

Feedback to Teachers

An analysis of the errors made by the students can be used to identify the facts, concepts, principles etc. with which the students are having difficulty. If majority of the students (say 60%) in a class are not able to master a particular concept it may be regarded as inefficiency of the instructional material or instructional process. In some cases errors are made by only a few students.

Following Remedial Measures can be taken by the Teachers

1. Teacher can attempt to reteach the particular concept, where low achievement have been found in majority of the students.
2. Where a few percentage of students failed to understand the concept, they may take help from the teacher, or they can even seek cooperation from more able students of the class.
3. Formative assessment material may be used by the teacher for quality control.
4. If content and objectives are similar, the teacher may compare the performance of one year to another (here children have changed but still general assessment will give overall picture).
5. Teachers should improve their knowledge and teaching techniques.
6. Inservice teacher training programme can be organised for the teachers at least once in five years.
7. Management/Head of the Institution should also check the quality and help the teachers as and when required.

Formative Assessment

The New Education Policy (1986) visualizes evaluation as an integral part of teaching-learning process. Emphasis has been laid on 'Formative role of evaluation', this will help to improve the teaching-learning process and also the process of curriculum construction at the formative stage. Assessment of a child starts right from the point when a child begins formal course of study.

Evaluation has three phases—entry assessment, formative assessment and summative assessment. In summative assessment children are to achieve the defined expected levels of competence on the basis of test administered.

Formative assessment on the other hand is basically utilised for purposes of guidance and is built into the transaction of the curriculum. It supplies a lot of diagnostic and achievement data about individual children. This achievement data can be used by the teachers to ensure that the minimum levels of learning are attained by all children. Formative assessment intervenes during the formation stage that is, when the process of teaching and learning is going on and not after it is completed. It seems two important purposes of evaluation.

— It points to the areas where corrective and remedial measures are needed.

— It evaluates the process of learning.

Objectives of Formative Assessment

Ralph Tyler in 1942 considered that the primary function of evaluation is to determine the extent to which students have or have not changed in relation to the set of desired behaviours. The emphasis in his approach was mainly summative. Investigators like Gagne, Glaser and Mager were interested to know why a set of desired objectives have or have not been achieved that is, why an instructional programme worked or failed to work. They, therefore, evaluated each step of the instructional programme, in relation to desired set of objectives. Such an approach would help to improve the instructional package in the development phase, rather than pondering over its failure after the programme is completed. Emphasis in this approach is primarily on the formative evaluation, that is, the formative stage.

Formative assessment determines how well the students are assi-milating various intermediate components. In formative assessment four components—concepts, skills/competencies, specific task/ behaviours and tools of evaluation are used. Detailing of every con-cept is made on these lines for effective teaching-learning process.

All the students can achieve the desired objectives of learning if scheme of formative assessment is properly used. When student is continuously evaluated and guided through formative evaluation scheme, there is no reason for the failure in the final summative evaluation/assessment.

Achievement Test

Frequency of a Score or Group of Scores

During practice teaching you are to construct achievement tests in various subjects and so in science, administer it, analyse it and submit the report. Let us discuss how to do all this.

Example–Let us start with a Diagnostic Test in Science for the students of DIET, Rajinder Nagar, N. Delhi.

The marks obtained by the ETE II year student in the Diagnostic Test for Science are as follows :

(Maximum Marks 100)

60	65	15	75	60	59	50	40
46	62	33	40	39	48	68	72
74	46	63	43	69	71	78	48
64	49	45	45	69	55	68	61
73	74	67	65	45	59	61	61
58	49	55					

The data from tests and experiments need to be classified and organised in a systematic way for understanding the meanings and deriving some useful conclusions.

For this purpose, the scores are distributed into groups of scores (classes) and each score is allotted a place in their respective group or class. It may also be carefully noted how many times a particular score or group of scores occur in the given data. This is known as the frequency of a score or group of scores.

Now, tabulate these scores in a Frequency distribution as follows:

Steps for Grouping Data into Frequency Distribution

Finding the range–First of all find out the range of the series. Range can be found as :

Range = Highest score—Lowest score

In the present example the Range is

Highest score = 78

Lowest score = 33

Range = 78 – 33 = 45

Determining the Class Interval or Grouping Interval–To have an idea of the size of the classes i.e. class-interval, the range is divided by the number of classes desired. Class-interval is usually denoted by the symbol 'i' and is always a whole number.

Therefore, class-interval is calculated as follows :

$$i = \frac{\text{Range}}{\text{Number of classes desired}}$$

Here range is 45. Scores are 43 in number and thus about ten classes are sufficient. Therefore

$$i = \frac{45}{10}$$

= 4.5 i.e. Nearest whole number is 5.

∴ Length of class interval = 5.

Making a Frequency Distribution–After deciding the size and number of class-interval and range, a frequency distribution is made as follows :

For writing the classes of distribution the class of scores are tabulated. First, decide the lowest class and then the subsequent classes according to class-interval. In the present example, 30-34 can be taken as the lowest class and then 35-39, 40-44 up to 75-79.

Tallying the scores into proper classes—The scores given in the data are taken one by one and tallied in the proper classes.

These tally marks are then totalled, which comprise the total frequencies or number of that class denoted by N (here N = 43). The tallies against each class are also totalled separately.

Checking the tallies— Check that the total frequencies or number is equal to the number of individuals whose scores have been tabulated.

Measure of Central Tendency

It can be seen that there are very few students who either score very high or low. The marks of the most of the students lie somewhere between the highest and the lowest scores of the whole class. Then this tendency of statistical data is called Central Tendency and the typical score lying between the extremes and shared by most of the students is referred to as a measure of Central Tendency. The most common measures of central tendency are mean, median and mode.

Mean

Mean gives us the 'average' and is the sum of all the scores in a series divided by the number of scores. But in the case of grouped data as in our case the mean is to be calculated as follows:

First find out the mid-point or X of the class-interval, for example for the class 30-34 the mid-point is found as follows:

$$X = \frac{30+34}{2} = \frac{64}{2} = 32$$

Similarly, the mid-points for the other class-intervals.

(a) Multiply X by 'f the frequency of the class-interval.

(b) Add up f X, the sum can be represented as E f X.

(c) N is the total of all the frequencies. Then calculate Mean by the formula.

The calculation for the present data for mean can be seen in this chapter.

The mean for the present scores is 57.58. The mean value gives us and idea of the level of average achievement by the students in the test. It also helps us to carry out the comparison with other students, the one who scores above the average and the one who scores below it.

Median

The median of a series may be defined as 'The point on the score scale below which one-half or 50 per cent of the scores fall.

Or in simpler terms it is that figure above and below which there are equal number of figures. But it is not the central score which is the median. Instead it is only the measure or value of the central item that is known as the median. The median for the grouped data can be calculated. It can be compiled as follows :

First determine the figure in which the median falls viz. the total of frequencies of N, in this case it is 43. The formula for determining it is as follows :

$$\frac{N+}{2}$$

$$=\frac{43+}{2}$$

$$=\frac{44}{2}=22$$

It means that we have to find out the figure which is at the 22nd place. The total of the frequencies from below comes to 21 (F) upto class-interval 55—59. But we have to find out the figure at the 22nd place. So we can say that the 22nd place will be the next to that which is compiled by finding the mean of the seven figures and adding it. Therefore, the median at the 22nd place will lie next higher to it viz. in the class-interval 60-64. This class interval is known as median class.

Where median can be calculated by the formula as follows :-

$$\text{Median} = L + \left[\frac{N/2-F}{fm}\right]\times i$$

where,

i → Length of class-interwal.

L → Exact lower limit of the median class.

N → Total of all the frequencies.

F → The total of all the frequencies before the median class.

fm → The number of the frequencies of the group in which the median lies in class-interval. Therefore median for the TABLE can be calculated as follows:

$$\text{Median} = L + \left[\frac{\frac{N}{2} - F}{fm}\right] \times i$$

Where $L = 59.5, \ \frac{N}{2} = \frac{43}{2},$

$F = 21, \ fm = 8, \ i = 5$

$$\textit{Hence Median} = 59.5 + \left[\frac{\frac{43}{2} - 21}{8}\right] \times 5$$

$$= 59.5 + \left[\frac{21.5 - 21}{8}\right] \times 5$$

$$= 59.5 + \frac{0.5 \times 5}{8}$$

$$= 59.5 + \frac{2.5}{8}$$

$$= 59.5 + 0.31$$

$$= 59.81$$

Therefore the median is 59.81.

The most frequently occurring number in the list is called the mode. In the case of grouped data it can be calculated as follows :

Mode = 3 Median-2 Mean In the present example :

Median is 59.81 and Mean is 57.58. Putting these values in the formula for mode, we get

Mode = 3 x 59.81–2 = 57.58

= 179.43–115.16 = 64.27

= 64.3 approximately.

Thus, the mark comes out to be 64.27 or 64.3. Hence, for the present list of scores the most frequently occurring Number is 64.3 or 64.

Graphical Representation of Data

The above data can also be represented graphically through graph by means of Histogram or Frequency Polygon. There are other ways of representing data graphically, but for our purpose we will take into account Histogram and Frequency Polygon.

The Histogram

It represents the bar graph of a frequency distribution. The histogram can be constructed as follows :

(i) The class of scores should be represented in the form of actual class limits, for example, 29.5—34.5, viz., for the class of scores 30—34 the lower limit of the class is to be written as 29.5 and for the higher limit 34.5. Thus, the actual limit of class is 29.5—34.5 and 34.5—39.5 and so on.

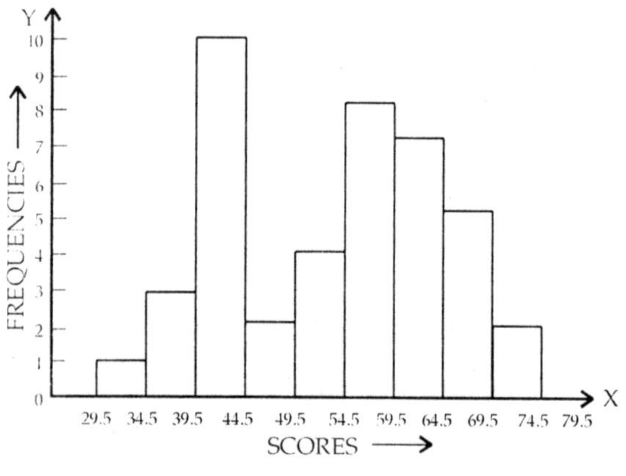

Histogram

(i) Plot the scores on the X-axis and the frequencies on the Y-axis.

(ii) Each class interval with its specific frequency is represented by a separate rectangle.

(iii) Select suitable units of representation for both the X-axis and the Y-axis.

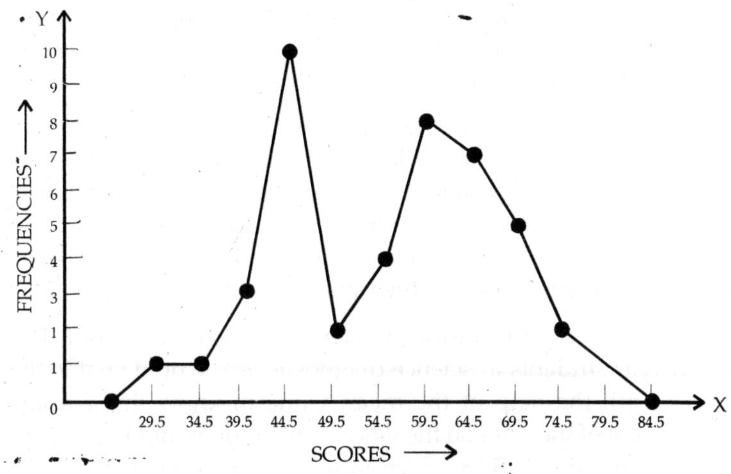

Thus, the histogram provides us a clear as well as accurate picture of the relative proportions of frequency from interval to interval. (The histogram as shown in Fig. is for the score as tabulated in TABLE).

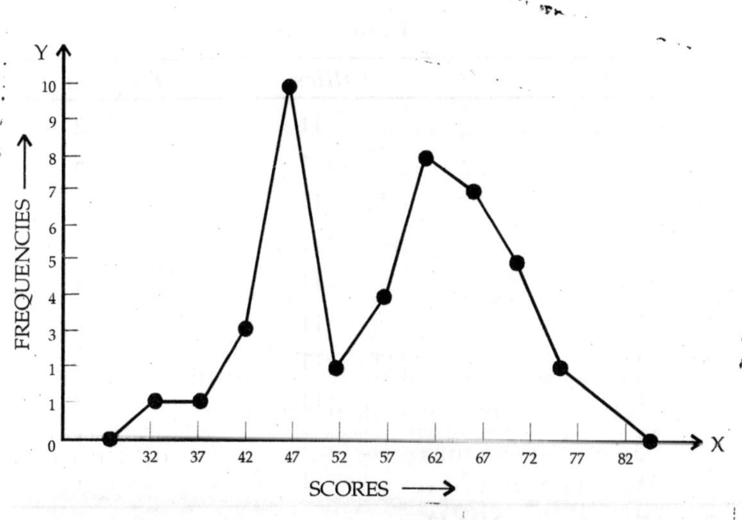

Frequency Polygon

Similarly, the frequency polygon can also be drawn but on the X-axis mid-points of the class-intervals are plotted and on the Y-axis the frequencies are plotted. Make this frequency polygon.

Thus, the frequency polygon is a line graph of the distribution and it shows the graphical relationship between the mid-points and the frequencies. It helps us to compare groups of class-interval in relation to the largest or smallest frequency. It also helps us to know the pair of groups or class-intervals which has the same frequency. It is easy to know the trend of the distribution.

In the present case, the data which has been analysed for E.T.E. second year students in science diagnostic test, would enable the teacher with the help of the mean value to know the average achievement of the class on the whole which comes out to be 57.58. The median value is 59.8 which indicates the point on the score scale below which one-half or 50 per cent of the scores fall viz. for the present test the score scale 59.8 is the score below which 50 percent of the scores fall while the mode is 64.3 viz. it is the most frequently occurring number in the list of scores for the given test. Thus, it would enable the teacher to know the score at which most of the students lie viz. most of them are setting a score of 64 or 65.

Table

Class of Scores	*Tallies*	*Frequencies*
75—79	11	2
70—74	~~1111~~	5
65—69	~~1111~~ 11	7
60—64	~~1111~~ 111	8
55—59	1111	4
50—54	11	2
45—49	~~1111~~ ~~1111~~	10
40—44	111	3
35—39	1	1
30—34	1	1
Total Frequencies N = 43.		

Table

Class of Scores	*f*	*x*	*fx*
75—79	2	77	154
70—74	5	72	360
65—69	7	67	469
60—64	8	62	496
55—59	4	57	228
50—54	2	52	104
45—49	10	47	470
40—44	3	42	126
35—39	1	37	37
30—34	1	32	32
	N = 43		Σ fx =2476

$$\text{Therefore Mean} = \frac{\Sigma fx}{N} = \frac{2476}{43} = 57.58$$

Table

Class of Scores	*f*
75—79	2
70—74	5
65—69	7
L = (59.5) 60-64 (64.5)	8 = (f m)

On analysing the marks (data) obtained by students on achievement tests given at regular intervals, you as well as your students will know their weak and strong points and thus you can give them necessary suggestions for further improvement. If necessary you can also give them remedial exercises. This shows how analysis of data give feedback to students and teachers, and how this feedback may be used for improving teaching learning process in science.

There are two types of evaluation—formative and summative. Formative evaluation of a child starts right from the point when a child begins formal course of study. Summative evaluation is done at the end of the course. We can say terminal testing is formative evaluation, and annual examination is summative evaluation. In summative evaluation it is generally presumed that all those who pass the final examination has achieved the defined expected level of competencies on the basis of the examination administered. Formative evaluation is basically utilised for the purpose of guidance and is built into the transaction of the curriculum. It supplies a lot of diagnostic and achievement data about individual children. This achievement data can be used by the teachers to ensure that the minimum levels of learning are attained by alt children.

During analysis of evaluation data 'MEAN', 'MEDIAN' and 'MODE' tell a lot about the children under study-MEAN gives the 'average'. MEDIAN is the point on the score scale below which one-half of score of 50% of the score fall. MODE is the most frequently occurring member in the list of scores.

'Histogram' and 'Frequency polygon' are the graphical representation of data. The HISTOGRAM represents the bar graph of frequency distribution. Scores are plotted on the axis and the frequencies on the Y-axis. The FREQUENCY POLYGON is drawn plotting mid-points on X-axis and class intervals on Y-axis.

Questions

1. How can the following types of data analysis help in effective science teaching :
   (i) subject wise
   (ii) topic wise

(iii) learning outcome wise

(iv) response wise

2. How can the data analysis give the feedback to (a) students, and (b) teachers for improving teaching-learning process in science ?
3. What is the difference between 'formative assessment' and 'summative assessment'?
4. What do you mean by 'MEAN', 'MEDIAN' and 'MODE'? What do they tell about the students and their achievements?
5. What are 'histogram' and 'frequency polygon' ? What do they communicate ?

15

Suggested Activities

For Primary (III-V) Classes

1. Direction (N, S, E, W) from Sunset, Sunrise, pole star and magnetic compass.
2. Formation of day and night with the help of globe and torch.
3. Formation of Solar eclipse, and lunar eclipse with a small ball, a big ball and torch.
4. Observation of phases of moon—No Moon, Crescent, Half Moon and Full Moon.
5. Shadows in the Morning, Noon and Afternoon.
6. Classification of objects—opaque, transparent and translucent.
7. Experiencing of muscular force, gravitational force and magnetic force.
8. Experiencing 'force causing motion and doing work'.
9. Experiencing 'different kinds of energy—mechanical energy, heat energy (solar energy) and electrical energy'.
10. Demonstration of one form of energy can be changed into another form of energy.
11. Discussion on 'how energy can be saved'.
12. Showing three states of matter—solid, liquid and gas.
13. Observing evaporation and condensation.

14. Observation of clouds, rains, hails, snow, fog and dew.
15. Experiencing breeze, wind and storm.
16. Showing 'Moving water has energy. Moving air has energy.
17. Measuring mass of a body in kg. by two pan balance.
18. Measuring weight of a body in Newton by one pan balnce spring balance, weighing machine.
19. Measuring volume of water in mili-litre by measuring jar.
20. Counting heart beat per minute and pulse per minute.
21. Use of five senses-touch, see, smell, taste and hear.
22. Counting teeth.
23. Recognising different internal parts of a human body in a diagram/model.
24. Measuring temperature of air, water and human body.
25. Classifying things into Living and Non-living.
26. Classifying things into natural and man made.
27. Identification of parts of a plant—root, stem, leaves, flower, fruit, seeds.
28. Classifying vegetables into root, stem, leaves, flower, fruit, seeds.
29. Classifying plants into herbs, shrubs, trees, climbers, creepers, twiners, water-desert-mountain plants, and explaining their characteristics.
30. Classifying animals into pet animals, domestic animals, wild animals, plant eating animals, flesh eating animals, land animals, water animals, birds, insects, crawling animals, desert and mountain animals.
31. Germinating seeds and observing various stages from seed to plant.
32. Reporting things obtained from plants-food, clothing, house material and wood.
33. Reporting things obtained from animals-food, silk, leather.

34. Collecting nests/pictures of nests.
35. Setting up an insect cage.
36. Preparing electral powder.
37. Making a herbarium.
38. Collecting things/their pictures used in the above activities, and paste them in scrap book, or display them on the display board.

For Upper Primary (VI-VIII) Classes

1. Weight of a body floating in water.
2. Use of convex lens-in camera, in projector, in microscope, in telescope, as a magnifying glass, as a burner.
3. Demonstration of eye model using convex lens, screen (retina) and beam of light.
4. Demonstration of defects of eye-shortsightedness and long-sightedness, and use of lenses for correction.
5. Making working Model of solar cooker.
6. Big demonstration models of thermometer and barometer.
7. Heating effect, magnetic effect and chemical effect of electric current.
8. Expansion of solids, liquids and gases on heating using improvised apparatus.
9. Heat Zinc Oxide (white) in a dry test tube (It changes to yellow). Cool it. (It changes to white again).
10. Add iron filings to a copper sulphate solution and observe copper deposit on iron.
11. Add zinc to copper sulphate solution (blue); it becomes colourless.
12. Add copper to silver nitrate solution (colourless), it changes to blue.
13. Mix acetic acid, sulphuric acid and alcohol. The mixture gives fruity smell.
14. Mix tartaric acid and baking soda (no reaction). Add water, we get effervescence.

15. Cobalt chloride is blue when dry and pink when wet.
16. Copper sulphate is white when dry and blue when wet.
17. Heat Ammonium Hydroxide. Bring a glass rod dipped in Hydrochloric Acid near it. White fumes are produced.
18. Chromatography with blue and red solutions.
19. Heat Magnesium metal. Add water. The mixture turns red litmus blue.
20. Make candles of "Napthalene, Benzoic Acid, Octadecanoic Alcohol and Cetyl Alcohol. See whether those candles burn with colourless, bright or soothy flames.
21. Make Tricolour Tube.

    (Water + red ink) + (oil) + (Spirit.+ blue ink).
22. Cheek squamous epithelial cells of man.
23. Squamous epithelial cells from frog's skin.
24. Onion peel.
25. Starch grains from potato/flour.
26. Epidermal layer of lilly leaf to study stomata.
27. Striped muscles from frog/cockroach leg.
28. Morphological study of plant, plant parts and their modifications—xerophytic plants.
29. Observation and identification of animals found in the locality from different habitats, e.g. garden slug, insects their larvae and zoo animals.
30. Setting up of an aquarium and observation of fish breathing, movements, eating, showing relationship of plants and fish. Observing snails in the aquarium.
31. Setting up of hay culture and observation of micro-organism (paramecium).
32. Study of pond water-(algae and other micro-organism).
33. Demonstration of transpiration using belljar.
34. Demonstration of evolution of oxygen during photosynthesis.
35. Demonstration of presence of starch in the leaf(coleus leaf and other soft verigated leaves).

36. Study of osmosis using unshelled egg as a whole (shell can be removed by keeping egg in concentrated Hydrochloric Acid).
37. Study of conduction of water through xylem of small soft plants using coloured water.
38. Mounting and study of xylem trachiels by meceration (put small soft pieces of stem in Nitric Acid/Pottasium Hydroxide pressed by cover slip).
39. Study of bread mold.
40. Study of the difference between exhaled and inhaled air using phenopthaline solution and few drops of sodium hydroxide pink solution (basic) turns white when acidic (carbonic acid).
41. Dissection of frog to study viscera, digestive system heart and blood vessels.
42. Using simple paper chromatography for the separation of plant pigments.
43. Demonstration of soil erosion and its conservation by comparing flow of water in two equal size slantingly placed trays one with soil, other with a patch grass in soil.
44. Demonstration of bending of shoot towards light.
45. Observation and feeling of exhaust from vehicles (polluted air) on us (recall of such experiences).
46. Effect of tea/coffee/alcohol/disprin/hot, cold water on breathing and heartbeat of frog.
47. Counting of pulse and heartbeat before and after exercise.

Unitwise Activities

Measurement

1. To measure regular and irregular objects
2. To measure volume
3. To measure temperature
4. To prepare a pan balance
5. To measure time

Materials Around

6. To group objects
7. To prepare models by plasticine/clay
8. To test for hardness
9. To show that no two objects can occupy same space
10. To observe differences when objects float
11. To examine density of different materials
12. To test for solubility
13. Experiments to show that some substances are magnetic

Separation of Substances

14. To separate a mixture
15. To demonstrate different methods of separation
16. Decantation
17. Loading
18. Filtration
19. Sieving
20. Winnowing
21. Distillation
22. Evaporation
23. Crystallisation
24. Sublimation
25. Centrifugation
26. Chromatography
27. Separation by a magnet

Changes Around

28. To observe growing seedlings
29. To examine changes in the mixture of sulphur and iron fillings on heating
30. Observation of changes in wax due to heating and cooling
31. Observation of rusting

Motion, Force and Pressure

Observation of a few moving objects and measurement of average speed

32. Measurement of average speed of a body in circular motion
33. To prepare and calibrate a spring balance
34. To observe effect of the point of application and magnitude of force
35. To compare the force of friction on different objects using spring balance
36. To observe the effect offeree on objects of different areas
37. To measure the time period of a pendulum
38. To observe effect of steam lining

Simple Machine

39. To observe and use simple machines
40. To construct a beam balance
41. To make the model of a screw

The Universe

42. To observe constellations
43. To prepare a scale model of the solar system
44. To observe the shadow of a stick
45. To observe the timings of sunrise and sunset
46. To observe a sun-dial

The Living World

47. To observe a variety of living objects and classify them
48. To study the growth in living and non-living objects
49. Setting the maintenance of an aquarium
50. To collect animals and plants from the locality, draw and label each

Structure and Function of Plants and Animals

51. To collect plants and study their preservation

52. To examine internal structures of animals
53. To examine external and internal structures of animal listing their functions
54. To examine modifications in plant parts and list their functions
55. To collect flowers and study of pollen grains
56. To study vegetative propagation in some plants
57. To identify and group different plants and animals

Food and Health

58. To examine food items of man and their major grouping
59. To list food habits in different animals Unit

Man's Dependence on Plants and Animals

60. To study man's dependence on plants and animals
61. To study food chain and balance in nature
62. To demonstrate soil erosion
63. To demonstrate plant's role in preventing the soild erosion

Adaptability of the Environment

64. To feel hot water
65. To study adaptation in different plants and animals

Water

66. To collect water from various sources and examine the residue
67. To examine water-content in plants
68. To taste water from different sources of drinking water
69. To study different processes of purifying water (decantation, loading, filtration, distillation etc.)
70. To test hardness of water from different sources
71. To study water as a solvent

Energy

72. To examine different sources of energy

73. To understand that light is a form of energy
74. To study the conversion of energy
75. To study heat energy
76. To examine the relationship of energy with movement
77. To observe conservation of energy
78. To show that moving water has energy

Motion, Mass and Friction

79. Experiment to demonstrate 'inertia'
80. To study mass
81. To find out the force of sliding and rolling friction
82. To examine ball and roller bearings
83. To study action and reaction
84. To determine relative density of kerosene oil

Pressure and Buoyancy

85. To demonstrate thrust and pressure
86. To demonstrate that water tends to remain at the same level
87. To demonstrate that water exerts lateral pressure
88. To study the pressure of water at different heights
89. To demonstrate that water exerts equal pressure on all sides
90. To explain the principle of hydraulic press
91. To demonstrate the method of measuring buoyant force
92. To determine relative density

Heat and Its Effects

93. To demonstrate conversion of mechanical energy into, heat
94. To demonstrate that quantity of heat required to heat a substance is proportional to the rise in temperature
95. To study the effect of heating two substances of same mass to same range of temperature
96. To determine the melting point of ghee

97. To determine the boiling point of water
98. To show the thermal expansion of solids
99. To show the expansion of a liquid
100. To show the expansion of a gas

Transfer of Heat

101. To demonstrate the conduction of heat through a solid
102. To demonstrate the convection of heat in liquids
103. To demonstrate the convection of heat in gases
104. To show that water and glass are bad conductors of heat
105. To study some radiations

Light and Optical Instruments

106. Oil perform experiments with light
107. To study reflection of light on different surfaces
108. To study the focal length of a convex lens and a concave mirror.
109. To study image formation by a convex lens and concave mirror
110. To study refraction through glass slab and prism
111. To make a model of human eye
112. To prepare a model of a pin hole camera

Vibrating Bodies and Sound

113. To study vibration
114. To study the passage of sound through water
115. To study the propagation of sound through solids
116. To study the high and low sound
117. To study resonance
118. To observe reflection of sound
119. To show that sound may be absorbed

Effects of Electricity

120. To study the parts of an electric cable
121. To study electrical circuits, conductors and insulators

122. To study the heating effect of electric current
123. To observe the effect of electric current on a magnetic compass
124. To study A.C and D.C

Electric Charges at Rest

125. To find the presence of electrical charges in the comb
126. To observe the repulsion in an electrically charged balloon
127. To demonstrate that there are two kinds of charges—like charges repel and unlike charges attract
128. To study the charging mechanism of a simple electroscope
129. To test for charges in conductors and insulators

Magnetism

130. To test for magnetism
131. To identify magnetic, north and south
132. To demonstrate that like poles repel and unlike poles attract each other
133. To demonstrate the use of magnetic compass to determine direction
134. To magnetise and demagnetise a piece of iron
135. Use magnetised needle or razor blade to locate north and south
136. To observe the effect of distance on magnetic force

Nature and Composition of Substances-I

137. To show the difference of intermolecular space in a gas and in a liquid
138. To study elasticity of some materials
139. To study plasticity of some substances
140. To show decomposition of copper carbonate
141. To show the electrolysis of water
142. To demonstrate some chemical reactions
143. To demonstrate some combination reactions

Nature and Composition of Substances-II

144. To demonstrate the addition of masses in a chemical reaction
145. To demonstrate conservation of mass during mixing
146. To determine the composition of compound

Air and Oxygen

147. To show that 1/5 of air is oxygen
148. To observe the effect of blowing exhaled air into lime water
149. To observe that oxygen is released by green aquatic plants
150. To prepare oxygen and study its properties

Water

151. To study water-content in some substances
152. To study the solubility of liquids and gases in water
153. To prepare hydrogen gas and study some of its properties
154. To prepare a saturated solution of sugar, salt and alum
155. To study some oxidation and reduction processes

Acids, Bases and Salts

156. To demonstrate some properties of sulphuric, nitric and hydrochloric acid
157. To test for acidity
158. To demonstrate some properties of bases
159. To demonstrate neutralization
160. To demonstrate the preparation of soap

Preservation of Self-I

161. To observe how food gets spoiled and study some causative organisms
162. To list the common parasites present in a locality
163. To study the food-chain in a pond
164. To study respiration in germinating seeds and to test for carbon dioxide evolved in this process

165. To examine the heart beat of a frog
166. To observe the veins of the lower arm
167. To determine the pulse rate
168. To observe the vascular bundles in the transverse section of stem
169. To observe the feeding activity of ants

Preservation of Self-II

170. To observe locomotion and movement in some animals
171. To observe movements in plants

Population

172. To list different types of habitat in the surroundings
173. To list characteristics of habitats like those of river, school garden etc.
174. To draw an outline map of a locality showing different habitats
175. To study the organisms and their habits in the locality

Pollution

176. To observe the effect of washing soda on fish
177. To observe the ingredients of smoke
178. To list the sources of noise in the environment
179. To list various environmental changes during various seasons and list the advantages and disadvantages of these changes
180. To list the common pollutants in the surroundings

Light

181. To observe the effect of temperature on the colour of a body
182. To observe the light is necessary to make objects visible
183. To observe reflection of sunlight
184. To verify that light travels in a straight line
185. To study formation of umbra and penumbra

186. To observe the reflection of light from a mirror and find the relationship between the angle of incidence and reflection
187. To study the passage of light through a glass slab and compare the angle of incidence and refraction

Light and Colour

188. To observe absorption light by different coloured sheets
189. To split sunlight into component colours
190. To make Newton's disc and to study mixing of colours
191. To study the effect of moving objects on our eye (Perception of eye)
192. To observe parallax between two objects (fingers)

More about Electricity

193. To study flow of water from higher to lower level
194. To study the parallel and series combination of cells
195. To study resistance in series
196. To study the factors on which the resistance of wires depend
197. To demonstrate magnetic effects of electric current

Electrical Energy

198. To observe the working of a fuse-wire
199. To observe a fuse-socket and grip (kit-kat)
200. To study the generation of electricity in dynamo

Electrical Magnetism

201. To make an electromagnet
202. To demonstrate the working of an electric bell
203. To show a simple transformer
204. To demonstrte the working of a simple model of an electric motor

Structure of Atom

205. To prepare simple models of atoms of helium, oxygen and sulphur

206. To draw models of nitrogen, magnesium and chlorine atoms

Nuclear Energy

207. To prepare chart for showing chain reactions
208. To prepare a chart showing some common uses of radio active isotopes using illustrations, newspapers and maga-zines cuttings

Carbon in Nature

209. To produce carbon dioxide by burning some materials
210. To observe different forms of carbon
211. To study the electrical conductivity of different forms of carbon
212. To demonstrate combustion
213. To study conditions for burning
214. To observe different types of combustions
215. To demonstrate different parts of a flame and their heating effects

Compounds of Carbon

216. To demonstrate preparation and properties of carbon dioxide
217. To test for carbonate and bicarbonate
218. To demonstrate distillation of crude oil
219. To study the presence of carbohydrates in food items
220. To test for fats in some common substances
221. To test for proteins in some common substances

Our Living World

222. To observe detailed structures of some micro-orgnisms

Cells and Tissues

223. To observe the growth in some plants
224. To examine some plant and animals tissues

Reproduction

225. To demonstrate the reproductive parts of the animals
226. To show reproductive parts of plants

Growth and Development

227. Germination of seeds

Heredity & Variation

228. To observe survival of plants
229. To study the variation in human beings

Organic Evolution

230. To study different evidence in support of organic evolution

Materials-I

231. To study physical properties of some metals
232. To study the use of some metals
233. To observe the phenomenon of corrosion and its prevention
234. To observe the oxidation process

Materials-II

235. To demonstrate the physical properties of some materials by their burning odours

Agricultural Practices and Implements

236. To observe the effect of depth on seed germination
237. To collect and study some crop plants and weeds
238. To collect and examine soils from different places

Our Crops

239. To select healthy seeds
240. To observe some common crops and classify them into different groups based on their use and seasons
241. To observe the stage of growth of some forms of common crops
242. To observe the nodules in some legumes

Improvement of Crop Production

243. To examine some samples of soils
244. To study the various components of soil
245. To study the water holding capacity of different soils
246. To test the acidity and alkalinity of soils
247. To demonstrate the process of emasculation
248. To collect and study different types of fertilizers used in the locality

Useful Plants and Animals

249. To test for adulteration of honey with sugar or gur
250. To separate larva and unhatched eggs of silk worm
251. To test the quality of an egg
252. To study the medicinal plants and plants which provide food

Animal Husbandry

253. To test the amount of water in milk
254. To observe different types of fibres

Conservation of Natural Resources

255. To study the soil-erosion
256. To examine samples of water from different sources.

16

Sample Lesson Plans

Lesson Plan No. 1

Pupil teacher's name : Class : III

Roll Number : Date :

Subject : Science Time : 40 min.

Topic : Things around us.

Specific Objectives

1. Students will be able to define and give examples of man-made and natural things.
2. Students will differentiate between living and non-living things.
3. Students could tell the characteristics of living and non-living things.

Introduction

	Questions	*Expected Answers*
1.	Children, tell the name of the things which you see in your school, at your home and in your environment.	Trees, Plants, Scooter, Bus, Tables, Chairs, Houses, Buildings etc.
2.	Name some natural things.	Trees, Plants, Sky, Sun etc.
3.	Name some things which are made by man.	Buildings, Clothes, Table, Chairs, Chalk etc.
4.	What do we call such things/articles?	Problemtaic Question

Man-made Things
Natural Things
Non-living Things
Living Things

Presentation

Content	*Pupil-teacher's Activity*	*Student's Activity*
Man-made and Natural things	Pupil-teacher will ask the following questions— (a) Name the things which you see around you in your environment. (b) Can you classify these things? Pupil-teacher will tell the students— Those articles which are made by man are called man-made things whereas the things which are found in nature are called natural things.	Students will answer the questions— Flowers, Trees, Scooter, Car, people etc. Yes, we can classify these things into man-made and natural things. Students will give some more examples of man-made and natural things.
Living and non-living things	Pupil-teacher will ask the following questions— (a) Can you classify these things into some other category? (b) Give some examples of living things. (c) Why are these things called living things? Pupil-teacher will explain the students by showing different living as well as non-living things— The things which can breathe, move, grow and reproduce are called living things. The things which do not move and do not breathe are called non-living things.	Yes, we can classify them into living and non-living things. Man, Cat, Trees, Plants etc. Because they can breathe, grow and move. Students will listen carefully and give some more examples.
Characteristics of living things	The above said qualities are the characteristics of living things. The Pupil-teacher will explain this through the strips of flannel board.	Students will tell the characteristics of living things (i) They breathe (ii) They eat (iii) They sleep etc.

Teaching Aids

Flannel Board, Different objects like Stone, Flower, Plant, Blackboard, Duster, Chalk etc.

Previous Knowledge

Students are aware of the different things around them and can name them/know their names.

Statement of Topic

"These things are called man-made or natural things and today we will study about the things around us."

Living Things	*Non-Living Things*
Breath	Do not Breathe
Move	Do not Move
Growth in Size	Do not Grow in Size
Give Birth to child	Don't Give Birth to Child

FLANNEL BOARD

Recapitulation

1. Pupil-teacher will ask the students to encircle the living things with red colour and non-living things with black colour on chart.
2. Pupil-teacher will ask to classify the living and non-living things from the given objects.

Home Work

Pupil-teacher will give the following homework to the students Observe the things in your environment and

1. list their properties,
2. draw their pictures in your copies.

On Blackboard

Pupil-teacher's Name :	Class: III
Roll No. :	Date :
Subject : Science	Time : 40 min.

Topic : Things around us

Man-made things	**Natural things**
Blackboard, chalk, chair, table	Tree, river, animals
Living things	**Non living things**
Human beings, cat, fish	Stone, book, table

Characteristics of Living things

(i) They breathe
(ii) They move
(iii) They grow
(iv) They reproduce young ones.

Lesson Plan No. 2

Pupil-teacher's name :	Date :
Subject: EVS	Class : IV
Topic : Matter and its Properties	Time : 35 min.

Objectives (in Behavioural Term)

1. Students will be able to differentiate between transparent and opaque objects with examples.
2. Students could distinguish between soft and hard objects with examples.
3. Students would differentiate between good conductors and bad conductors of heat.

4. Students will be able to classify the soluble and insoluble materials.

Teaching Aids

Table, sponge, cotton, stone, iron-rod, dough, polythene, cardboard, glass, matchbox, sand, chalk, salt, sugar, candle, wooden cube, wooden rod, pin, torch.

Previous Knowledge

Students know about the three states of matter.

Introduction

Pupil-teacher will ask the following questions to test the previous knowledge :

Questions	Expected Answers
1. What are the three states of matter?	Solid, liquid and gas.
2. Name some solid things/ materials.	Iron, wood etc.
3. Name some liquids.	Water, milk, tea.
4. Name some gases.	Oxygen, Hydrogen, Air.
5. These matters have some properties. Can you name some of them?	**Problematic question.**

Statement of the Topic

Today we will study about these properties of matter:

Hard and soft materials

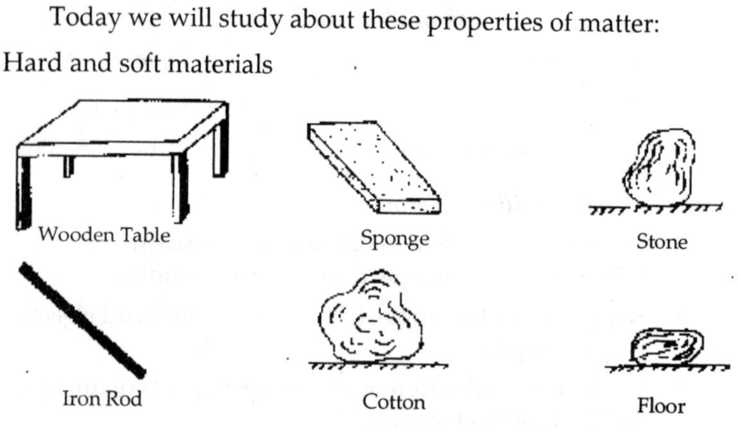

Introduction

Content	*Pupil-teacher's Activity*	*Student's Activity*
Identification of properties of (materials)	Pupil-teacher will teach through child centred method and will ask the following questions— How will you identify a material? Yes, these are the properties through which we can identify the materials. These are called the properties of materials.	Students will reply— By touch, vision, colour and smell etc. Students will listen carefully.
1st Property some materials are hard whereas some are soft.	Pupil-teacher will explain this concept with the help of some experiments e.g., she will ask one student to come and touch the cotton and the stone. Then she'll ask the student how did he feel. Besides, she will ask some more examples.	Students will answer—Stone is hard and cotton is soft.
2nd Property Transparent and opaque materials	Pupil-teacher will explain this concept with the help of the following experiment— Light can pass through the polythene whereas light cannot pass through a cardboard. Therefore the materials through which light can pass are called transparent materials. The materials through which light cannot pass are opaque materials. Besides, Pupil-teacher will give some examples.	Students will listen carefully and will answer the questions.
3rd Property Good conductors and bad conductors of heat.	Pupil-teacher will explain this concept with the help of an experiment— Take an iron rod. On heating its one end we find that the other end also gets heated up. Therefore such materials are called good conductors of heat.	Students will listen carefully. They will do the experiment and observe it.

Contd.

Content	*Pupil-teacher's Activity*	*Student's Activity*
	In the same way if we heat up wooden stick we find that its other end is not heated.	
4th Property Soluble and insoluble materials	Teacher will try to dissolve sand, chalk, salt and sugar in water.	Students will listen, experiment, observe and will give reply to the questions asked.

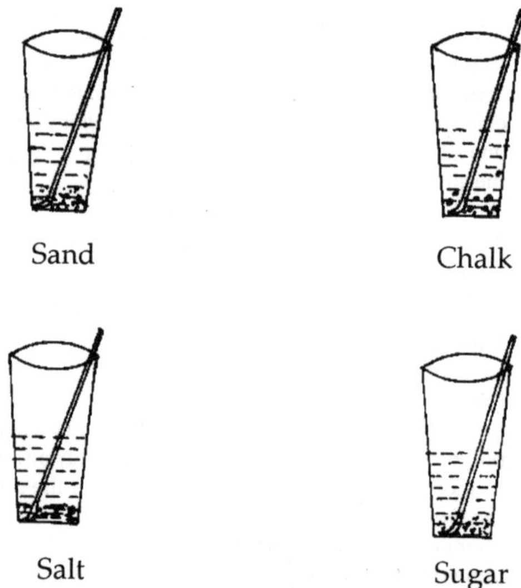

Sand Chalk

Salt Sugar

Recapitulation

From the following classify—

1. Hard and soft material (iron and sponge)
2. Transparent and opaque materials (polythene and card-board)
3. Good conductor and bad conductor of heat (copper and wood)
4. Soluble and insoluble materials (sugar and stone)
5. Distinguish between transparent and opaque materials.
6. Differentiate between soluble and insoluble materials.

Home Work

List the names of 10 materials and from the properties given below list their properties :

1. Hard
2. Soft
3. Transparent
4. Opaque
5. Good conductor of heat
6. Bad conductor of heat
7. Soluble
8. Insoluble

Black Board Summary

Date :	Subject : EVS
Pupil Teacher:	Class : IV
Topic : Matter and its Properties	Time : 35 min.

1st Property : Soft and hard materials

2nd Property : Transparent and opaque objects

3rd Property : Good conductors and bad conductors of heat

4th Property : Soluble and insoluble materials

Lesson Plan No. 3

Subject : Science (Physics)

Topic : Different Types of Motion (Lecture-Cum-Demonstration Method)

Class : VI

Time : 35 Minutes

Specific Objectives (Written in Behavioural Terms) This lesson will enable the students to :

(1) understand the meaning of motion.

(2) give the definition of speed.

Circular Motion.

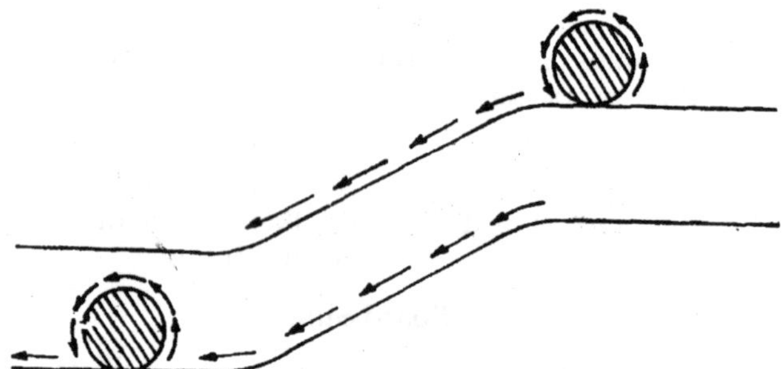

Fig. Linear and Circular Motion.

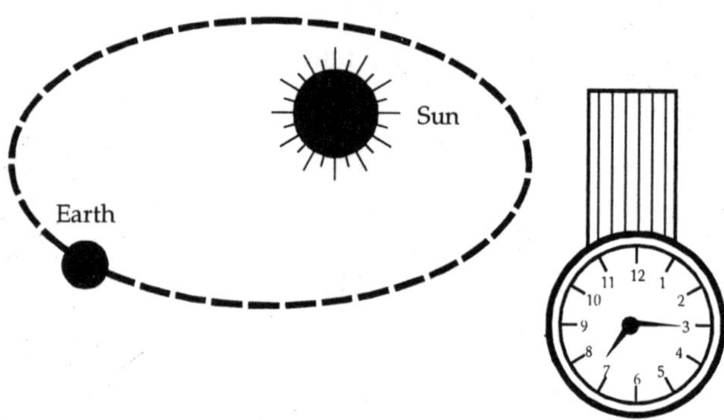

(Approximately) Circular Motion

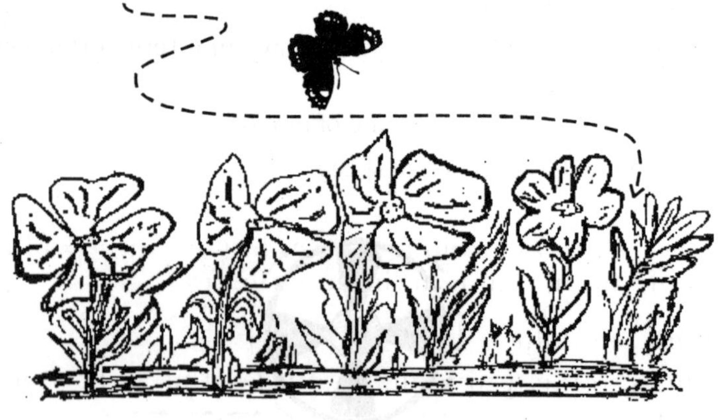

Irregular Motion

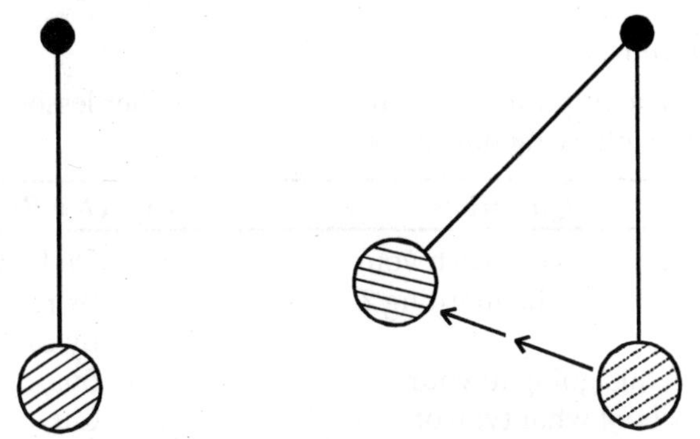

No Motion (Body at Rest). To and Fro Motion (One Side).

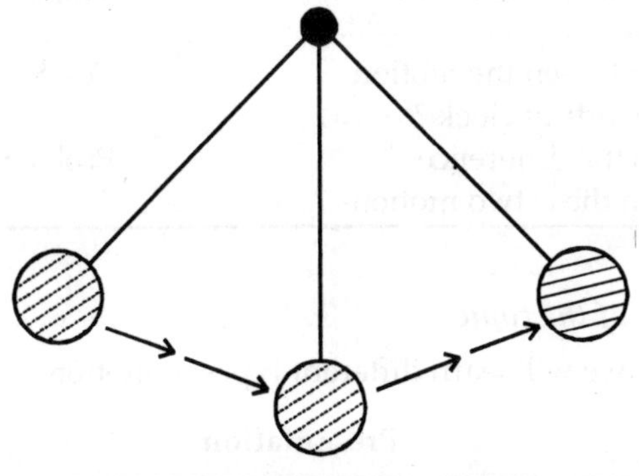

Oscillatory Motion.

(3) define regular and irregular motions with examples.

(4) explain linear motion with examples.

(5) can differentiate between circular and oscillatory motions.

Teaching Aids

Some self-developed instruments as shown in Figs. to explain oscillatory, linear, circular and irregular motions.

Previous Knowledge

Students can give some simple examples of motion from their daily life.

Introduction

The pupil-teacher will introduce his/her lesson with the help of the following questions :

Questions	*Expected Response*
1. How do you reach your school in the morning ?	(i) On foot, or (ii) By rickshaw, or (iii) By car or bus.
2. While going to your school what type of vehicle you see on the roads ?	(i) Bus, or (ii) Car, or (iii) Scooter
3. Have you seen the motion of swing ?	Yes, Sir/Madam
4. Have you seen the motion of the hands of clock ?	Yes, Sir/Madam
5. What is the difference between these two motions ?	Problem/Question

Statement of the topic

Today we will learn different types of motion.

Presentation

Content	*Pupil-teacher's Activity*	*Student's Activity*
Motion: When a body changes its position with time in comparison to other body at rest, the body is said to be in motion.	***Pupil-teacher*** will roll the ball and ask the following questions— 1. Is there any change in the initial position of the ball? 2. Did the ball take any time to change its position? ***Teacher's statement.*** Teacher will define motion as given in content.	 Yes, its position has changed. Yes.
Linear Motion: When a body moves in a straight line then its motion is known as a linear motion.	1. Is the ball moving in a straight line ? 2. What do we call such type of motion ?	Yes, it is moving in a straight line. (No response)

Contd.

Content	*Pupil-teacher's Activity*	*Student's Activity*
	Teacher's Statement: Teacher will dcfinite the linear motion as given in content.	
Irregular Motion: When an object moves in different directions then it is said to be in irregular motion.	1. Have you ever seen a flying bee ?	Yes.
	2. Is its movement in a straight line ?	No, it moves here and there without any regularly in its directions.
	Teacher's statement: Teacher will definite irregular motion as given in content.	
Oscillatory Motion: When an object moves to fro and from its initial position, then the motion is known as oscillatory motion e.g. swing and pendulum.	The teacher will tie a stone with a thread and move the stone to and fro from its initial position and will ask the following questions:	
	1. Have you ever seen a swing ?	Yes.
	2. How does it move ?	To and fro from its position.
	3. Is there any difference between the motion of the swing and the motion of the pendulum.	No, they are same.
	4. What do we call such type of motion ?	(No response)
	Teacher's statement: Teacher will explain the oscillatory motion as given in content.	
Circular Motion: When an object moves in a circle its motion is known as a circular motion, e.g. motion of Moon round the Earth, motion of wheel, motion of hands of clock, motion of electric fan etc.	1. Does the earth revolve round the Sun ?	Yes.
	2. How does the electric fan move ?	In circle.
	3. Have you observed the motion of the arms of the clock ?	Yes.
	4. How do they move ?	In circle.
	5. What is the scientific name of this motion ?	(No response)
	Teacher's Statement: Teacher will explain that such type of motion is called a circular motion.	

Recapitulation–Teacher can ask the following questions to know whether the objectives of this lesson are achieved or not:

Some examples are given below, classify the type of motion.

(a) Rotation of the earth around its axis.
(b) Motion of top.
(c) Arms of clock.
(d) Rolling of ball on the floor.
(e) Motion of needle of the sewing machine.
(f) Motion of swing.
(g) Motion of train.
(h) Motion of player of hockey.

Home Assignment

1. Differentiate between oscillatory and circular motions. Give some examples also.
2. How will we differentiate between body in motion and body at rest ?

On Black Board

Subject : Science   Date :

Topic : Motion

Class : Sixth

—Circular Motion   Circular Way

C

—Linear and Circular Motion   Line Parallel

Simple and Circular Way

—Oscillatory Motion   Oscillatory

—Irregular Motion   Irregular

Lesson Plan No. 4

Subject : Science (Biology)

Topic : Transport system in the body of animals (man) (Lecture-Cum-Discussion Method)

Class : VIII Time : Two class periods

Specific Objectives (Written in Behavioural Terms)—Students will be able to :

1. describe and appreciate the need for transportation system in higher animals.
2. explain that circulatory system helps in transportation of different materials within the body of the organisms.
3. identify various components of circulatory system—heart, arteries, capillaries and veins.
4. describe the structures and explain the functions of various organs of circulatory system very briefly.

Teaching Aids

Regular classroom aids like chalkboard, chalks (coloured). Chart of circulatory system of man. Diagram of with connected main arteries and veins.

Previous Knowledge

Students have studied the digestive and respiratory system. They know that food and oxygen are needed by each cell to get energy. They have a general idea of blood circulation.

Introduction

The lesson will be introduced by asking questions based on their previous knowledge and experiences and then it will be related to the new knowledge of this lesson. Some questions like these will be asked and discussed.

1. What happens to the food we eat?
2. In which part of the body the food is digested and absorbed?
3. How does it reach to different parts of the body? It will be concluded from this discussion, Teacher-Learner

Interaction (TLI) that transport of material is required in higher organisms.

Presentation

Content	*Procedure*
Circulatory system is the transport system in higher animals (man).	The lesson will be developed by discussing (TLI) the following questions : • What transport mechanisms is used within the body of man ? • What do you call this system ? The term blood circulation or circulatory system will be emphasised. • Is there any special circulatory system in amoeba or other single celled organisms ? • Why there is no need of circulatory system in amoeba ? • How does the transport of material take place in amoeba ? • How do all cells get food and oxygen in higher animals ?
Oxygen and food needed by each cell is transported through blood.	With the help of a chart of circulatory system, it will be discussed and explained (TLI) that food is absorbed by the blood while passing through the elementary canal and this food is distributed to various parts of the body and its tissues. • What happens to the blood when it passes through the lungs ? 2. What happens to the oxygen when blood containing more oxygen passes through various parts of the body ? 3. What is the transporting media in man ? By asking and discussing such questions it will be clarified that blood is the transporting media in higher organisms.
Circulatory system consists of the heart, arteries, capillaries and veins.	1. By showing the chart of blood circulation again and drawing the diagram of connection of arteries and veins through capillaries and by relevant questioning a simple idea of closed circulatory system will be given to them. Students will also be asked to draw simple diagrams. 2. Look at the chart and tell where is the heart situated ? 3. What is the function of heart ?

Contd.

Content	*Procedure*
	• The heart keeps on pumping all the time. • What kind of walls should it have ? Thick or thin ? Half cut diagram of heart will be shown to students. The shape and structure of heart will be explained by TLI in a very simple way. (Pointing to aorta) Locate this vessel in the chart and follow its path. By drawing T.S. of an artery and a vein structure and function of arteries and vein will be explained by TLI. • How does blood go from arteries to veins ? It will be explained with the help of the diagrams. Some animals have open cir-culatory system, some have close circulatory system. • Which kind of circulatory system is found in man? • Why do you think it is called closed circulatory system. All higher animals have closed cir-culatory system.

Recapitulation

The lesson will be recapitulated by asking the following questions:

1. Which system is called transport system in higher organisms?
2. What is the function of transport system in man?
3. Why is there no need of a special circulatory system in amoeba?
4. What are the various components of circulatory system in man?
5. Why are the walls of arteries thicker than veins?

Assignment

Do this activity at home, bring its results and answer the questions.

Activity

Take your pulse rate per minute. Jump for two minutes and at once take your pulse rate again. Repeat the procedure three times and fill your results in a table as shown below :

Sl. No.	*Pulse Rate*	*Pulse Rate After Exercise*
1.	....	....
2.	....	....
3.	....	....
Average	....	....

1. While exercising, do you need more energy or less energy than normal?
2. While exercising, will you be needing more oxygen or the same as normal?
3. Pulse rate has increased just after exercise. Why?

On Black Board

Circulatory System

Circulatory system is the transport system in higher animals including man.

Blood is the transporting media in man and other higher animals.

Oxygen and food is transported through blood in different parts of the body.

Circulatory system consists of :

(i) Heart-pumping organ of the body.

(ii) Arteries—Carry oxygenated blood from the heart to different parts of the body. They are thick walled.

T.S. of Artery

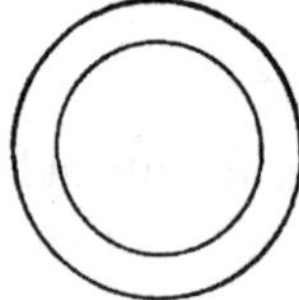

T.S. of Vein

(iii) Vein—brings deoxygenated blood back from the various parts of the body to the heart. They have thinner walls than arteries.

(iv) Capillaries—Very small branches of blood vessels which spread in various tissues and connect the arteries to the veins.

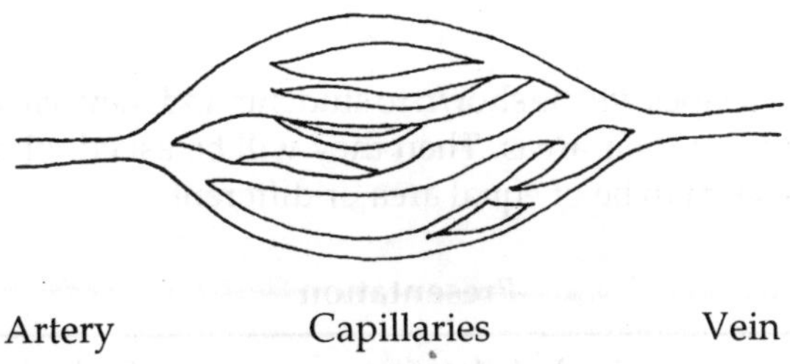

Artery Capillaries Vein

Lesson Plan No. 5

Subject : Science (Physics)

Topic : Area (4.3—Scientific Method)

Class : VI

Time : Two class periods

Specific Objectives (Written in Behaviourist Terms) Given out geometrical shapes students will be able to

1. predict whether their areas are same or different.
2. compute their areas and see how far their predictions are right.

Teaching Aids

Four cut shapes (thick chart paper or card board)

1. circle of 7 cm radius (marked A).
2. triangle of base 28 cm and height 11 cm (marked B).
3. rectangle of length 14 cm and breadth 11 cm (marked C).
4. rectangle of length 22 cm and breadth 7 cm (marked D).

Note : Do not write dimensions on cut shapes and also do not tell these dimensions to students.

Previous' Knowledge

Students know

1. area of circle = πr^2
2. area of triangle = ½ x base x height
3. area of rectangle = length x breadth

Introduction

The cut shapes will be shown to students and they will be asked how to find out their areas. Then they will be asked whether the cut shapes seem to be of equal area or different.

Presentation

Content	*Teacher's Activity*	*Student's Activity*
Concept of Area	The teacher will divide the students in groups of 4-5 students per group, and will give one set 4 (marked A, B, C, D) cut shapes to each group. He/she will then ask :	
	1. Guess whether their areas are equal or different. 2. If different, which is largest and which is smallest.	Groups will guess without measuring and tell the teacher what they
	This is PROBLEM. Teacher will write the responses on the blackboard. These responses are the HYPOTHESES.	Groups will see the blackboard.
	Teacher will then ask the groups to measure the required lengths of the cut shapes and compute their areas.	Groups will measure and compute as asked by their teacher.
	This is EXPERIMENT. Teacher will ask the groups their results. Teacher will write down down the results of the groups on blackboard.	Group will tell their results, areas of each shape.
	Teacher will ask, whether the areas of shapes are same or different. This is CONCLUSION.	Groups will see the blackboard. Groups will say areas of all shapes are same.

Blackboard Summary

Group	*Predictions (Hypotheses)*
I	
II	
III	
IV	

Area of circle = πr^2 = ...cm^2

Area of triangle = ½ x base x height = ...cm2

Area of rectangle = length x breadth = ...cm2

Results (CONCLUSION)

Area of shape A (circle) =

Area of shape Â (triangle) =

Areas of shape (1st rectangle) =

Area of shape D (2nd rectangle) =

Areas of all shapes are same.

Lesson Plan No. 6

Subject : Science (Chemistry)

Class : VIII (Enrichment Lesson)

Time : Two class periods (4.4 Use of Programmed Instruction-Self-Learning Method)

Previous Knowledge

Students recall that atom is the smallest particle of an element.

Introduction

The lesson will be introduced with the questions like :

1. What is matter?
2. What is element?
3. Is element matter?

4. What is the name of the smallest possible particle of an element?
5. Can an element be further sub-divided?

Presentation

A programme 'Structure of Atom' will be given to students. Students will work on it individually. This is a self-learning unit. Most of the students will not have any difficulty. Teacher will guide only those students, who really need his help.

Note—When students complete the self-learning unit 'Structure of Atom', a multiple choice test.

Assignment

Students can take the Unit 'Structure of Atom' at home to complete it, if they are unable to complete it in class.

Lesson Plan No. 7

Subject : Science (Biology)

Topic : Digestive System of Man

Class : VII

Time : Two class periods

Specific Objectives (Written in Behavioural Terms)

1. Given the (i) diagram of Digestive System of Man and (ii) Taking Stomach-Script, the pupil teachers will develop Multimedia Package—Digestive System of Man.
2. Using the Multimedia Package "Digestive System of Man" the Students will recognise and describe as below:

Recognise

(i) Alimentary canal (Food Pipe) from Mouth to Anus viz. Stomach.

(ii) Teeth and Tongue (Can also be recognised by observing actual Teeth and Tongue)

(iii) Stomach

(iv) Small Intestine

(v) Large Intestine

(vi) Rectum and Anus

Describe

(i) The functions of Teeth, Tongue, Salivary Glands, Wall Muscles of Food Pipe, Stomach, Small Intestine, Large Intestine, Rectum and Anus.

(ii) The functioning of Digestive System of Man.

Teaching Aids : Multimedia Packages

"Digestive System of Man", Comprising

(i) Textbook

(ii) "Digestive System of Man" Chart

(iii) "Talking Stomach" Script

(iv) Audio Tape of Talking Stomach

Development of Multimedia Package: "Digestive System of Man"

(i) Make a Colourful Chart of Digestive System of Man with the help of Fig.

(ii) With the help of your Textbook prepare yourself for Teacher—Learner Interaction and Teacher—Material (Chart) Interaction.

(iii) Prepare an Audio-Tape with Talking Stomach Script, Using a Cassette Tape Recorder.

Previous Knowledge

Students recognise teeth, tongue, food pipe, stomach, small intestine, large intestine, rectum and anus in a chart of the Digestive System of Man.

Introduction

Students will be asked to bring one fruit each. Then they will be asked to eat it, following a question where this food is going. Students may answer. This is going to our stomach". Then students will be shown the chart, and will be asked to describe in the Chart Diagram where the food goes from mouth. Thus Digestive System of man will be introduced.

Presentation

Alimentary Canal

Tr. When you eat, where does the food go?

Sts. It goes to our stomach.

Tr. Point out the tube in the chart through which food goes from mouth to anus viz. stomach.

Sts. Show the path of food from mouth to anus viz. stomach in the Digestive System of Man. Chart—from mouth to food pipes to stomach, to small intestine, to large intestine, to rectum and to anus.

Note: *Teacher* will facilitate the *students*, to show this path, and will tell the students "the name of this tube (path) is *Alimentary Canal*".

Digestion Begins in the Mouth

TR. When you ingest food into your mouth what do your teeth do?

Sts. Our teeth break the food into smaller pieces.

Tr. Your Mouth has *Salivary Glands*, which secrete *Saliva*. This *saliva* moistens the food and converts some *starch* into *sugar*. Does your tongue help in chewing by moving the food in various directions?

Sts. Yes, our tongue helps in chewing the crushed moist food in our mouth, but how do we know the *saliva* converts *starch* to *sugar*.

Tr. Teacher gives a piece of bread to each student and asks them to put it in their mouths. Then asks, *how does it tasted.*

Sts. No taste.

Tr. Now chew it. How does it taste now?

Sts. Sweet.

Tr. Sweet because bread *(starch) tasteless* is changed into *Sugar (sweet). So in the mouth digestion begins.*

From Mouth to Stomach through Food Pipe

Tr. Where does this food go from your mouth when you swallow?

Sts. It comes to our *food pipe*.

Tr. Yes. This *food pipe* is also called *Oesophagus*. When food comes in *food pipe its walls muscles* start contraction and expansion movement, which pushes the food into your *stomach*. The *stomach* chums this food, and partly digests it, and sends the remaining semi-solid food into your small intestine. Do you think your *stomach is your food reservoir?*

Sts. It looks like that, because all the food from our mouth is first stored here, and then it goes to *small intestine*. As we have *salivary glands* in our mouth, which secretes *saliva*, and *this saliva begins digestion*. Do we also have some *glands in our stomach* which also *secrete* some liquid helping digestion in the *stomach*?

Tr. Yes. *your stomach lining contains about 35 million glands* which *secrete* about *three litres of gasteric juice per day*, mainly *hydrochloric acid*.

Sts. Does this acid digest the food in stomach.

Tr. Yes.

Sts. You said, our *stomach just partly digest our food*, and the remaining goes to our *small intestine*.

(i) How much food can our stomach store?

(ii) How does the stomach digest the food it stores?

(iii) Our food contains *proteins, carbohydrates and fats etc.* Which are digested in our *stomach*, and how much time does our stomach take to digest all this?

Tr. *(i)* Your stomach resembles a deflated balloon when empty. It slants across your body, big at top, small at bottom like a letter-J. Its *capacity* is about *two litres*, where your dog holds three times as much.

(ii) When you eat food, it is deposited in layers (one layer over the other). Muscular contractions of your *stomach mix* these food layers thoroughly with *digestive juices mainly hydrochloric acid*. Pretty soon they are a thick *gruel*. *This is how food is digested in the stomach.*

(*iii*) Stomach digests proteins, breaking it down into *polypeptides,* but the final job is done by your *small intestine, which also takes of carbohydrates fats and other foods.* The *mashed potatoes take the stomach only few minutes to digest, meat takes longer, and leafy vegetables still longer. For spinach, it takes as long as 24 hours to digest.*

What Happens in Small Intestines?

Tr. Where does the food from stomach go?

Sts. It goes to our small intestine.

Tr. Is it digested, undigested or semidigested?

Sts. Semi digested. What happens to this food here?

Tr. Your small intestine serves two purposes—digestion and absorption of the digested food. The absorbed food enters your Blood Stream and is carried away to various parts of your body for assimilation.

Sts. Oh! so the digested food is absorbed in our small intestine, and this absorbed food enters our blood stream which carries it to various parts of our body for assimilation. Then what happens to undigested found?

Undigested Food, Large Intestine, Rectum and Anus

Tr. Where the undigested food from small intestine can go?

Sts. To Large intestine.

Tr. Yes, this undigested food moves from your small intestine to your large intestine, where the undigested food passes to your rectum which pushes it out of your body through your anus. So what did you learn today?

Sts. We learned, "When we eat food, how is it digested by our Digestive System"

Recapitulation

(i) Students will involved in explaining the functioning of Digestive System of Man with the help of Chart.

(ii) Students will be asked to listen to the Audio taped Talking Stomach.

(iii) Photocopies of speaking stomach—Audio tape script may also be given to students for reading.

Assignment

In the photocopy of Digestive System of Man, colour the digestive system and show by arrows the direction of food from mouth to anus. Label

(a) Mouth (teeth, tongue; Sdiiyafy glands)

(b) Food Pipe or Oesophagus (Wall muscles)

(c) Stomach (35 million glands)

(d) Small Intestine (6 metres long)

(e) Large Intestine

(f) Rectum

(g) Anus

Note : Paste it into your Scrap Book.

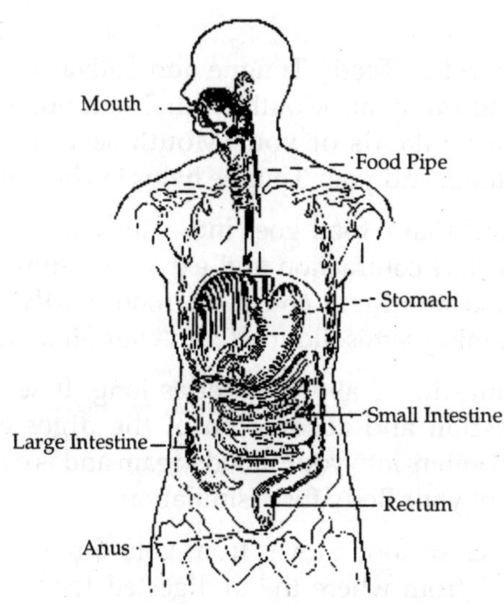

Fig. Digestive system of man.

Talking Stomach : A Script

On Black Board

— Alimentary Canal extends from mouth to anus through stomach.

— Salivary glands of the mouth secrete saliva, which moistens the food, and so the tongue helps in chewing.

— Stomach lining contains about 35 million of glands, which secrete about 3 litres of gastric juice per day—mainly hydro-chloric acid. This helps in digesting food.

— Small intestine is about 6 metres long.

— The absorbed digested food in small intestine enters into blood stream and is carried away to various parts of the body.

I am your Stomach. I am a part of your Digestive System. When you are hungry, you eat food. When you are thirsty, you drink water. Sometimes you eat and drink even when you are not hungry and thirsty. How do I know? I do not see, but it comes to Me through your Alimentary Canal which extends from your Mouth to your Anus viz. Me.

Your Mouth has Teeth, Tongue and Salivary Glands. When you ingest food into your Mouth, your Teeth break it into small pieces, Salivary Glands of your Mouth secrete Saliva which moistens the food, and your Tongue helps in chewing.

From your Mouth, food goes into your Food Pipe, where its Wall Muscles start contraction and expansion movement, which pushes the food into Me. I churn the food, partly digest it, and send the remaining semisolid food into your Small Intestine.

Your Small Intestine is about 6 metres long. It serves two purposes— digestion and absorption of the digested food. The absorbed food enters into your Bloodstream and is carried away to various parts of your Body for assimilation.

The undigested food moves from your Small Intestine to the Large Intestine from where the undigested food passes to your Rectum which pushes it out of your Body through your Anus.

People think I am terribly important. Actually, I am just a Convenience—your Food Reservoir. So far as your digestion is concerned, your Small Intestine is the real champ. I work on protein, breaking it down into polypeptides, but even here final job is done by your small Intestine, which also takes care of carbohydrates, fats and other food stuff.

I am glossy pink outside. Inside, I resemble a deflated balloon when I am empty. When I am full, I slant across your Body, big at top, small at bottom like the letter J. My Capacity is a little under two litres. Your dog can hold three times as much.

I am not as important as people think I am. I perform a number of jobs that make your life pleasant. My lining contains some 35 million glands that may secrete about three litres of gastric juice per day—mainly hydrochloric acid.

Everyone thinks of me a violent churn, which manhandles every thing that you swallow. Not so. As you eat dinner, the food is deposited one layer at a time. My muscular contractions mix these food layers thoroughly with digestive juices. Pretty soon they are a thick gruel. The meshed potatoes take me only a few minutes to handle. Meat takes longer, and leaf vegetables still longer. How long? It all depends on your mood—tense or relaxed. Four hours is average for a normal meal. For spinach it may take as long as 24 hours. Fatty meals pose special problems for me. A heavy fatty breakfast taken by you becomes a heavy load for Me, with the result when you sit down for lunch, I may still be working on as much as a fourth of your breakfast.

In fact, I lead a pretty relaxed life. While my neighbours (Liver, Heart, Lungs and Kidneys) are busy 24 hours a day. I can finish my work on a normal dinner by the time you go to bed. So I also go to sleep when you do.

I have a remarkable attribute : the way I reflect your moods. When your face turns red with anger, I turn red. When you get pale with freight, I get pale too. When you get excited, my secretions triple in volume. I share your depressions too, my muscular waves stop and so does Secretion of gastric juice.

17

Model Lesson

Instructions to Students

This is not a test. This is a PROGRAMME designed for you to learn the "Structure of Atom".

In this Programme you will find numbered paragraphs. These paragraphs are called FRAMES. Read each Frame carefully and answer the questions given after each Frame.

Check your answers from the ANSWER KEY given at the end of the programme.

Frame 1

Matter is made up of very small particles called atoms. The smallest particle of matter is..........

If answer is correct go to Frame 2, otherwise Repeat Frame 1.

Frame 2

Atom is made of various particles called electrons, protons and neutrons. Electrons are negatively charged particles. Protons are positively charged particles. Neutrons have no charge,.that is, they are neutral.

Complete the following sentences :

(a) The positively charged particle of an atom is..........

(b) An electron has .... charge.

(c) A neutral atomic particle is called ....

If answers are correct go to Frame 3 otherwise repeat Frame 2.

Frame 3

Check the statement below that is true. A proton is :

(a) positively charged.

(b) negatively charged.

(c) neutral.

(d) sometimes positive, some times negative.

If answer is correct go to Frame 4, otherwise repeat Frames 2 and 3.

Frame 4

Check the statement below that is true. A neutron is :

(a) positively charged.

(b) negatively charged.

(c) neutral.

(d) sometimes positive, sometimes negative.

If answer is correct go to Frame 5, otherwise repeat Frames 2 and 4.

Frame 5

Check the statement below that is true :

An electron is :

(a) positively charged.

(b) negatively charged.

(c) neutral.

(d) sometimes positive, sometimes negative.

If answer is correct go to Frame 6, otherwise repeat Frames 2 and 5.

Frame 6

The weight of a proton is approximately equal to the weight of a neutron, and the weight of an electron is so small compared to the weight of a proton or a neutron that it can be neglected. Check the statement below that is true.

The weight of a proton is approximately equal to the weight of

(a) electron (b) neutron

(c) each of them (d) none of them.

If answer is correct go to Frame 7, otherwise repeat Frame 6.

Frame 7

The charge of an electron is equal and opposite to the charge of a proton. If the charge of an electron is-x units, then the charge of a proton should be :

(a) – x units (b) + x units

(c) more than x units (d) less than x units.

If answer is correct go to Frame 8, otherwise repeat Frame 7.

Frame 8

If the charge of a proton is +x units, the charge of an electron should be..........

If answer is correct go to Frame 9, otherwise repeat Frames 7 and 8.

Frame 9

An atom can be assumed to be spherical in shape. At its centre there is a very small space (compared to the atom as a whole) containing protons and neutrons. This space is called nucleus as shown in given figure :

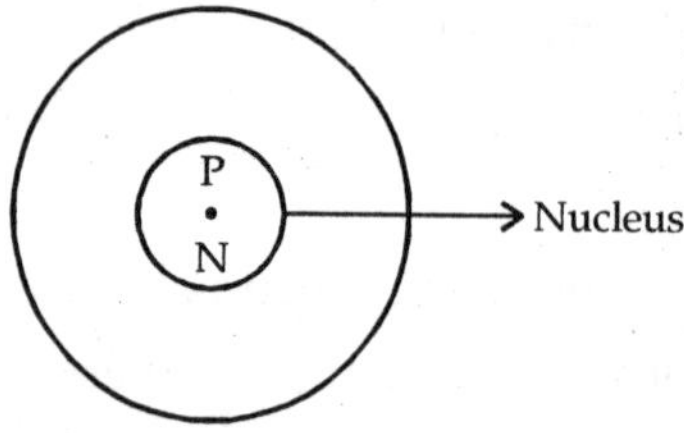

Check the statement below that is true.

The nucleus of an atom contains :

(a) protons only. (b) neutrons only.

(c) protons and neutrons both. (d) none of them.

If answer is correct go to Frame 10, otherwise repeat Frame 9.

Frame 10

Around the nucleus some hollow spheres of different sizes can be assumed. The space between any two of such hollow spheres is called a shell as shown in given figure :

Check the statement that is true.

(a) A is a shell, (b) B is a shell.

(c) Both A and B are shells, (d) None of them are shells.

If answer is correct go to Frame 11, otherwise repeat Frame 10.

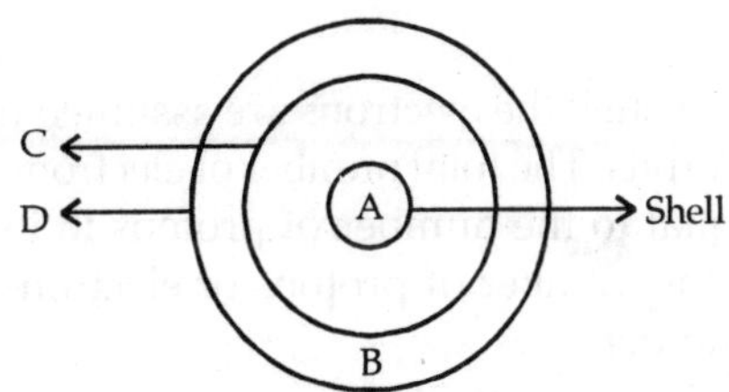

C-boundry of first hollow sphere D-boundry of second hollow sphere.

Frame 11

As the number of electrons is equal to the number of protons and the charge of an electron is equal and opposite to the charge of a proton the atom as a whole is neutral.

Example-Sodium atom has 11 electrons and 11 protons. If charge of an electron is-x units, the charge of a proton will be + x units.

Charge of 11 electrons =-11 x units

Charge of 11 protons = + 11 x units.

Therefore total charge of sodium atom is equal to

–11x plus + llx= 0.

Complete the following statements :

(a) A neutral atom has 40 electrons, then it should have .... protons.

(b) If an atom has 10 electrons but only 9 protons, then the atom .... neutral (will be, will not be).

If answers are correct go to Frame 12, otherwise repeat Frame11.

Frame 12

Nucleus has protons and neutrons. Around the nucleus there exist electrons in various spherical shells. Complete the following statements :

(a) Electrons exist in the ....

(b) Protons exist in the ....

(c) Neutrons exist in the ....

If answer is correct go to Frame 13, otherwise repeat Frame 12.

Frame 13

In a particular shell the electrons are assumed to be moving in various circular orbits. The total number of electrons in all the shells of an atom is equal to the number of protons in its nucleus. This number, that is the number of protons or electrons in an atom, is called atomic number.

(a) Sodium has 11 protons in the nucleus. The total number of electrons in all the shells of sodium will be ....

(b) The atomic number of sodium is ....

If answers are correct go to Frame 14, otherwise repeat Frame13.

Frame 14

The atomic number of oxygen is 8. What will be the number of protons in the nucleus, and the number of electrons in the shells ?

(a) Number of protons is ....

(b) Number of electrons is ....

If answers are correct go to Frame 15, otherwise repeat Frames 13 and 14.

Frame 15

The sum of the number of neutrons and protons is equal to the atomic weight of an atom.

Example-Oxygen has 8 protons and 8 neutrons. Thus the atomic weight of oxygen is 8 + 8 = 16.

Sodium atom has 11 protons and 12 neutrons. Check the statement below that is true. Atomic weight of sodium is :

(a) 11 (b) 12

(c) 23 (d) 1

If answer is correct go to Frame 16, otherwise repeat Frame 15.

Frame 16

Nitrogen atom has 7 protons and 7 neutrons. The atomic weight of nitrogen is ...

If answer is correct go to Frame 17, otherwise repeat Frames 15 and 16.

Frame 17

The atomic weight of hydrogen is 1. It has 1 proton, then the number of neutrons in hydrogen atom is ..... .

If answer is correct go to Frame 18, otherwise repeat Frames 15, 16 and 17.

Frame 18

The number of shells in an atom may vary from 1 to 7, that is the number of shells in an atom cannot exceed 7, though it can be less than 7 (6, 5, 4, 3, 2, 1) depending upon the total number of electrons in a particular atom.

The number of electrons present in each shell is governed by 2 rules.

Rule 1-The nth (n is the number of shell) shell cannot have more than 2n2 electrons.

Example-For the first shell n = 1

Therefore $2n^2 = 2.1^2 = 2$

It means 1st shell cannot have more than 2 electrons (if the atom has more electrons, they will be in the other shells), though it can have less than 2 (if there are not enough electrons in a particular atom).

For the 2nd shell n = 2

Therefore $2n^2 = 2.2^2 = 2.4 = 8$

It means 2nd shell cannot have more than 8 electrons though it can have less than 8 (as explained above).

According to this rule, there should not be more than

(a) .... electrons in 3rd shell.

(b) .... electrons in 4th shell.

(c) .... electrons in 5th shell.

(d) .... electrons in 6th shell.

(e) .... electrons in 7th shell.

If answers are correct go to Frame 19, otherwise repeat Frame18.

Frame 19

Oxygen has 8 electrons. According to the above mentioned rule write down the number of electrons in different shells.

Shell 1 .... Shell 2 .... Shell 3 ....

If answers are correct go to Frame 20, otherwise repeat Frames 18 and 19.

Frame 20

The atomic number of chlorine is 17. Write down the number of electrons in different shells.

Shell 1 .... Shell 2 ....

Shell 3 .... Shell 4 ....

If answers are correct go to Frame 21, otherwise repeat Frames 18, 19 and 20.

Frame 21

Rule 2-Last shell cannot have more than 8 electrons in an atom, and the last but one shell cannot have more than 18 electrons.

Complete the following statements :

(a) An atom has 5 shells. The number of electrons in its 5th shell should not exceed ....

(b) The number of electrons in its 4th shell should not exceed ....

If answers are correct go to Frame 22, otherwise repeat Frame21.

Frame 22

The atomic number of sodium atom is 11 and its atomic weight is 23. Write down the number of the following items of a sodium atom :

(a) Electrons ....

(b) Protons ....

(c) Protons and neutrons ....

(d) Neutrons ....

(e) Electrons in 1st shell ....

(f) Electrons in 2nd shell ....

(g) Electrons in 3rd shell ....

(h) Electrons in 4th shell ....

If answers are correct go to Frame 23, otherwise repeat Frames 13-22.

Frame 23

The atomic number of carbon is 6 and its atomic weight is 12. Complete the following diagram of carbon atom by putting at proper places the number of electrons, protons and neutrons.

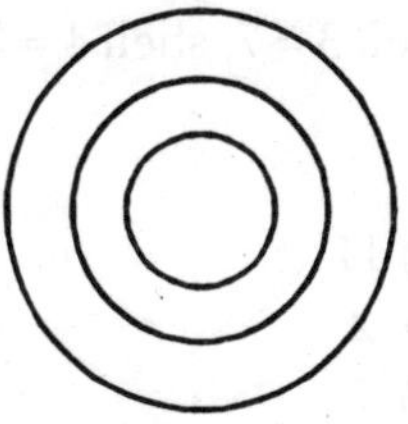

Fig.

If answer is correct CONGRATULATIONS, you have learned what we wanted to teach you through this PROGRAMME. IF NOT please repeat Frames 13-23.

Answers

Frame 1	*Frame 2*	*Frame 3*
atom	(a) proton (b) negative (c) neutron	(a) positively charged
Frame 4	*Frame 5*	*Frame 6*
(c) Neutral	(b) negatively charged	(b) Neutron

Frame 7

(b) + x units

Frame 8

– x units

Frame 9

(c) Protons and Neutrons both

Frame 10

b) B is a shell

Frame 11

(a) 40 Protons

(b) will not be

Frame 12

(a) shells

(b) nucleus

(c) nucleus

Frame 13

(b) 11

(a) 11

Frame 14

(a) 8 protons

(b) 8 electrons

Frame 15

(c) 23

Frame 16

14

Frame 17

0

Frame 18

(a) 18

(b) 32

(c) 50

(d) 72

(e) 98

Frame 19

shell 1 = 2

Shell 2 = 6

shell 3 = 0

Frame 20

shell 1 = 2 shell 2=8

shell 3 = 7, shell 4 = 0

Frame 21

(a) 8

(b) 18

Frame 22

(a) 11 (b) 11 (c) 23

(d) 12 (e) 2 (f) 8

(g) 1 (h) 0

Frame 23

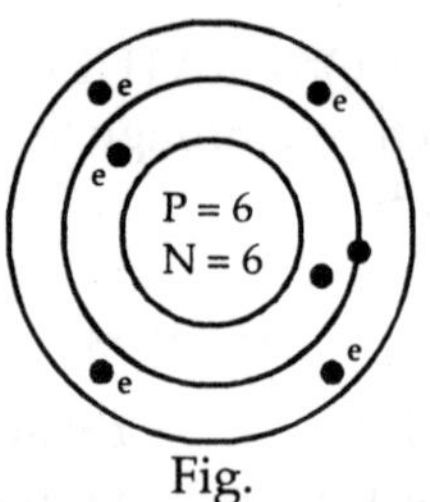

Fig.

18

Sample Questions

Section-A

1. What is air ? What are its important characteristics ?
2. How can you show that air is a mixture ?
3. Name the main constituents of air. How do you find their proportion in air ?
4. What is the composition of air ?
5. How can you show the presence of water vapour in air ?
6. Biscuits left in open in rainy season become soft. Why ?
7. (a) Why is fire extinguished by throwing sand or water on it?

   (b) If you boil water and cool it and then put a fish into it. Will the fish remain alive or die ? Why ?
8. State five important uses of air.
9. Fill in the following blanks :

   (i) Storm is a .... of air.

   (ii) Air occupies .... and possesses ....

   (iii) Air mainly contains (1) nitrogen, (2) oxygen and (3) ....

   (iv) Common salt becomes wet in the open in rainy season because air ....

   (v) Plants breathe in .... at................

(vi) Fish can breathe under water, because some .... is dissolved in water.

10. Write a brief answer against each of the following questions.
    (i) How can you get energy from air ? ....
    (ii) Does the lime water turn milky with nitrogen, oxygen or carbon dioxide ? ....
    (iii) Do the plants breathe in oxygen or carbon dioxide at night? ....
    (iv) What is the percentage of nitrogen in air ? ....
    (v) From where does dust come in the air ? ....
    (vi) How much is water vapour present in air ? ....

Section-B

1. Describe an activity to show that water is very essential for plants.
2. What are the functions of water in the bodies of animals?
3. Give names of 5 important sources of water in nature ?
4. How are rivers and springs formed in nature ?
5. How does water go from place to place and finally come back to the sea ? What is this process called ?
6. State any four physical properties of water.
7. Show experimentally that water is a bad conductor of heat.
8. How will you find the two fixed points on a Celsius thermometer ?
9. Water is a universal solvent. Prove it experimentally.
10. Which processes are involved in purification of drinking water ?
11. What is the use of water in industry ?
12. How will you find whether a given sample is of hard or soft water ?
13. What are the disadvantages of using hard water ?

14. What are the main causes of water pollution ? Give two methods of checking this pollution.

15. What do you mean by conservation of water ? How will you apply it in your house ?

16. What would happen, if :

    (i) water had a sour taste,

    (ii) water had a deep red colour,

    (iii) water were as thick as mobil oil,

    (iv) there were no water cycle in nature.

17. Give one word for each of the following :

    (i) Hot water spring ....

    (ii) Killing of germs in water. ....

    (iii) Drain water carrying filth. ....

    (iv) Settling down of insoluble solids in water on standing. ....

    (v) A house made from ice by Eskimos. ....

18. Fill in the following blanks :

    (i) Rain water contains very little..................

    (ii) Sea-water is saline, because it contains..................

    (iii) .... part of an iceberg remains hidden under water.

    (iv) Hard water can be softened by mixing .... with it.

    (v) Sub-soil water is usually .... for drinking.

19. Write a brief answer against each of the following questions:

    (i) Do green plants absorb carbon dioxide in day-time?

    (ii) What is the use of sand in purifying drinking water ?

    (ii) How do sea-animals breathe under water ?

    (iv) Which is the softest water in nature ?

(v) What happens when some water is left in a drinking glass for a week?...........

20. Write a, b, c, or d as you find the correct word or words, against each of the following :

(i) Sea-water is the hardest natural water, because ....

(a) It injures our skin.

(b) It is not fit for irrigation.

(c) It contains calcium and magnesium salts.

(d) It cuts away the sea-shore.

(ii) Water of a shallow well is called...........

(a) ground water.

(b) surface water.

(c) mineral water.

(d) sub-soil water.

(iii) Fish remain alive inside water because they ....

(a) can live without air.

(b) can decompose water and take up oxygen.

(c) can breathe in air dissolved in water.

(d) carry air in their gills from outside.

(iv) Eskimos build houses from ice, because ice.............

(a) is a bad conductor of heat.

(b) can float on water.

(c) is very hard.

(d) preserves their food.

(v) Hard water is unfit for its use in steam boilers, because it

(a) softens the boiler plate.

(b) forms a thick solid crust inside the boiler, because it.............

(c) does not form steam.

(d) cannot flow easily in the boiler tubes.

Sections-C

1. Explain the term 'Work'. How is it measured ?
2. Name different types of energy.
3. Distinguish between potential energy and kinetic energy. Give two examples of each type.
4. Suspend a small piece of stone tied to a thread from a rigid support as shown in the following figure. Pull the stone on one side and then release it. Discuss the energy transformation taking place during the motion of stone.
5. Discuss the energy transformations taking place in the following cases :
   - (a) In a steam engine.
   - (b) At hydro-electric power station.
   - (c) A stone released from a catapult hits a metal object.
   - (d) In a fire cracker.
6. Why should we use natural sources of energy with care and economy ? Name two methods to economise consumption of fuels.
7. Fill in the blanks :
   - (i) Work = ... x Distance moved.
   - (ii) A man merely supporting a bucket full of water .... work.
   - (iii) The capacity to do work is called ....
   - (iv) The wound up spring in a watch possess .... energy.
   - (v) Strong wind possesses .... energy.
   - (vi) At thermal power station heat energy is converted into .... energy.
   - (vii) Petrol possesses .... energy.

8. Match the items given in column A with the items given in column B :

Column A	*Column B*
(1) Light energy	(a) Water stored in a dam.
(2) Solar energy	(b) Energy spent in playing football.
(3) Muscular energy	(c) A car run by petrol fuel.
(4) Energy transformation	(d) Nuclear reactor.
(5) Potential energy	(e) Solar cooker.
(6) Atomic energy	(f) Tail of a comet.

Section-D

Answer the following questions in one or two words.

1. Give two examples of renewable sources of energy.
2. Give two examples of non-renewable sources of energy.
3. Give two quantities on which kinetic energy of a body depends.
4. Give two quantities on which potential energy of a body depends.
5. What type of energy does the water in a reservoir have ?

Answer the following questions in one or two sentences.

1. Define the term 'energy'. Name six different forms of energy.
2. Explain the energy transformation taking place during the motion of a Maxwell wheel.
3. Discuss the energy transformation taking place in the following cases :
   (a) A body swinging on a swing.
   (b) Hydroelectric power station.
   (c) A toy car moving with a battery.
   (d) Headlight bulb of a bicycle glowing with the help of a dynamo.
   (e) When a stone is dropped from the top of a cliff.

4. Why should we use the renewable sources of energy judiciously ?
5. Suggest different ways to conserve renewable sources of energy.

Answer the following questions in detail.

1. Distinguish between kinetic energy and potential energy. Give two examples of each type of energy.
2. Describe an experiment to show that kinetic energy of a body depends upon : (1) mass of the body, (2) speed of the body.
3. Describe an experiment to show that potential energy of a body depends upon :

   (1) mass of the body, (2) height to which the body is raised.
4. Explain the principle of conservation of energy with the help of an example.
5. Explain the cause of dissipation of energy in mechanical devices. How can dissipation of energy be reduced ?
6. Distinguish between renewable and non-renewable sources of energy. Give two examples of each type of source.

Fill in the blanks

(i) The wound up spring in a toy car possesses .... energy.

(ii) Our food possesses .... energy.

(iii) The potential energy possessed by a body depends upon .... of the body and the .... to which it is raised from the ground.

(iv) In an electric stove .... energy changes into .... energy.

(v) A cycle dynamo converts .... energy into .... energy.

(vi) Coal is .... source of energy.

(vii) In a solar cooker .... energy changes into .... energy.

Tick (V) mark the correct statements :

(i) When a stone is thrown upward, the potential energy changes into kinetic energy.

(ii) Energy can neither be created nor destroyed by a process.

(iii) In a vibrating tuning fork, mechanical energy changes into sound energy.

(iv) The loss of energy in machines can be minimised by lubrication.

(v) The flowing river water is a non-renewable source of energy.

(vi) A body cannot possess kinetic and potential energy simultaneously.

(vii) A cricket ball, moving along the ground possesses zero potential energy with respect to ground.

Match the following :

(i) The kinetic energy of a body depends on

(ii) Gobar gas is

(iii) Compressed spring of a sofa possesses

(iv) Air blowing with high speed is

(v) Cause of dissipation of energy in machines is

(vi) A ball moving at a height of 1m about the ground possesses

(a) potential energy.

(b) kinetic and potential energy simultaneously.

(c) friction.

(d) the mass and the speed of the body.

(e) non-renewable source of energy.

(f) renewable source of energy.

Section-E

Answer the following questions in one or two words.

1. What products do you get when water is electrolysed ?

2. How much salt is generally present in one litre of sea-water?
3. Name two types of hard water.
4. Write down freezing and boiling points of water.
5. Which one has less density-water at 40°C or ice at 0°C ?

Answer the following questions in one or two sentences.

1. How does a water cooler work ?
2. What should be done at very cold places during winter to prevent the water pipes from bursting ?
3. How is salt prepared from sea water ?
4. Which salts are responsible for hard water ?
5. Give two disadvantages of using hard water ?
6. Why is sodium metal placed in kerosene oil ?
7. What is mineral water ?

Answer the following questions in detail.

1. How are industries polluting water ?
2. Describe the experiment for the electrolysis of water with the help of a diagram.
3. Describe the importance of the unique nature of water.
4. What is rust ? How is it used ?How does it harm ? How can it be presented ?
5. What is salinity of water ? How does it remain constant?

Fill in the blanks :

(i) When a saturated solution is heated it becomes ....

(ii) Sodium reacts with water to give sodium hydroxide and ....

(iii) Water has the maximum density at .... °C.

(iv) The truck radiator cools the engine by circulating .... around it.

(v) Hydrogen burns in oxygen to give .... vapour.

Section-F

Answer the following questions in one or two words.

1. Name three chief constituents of air.
2. Give two uses of inert gases.
3. Give four uses of nitrogen gases.
4. What is dry ice ?
5. Name two nitrogenous fertilizers.
6. Which gas is used for filling electric bulb ?
7. Name three air pollutants ?

Answer the following questions in one or two sentences.

1. How does oxygen occur in nature ?
2. Why is CO_2 gas used for extinguishing fire ?
3. Why is CO_2 gas used in aerated drinks ?
4. What do you mean by acid rain ?
5. How do automobiles cause pollution ?

Answer the following questions in detail.

1. How is oxygen manufactured on large scale ?
2. How do factories cause air pollution ?
3. What makes the air polluted ? What are major causes of pollution ? How can air pollution be minimised ?
4. What are the uses of oxygen ?
5. How is acid rain formed ? How does it harm living and non-living things.

Fill in the blanks :

(*a*) Nitrogen forms .... % of the volume of dry air.

(*b*) The content of water vapour in air is called the ....

(*c*) Air also contains tiny solid ....

(*d*) Nitrogen compounds are essential for the growth of..........

(*e*) Helium is used to obtain very low ....

(*f*) Coal and petrol contain small amounts of..........

(g) All fuels contain ....

(h) Nitrogen reacts with atmospheric oxygen to give various .... of nitrogen.

Section-G

Answer the following questions in one or two words :

1. Name two animals who do not chew their food ?
2. Which test would you conduct to test starch in a food item ?
3. In which form animals store carbohydrates in their body?
4. How much leafy vegetables should one take daily in his balanced diet ?
5. Which one provides more energy-one banana or 100g of spinach ?
6. Name two food items which can provide us roughage.

Answer the following questions in one or two sentences :

1. List five nutrients which we obtain from food.
2. Name two functions of water.
3. Define a balanced diet.
4. Why do growing children need more proteins ?
5. What are food fads ?

Answer the following questions in detail :

1. What are the functions of food ?
2. How can you test presence of the following nutrients in a sample of food ? Glucose, starch, fats and proteins.
3. What are the functions of following nutrients : Proteins, Vitamins and Carbohydrates.
4. Why should we not believe in food fads ? Give four examples of food fads prevalent in your locality.
5. Why is it recommended to plan a balanced diet ? Should a balanced diet contain costly food items ? Explain.

Objective type questions :

1. Write T for true and F for false statements.
   - (i) Carbohydrates are body building nutrients.
   - (ii) Vitamins are body protective nutrients.
   - (iii) Proteins are energy giving nutrients.
   - (iv) Eating ghee makes our brain sharp.
   - (v) Minerals protect our body from diseases.

	Column I		*Column II*
(i)	Carbohydrate	(a)	Water soluble
(ii)	Joule	(b)	Plants
(iii)	Staple food	(c)	Wheat
(iv)	Autotroph	(d)	Unit of heat
(v)	Vitamin Bcomplex	(e)	Starch

Section-H

Answer the following questions in one or two words :

1. Production of which cereals increased after the Green Revolution in India ?
2. Name two food items which you would suggest to a person who is not able to see in dim light.
3. Deficiency of which mineral causes anaemia ?
4. Name two food items which are rich in calcium.
5. Name two diseases caused by contaminated food.
6. Name two ways through which communicable diseases spread.

Answer the following questions in one or two sentences :

1. What is the meaning of green revolution ?
2. Give one difference between malnutrition and under-nutrition.
3. Name the diseases caused due to deficiency of Vitamin B, Vitamin A, iron and calcium.

4. How is kerosene helpful in killing insect larvae ?
5. Why should you get vaccinated, if available, against a spreading disease.

Answer the following questions in detail :

1. Write deficiency diseases and their symptoms caused due to the deficiency of following nutrients. Also write their sources. Vitamin B, Vitamin C, protein, phosphorus and iodine.
2. What is the need of preservation of food ? Explain four methods by which you can preserve vegetables.
3. Explain three methods by which water can be made safe for drinking.
4. How does a house fly spread diseases ? What measures would you take to prevent spread of diseases through flies?
5. What are the general methods for prevention of a disease?

Match the following

Column I	*Column II*
(i) PEM	(a) Goitre
(ii) Milk	(b) Tuberculosis
(iii) Flies	(c) Chlorine
(iv) Water	(d) Pasteurisation
(v) Iodine	(e) Kwashiorkor

Tick (✓) Mark the correct one

(i) Green revolution in India has increased the production of

(a) cotton and sugarcane ☐ (b) Wheat and rice ☐

(c) wheat and sugarcane ☐ (d) rice and maize ☐

(ii) Night blindness in caused by the dificiency of

(a) vitamin C ☐ (b) Vitamin D ☐

(c) vitamin A ☐ (d) Vitamin B ☐

(iii) Our skin can synthesize

(a) vitamin A ☐ (b) vitamin B complex ☐

(c) vitamin C ☐ (d) vitamin D ☐

(iv) Milk can be preserved by

(a) pasteurisation ☐ (b) adding sodium metabisulphite ☐

(c) freezing ☐ (d) storage in dry and place ☐

(v) Malaria spreads through

(a) contaminated food ☐

(b) contaminated water ☐

(c) flies ☐

(d) mosquitoes ☐

Section-I

Answer the following questions in one or two words :

1. Name one non-renewable natural resource.
2. What term is used for the removal of the top soil by water or wind ?
3. Name the areas in which wild life is conserved.
4. Which two gases are released from automobiles that cause air pollution ?
5. Name two water pollutants.
6. In which one way does extremely loud sound cause us harm ?

Answer the following questions in one or two sentences :

1. What is water pollution ?
2. Although the forests are renewable resources yet their cutting is not advisable.
3. Why is the fertility of soil important ?
4. Why should we conserve natural resources ?
5. In which areas is terrace farming essential ?

Answer the following questions in detail :

1. What are the various kinds of natural resources ? Why is there a need to conserve these resources ?
2. What are the four ways that can help us in conserving non-renewable resources ?
3. Define pollution. How does pollution disturb the balance of nature ?
4. Write short notes on :

(a) Soil erosion, (b) Conservation of wild life.

Match the following

	Column I	*Column II*
(i)	Renewable	(a) Lions
(ii)	Soil erosion	(b) Coal
(iii)	Gir forest	(c) Rhinoceroses
(iv)	Non-renewable	(d) Reduced fertility
(v)	Khaziranga	(e) Animals

Fill in the blanks :

(i) Jim Corbett National Park is famous for ....

(ii) Uranium .... be recycled.

(iii) The substances which cause pollution are called ....

(iv) Micro-organism .... disintegrate DDT.

(v) Terracing in hilly areas .... soil erosion.

Section-J

Answer the following questions in one or two words :

1. Give two examples of the renewable sources of energy ?
2. Give two examples of the non-renewable sources of energy.
3. Give two reasons for the increasing demand of energy.
4. What is the source of energy for our food ?
5. Name two main types of power plants.

Answer the following questions in one or two sentences :

1. Give two uses for each of the following sources of energy: (i) The Sun (ii) Fuels (iii) Electricity (iv) Bio-gas (iv) Wind (v) Moving water.
2. Why should we increase the use of renewable sources of energy?
3. Why is energy essential for our living ?
4. What are the important factors responsible for the increase in the demand for energy?
5. How can we overcome the energy crisis ?

Answer the following questions in detail :

1. Define renewable and non-renewable sources of energy. Give three examples for each of them.
2. How is energy wasted at home ? Give remedial measures to avoid wastage of energy.
3. What is energy crisis ? How can you help in solving energy crisis ?
4. Energy saved = Energy produced. Discuss.
5. Write a short essay on 'Energy and Its Sources.

Match the items given in column A with the items given in column B :

Column A	Column B
1. Source of food	(a) Cattle dung
2. Solar energy	(b) Wind
3. Bio-gas	(c) Dependence on non-renewable sources of energy
4. Fossil fuel	(d) Plants and animals
5. Renewable source of energy	(e) Solar cooker
6. Non-renewable source of	(f) Use of car instead of public energy transport
7. Energy crisis	(g) Diesel
8. Wastage of energy	(h) Petroleum.

Write T for True and F for False against the following statements:

(i) Petroleum is formed inside the earth as a result of transformation of solar energy into chemical energy. ☐

(ii) The renewable sources of energy get exhausted as we use them. ☐

(iii) Tidal energy can be used to generate electricity. ☐

(iv) Poor maintenance of machines causes wastage of energy. ☐

(v) Use of pressure cooker to cook food saves energy and time. ☐

(vi) The demand of energy is decreasing with expansion in the activities of man. ☐

Fill in the blanks with suitable words given in brackets :

(1) Liquified petroleum gas is .... source of energy. (renewable, non renewable)

(2) Bio-gas is obtained from .... (petroleum, dumped waste products).

(3) Non-renewable sources of energy are .... (exhaustible, inexhaustible).

(4) The energy consumption .... with the increase in members of a family, (increases, decreases).

(5) The cheapest method to trap energy is to .... fast growing trees, (grow, fall down).

19

Model Papers

Paper No. 1

Time : 3 hrs. *M.M. : 70*

Note : All Questions are compulsory.

1. Identify a topic of your choice from class VI-VIII Science. Make a lesson plan to teach by scientific method in a 40 minutes period. 15

2. Identify any topic from class VI-VIII Science. Write 5 behavioural objectives. Construct one multiple choice test item for each objective. 15

3. Why audio-visual aids are used in upper primary classes? Answer this question taking into consideration the cognitive stages of students, and cone of experiences. 15

4. What is the importance of field trips/excursions/visits in science teaching ? What points you will keep in mind while organising an educational field trips/excursions of upper primary students. 15

or

Suppose you are an upper primary teacher, then how will you organise a science club in your school ? What difficulties do you expect in it ? What measures you would take to overcome these difficulties ?

5. If you identify some mentally/physically handicapped children in your class, what suitable strategies would you adopt to help such children ? 10

or

'Write a short note on any two of the following innovative experiences in science education at the elementary level :

(i) Nehru Science Exhibition.

(ii) Hoshangabad—Ekalavya Experiment.

(iii) Vikram Sarabhai Community Science Centre.

(iv) Urban Marginal Project. (UNESCO) NCERT, DESM

Paper No. 2

Time : 3 hrs. ***MM. : 70***

1. "Most substances expand on heating and contract on cooling". How will you use scientific method in teaching this concept to the students of VIIth class ? 10
2. How would you organize a field trip for class VIth students and to which place ? Explain which topics you would cover under this and how ? 10
3. Construct an achievement test for testing knowledge, under-standing, application and skill for class VIIth of 50 marks. How will you use the analysis of this test in providing feedback to the students ? 10
4. Identify a topic of VIIIth class science. Develop a programmed instructional unit on this topic. 10
5. Mention at least four competencies which can be developed in students through teaching of science. 2

   (i) What do you understand by minimum levels of learning? 2

   (ii) How will you identify the children with special needs ? 2

   (iii) What are the needs of children with special needs? 2

(iv) What are the various kinds of aids which can be used in teaching science ? 2

(v) How can you utilize educational television programmes for your class as a science teacher ? 2

(vi) What are the secondary sources of information ? 2

(vii) Explain the role of teacher in "Child-Centred Approach" ? 2

(viii) How can you use effectively the creativity of students in science club ? 2

(ix) What is the importance of improvising equipment in science teaching ? 2

Explain the Following 10

(1) Group activities.
(2) Teacher centred approach.
(3) Nature of Science.
(4) Importance of Science fair.
(5) Multi-media package.
(6) Community resources.
(7) Educational resources.
(8) Evaluation.
(9) Validity of a test.
(10) Steps of scientific method.

Paper No. 3

Time : 3 hrs. ***M.M. : 70***

Note : *All questions are compulsory. Q. Nos. 1 to 10 carry one mark each. Q. Nos. 11 to 20 carry two marks each and Q. Nos. 21 to 24 carry 10 marks each.*

1. Define minimum levels of learning in science teaching at elementary level.
2. Give full form of M.L.C. and M.L.L.
3. What is E.V.S. ?
4. Define hypothesis.
5. Name two roles of a teacher in curriculum transaction.
6. Is a slide tape programme a multi-media package ?
7. Define self-learning materials.
8. Is the use of low cost teaching aids educational technology ?

9. Where is Vikram Sarabhai Community Science Centre located?
10. Define the term objectivity of a test.
11. What do you mean by mobile science exhibition ?
12. What are the objectives of Ekalavya Experiment ?
13. Is there any relation between Nehru Birth Anniversary and Nehru Science Exhibition ?
14. Define the terms reliability and validity.
15. What are the characteristics of a good test ?
16. Name two improvised apparatus which you have used during your practice teaching.
17. What is the importance of community resources in teaching of science at elementary level ?
18. State two reasons for using audio-visual aids in teaching science at elementary level.
19. Write 10 items of a primary science kit.
20. State two differences between programmed instruction package and multi-media package.
21. Prepare a lesson plan of any topic for the students of class VII for 30 minutes duration through Lecture demonstration method.

    or

    Identify a topic from VIIIth class science syllabus. Develop a programmed instructional material on this topic.
22. Explain the competencies to be developed among children through teaching of science at elementary level.

    or

    Explain how will you utilize the achievement test information for providing feedback to the students and teachers.
23. How will you identify slow learner in your science class? As a science teacher what suitable strategy will you adopt to help such children?

24. You have to construct an achievement test in science. How will you make a plan for it ? Construct out achievement test using your plan on any topics of class VIII science for a duration of one hour and maximum marks 50.

Paper No. 4

Time : 3 hrs. ***M. M. 70***

Note : *All questions are compulsory.*

PART-A 10 x 4 = 40

1. Explain the method of teaching science using the following steps : problem, hypothesis, experiment and conclusion. Illustrate each step to teach the concept 'air has weight' in elementary classes using these steps.

or

Identify a topic of your choice from classes VI-VIII science. Make a lesson plan to teach this topic by lecture-demonstration method in a 30 minutes period.

2. Write three roles of a science teacher. Explain any one of them which you played during your practice teaching.

or

List ten experiences which you give to your students when teach-ing science starting from most concrete to most abstract. What is the position of the 'FIELD TRIP' in this list ? Make a 'Field Trip Plan' of a place of scientific interest in Delhi.

3. Identify a topic of your choice from class VI-VIII science. Write five behavioural objectives covering the topic. Construct one multiple choice test for each objective. Out of these five test items two should be of knowledge, two of understanding and one of application.

or

You have constructed an achievement test on some VI-VIII science content. Explain, how has it helped you to get feedback for students and teachers for effective science teaching.

4. List five resources of science teaching at elementary level. Explain the use of any one of them for effective science teaching.

or

How school T.V. programmes in elementary science are being used in Delhi schools ? What is the role of classroom teacher ? Does he do pre-and post-telecast activities ? How will it affect if he does or does not do these activities ?

PART-B 2 x 10 = 20

5. *Do any ten of the following :*

(a) Name a programmed instruction unit developed or used in your science course. Write two of its strengths.

(b) State two differences between multi-media package and pro-grammed instruction package.

(c) Define scientific temper. How can it be developed?

(d) A physically handicapped child has an IQ = 120. He cannot speak clearly but he can understand, what you speak. He cannot write and handle scientific equipment, but he can type. Which method will you use to teach him science and why?

(e) You want to teach a child 'how to read a thermometer'. Which approach will you use—teacher centred or learner centred, and why ?

(f) You want to teach a child 'concept of temperature'. Which approach will you use—teacher centred or learner centred, and why ?

(g) Is a package of the three NCERT science textbooks for classes VI-VIII an integrated science package? Give two reasons to justify your answer.

(h) State two reasons for using audio-visual aids in teaching science at elementary level.

(i) Write eight items of a primary science kit.

(j) How will you teach 'BIRDS' by EVS approach ?

(k) State two philosophic bases of Hoshangabad Science Project.

(l) Write two methods to mobilise community resources in science teaching.

PART-C 1 x 10 = 10

6. *Do any ten of the following :*

(a) Is a slide-tape programme a multi-media package?

(b) Is use of low cost teaching aids educational technology?

(c) Is there any relation between Nehru Birth Anniversary and Nehru (National) Science Exhibition?

(d) What do you mean by EVS ?

(e) Which method did you mostly use in teaching science ? Give one reason for using it mostly.

(f) Where is Vikram Sarabhai community science centre located.?

(g) What do you mean by mobile science unit ?

(h) Can you test interests and attitudes ? Give one strong argument in support of your answer.

(i) State the difference between a concept and skill.

(j) State the difference between integrated science and disciplined science.

(k) Define self-learning material.

Paper No. 5

Time : 3 hrs. **M. M. : 70**

Note *: All questions are compulsory.*

1. Write five steps of a Scientific method. Identify a topic of your choice from class VI-VIII science. Develop a lesson plan to teach this topic in a 40-minute's period using all the five steps listed by you. 15

or

Select a topic of your choice from class VI-VIII science and develop a lesson plan of 40-minute's period under the following heads:

(a) Specific objectives to be achieved.

(b) Major concepts to be developed.

(c) Teaching learning activities te be followed.

(d) Mode of evaluation to be undertaken. 15

2. (a) What is the difference between the Teacher-Centred Approach and the Child-Centred Approach in teaching science? Which approach will you use for developing the concept? 10

(b) Write 5 competencies which you feel should be developed while teaching science. 10

or

Write 5 objectives of teaching science at upper primary level.

3. In NCERT class VI science textbook, there are 4 lessons of Physics, 5 of Chemistry and 4 of Biology. In class VII there are 7, 5 and 6, in class VIII 5, 5 and 6 respectively. Do you think that this is a package of integrated science course, and one science teacher can teach the whole course? Discuss. 10

or

You must have taught 10 science lessons in your practice teach-ing school in upper primary classes. Select any one of them, and describe briefly how you taught it. 10

4. Write three methods of teaching science. Which method was mostly used in your practice teaching in schools ? Explain briefly how did you use that method while teaching science. Mention the topic and the class. 10

or

Name a programmed instruction unit which you used in your science course. Write down its strengths and weaknesses. How will you evaluate its effectiveness using pre-test and post-test scores ? 10

5. Identify any topic from class VI-VIII science. Construct 5 test-items one knowledge, two understanding and two of application. 10

or

Identify any topic from class VI-VIII science and construct five multiple choice test items each testing different objective (ability). 10

6. Write 5 resources which you can use for effective science teaching. 5

or

Why audio-visual aids are considered important for teaching science in upper primary classes ? 5

7. How will you ensure that your students have learned what you have taught them ? Explain with some concrete examples from science. 5

or

How can continuous and comprehensive evaluation help in effective teaching and learning of science ? 5

8. What is the purpose of organising Nehru Science Exhibition? How is it related with school, zonal and state science fairs? 5

or

Write the story 'From Science is Doing to EVS in the Union Territory of Delhi. 5

Paper No. 6.

Time : 3 hrs. ***M. M. : 70***

General Instructions :

(i) All questions are compulsory.

(ii) There are three parts in the question paper.

(iii) In Part A, question numbers 1 to 10 are very short answer type questions of 1 mark each.

(iv) In part B, question numbers 11 to 20 are short answer type questions of 2 marks each.

(v) In Part C, question numbers 21 to 24 are long answer type questions of 10 marks each.

Part-A

1. What do you understand by Hypothesis? 1
2. Name any three core components of primary science curriculum. 1
3. What should be the qualification of a primary science teacher? 1
4. Where is 'Ekalavya Project' located in our country ? 1
5. State yes or no whether a 'Science Laboratory' essential for teaching of science in upper primary classes ? 1
6. What is the most suitable method of teaching science at the elementary level ? 1
7. Name any two community resources for teaching science. 1
8. State the difference between concept and skill. 1
9. What do you understand by feedback to a student ? 1
10. What is a Mobile Science Unit ? 1

Part-B

11. What do you understand by the concepts of Science ? 2
12. Explain the criteria for identifying the "children with special needs". 2
13. What do you understand by Minimum Levels of learning in science ? 2
14. State the need and importance of establishing science clubs. 2
15. Explain with the help of two examples 'the role of teacher as facilitator'. 2
16. What do you understand by Educational Technology ? 2
17. Discuss the meaning of continuous evaluation. 2

18. State the principle of selecting audio-visual aids for teaching science at the upper primary level. 2

19. State five steps of the scientific method. 2

20. Briefly state two main objectives of Vikram Sarabhai Community Science Centre. 2

Part-C

21. Explain the characteristics of a good lesson plan in the teaching of science. Develop a lesson plan of 40 minutes, duration on any topic of your choice from science textbooks for classes VI-VIII

or

"The real spirit of teaching science lies in placing the students in the position of original investigators." What is the method towards which the above statement hints? Write the strengths and weaknesses of this method.

10

22. What is Scientific Attitude ? What is its importance in daily life ? With the help of three suitable examples, discuss the ways in which you would develop scientific attitude amongst your students through teaching of science.

or

Discuss the superiority of Child Centred Approach of teaching science over the Teacher Centred Approach.

10

23. What are the steps to be taken in the construction of an objective type test ? Explain with the help of suitable example. 10

24. What do you understand by innovative experiences in science education ? Describe any two of your innovative experiences in the teaching of science. 10

Paper No. 7

Time : 3 hrs. ***M. Marks : 70***

Note : *All questions are compulsory.*

1. 'Air has weight'. Make a lesson plan to teach this concept in class III in a period of 30 minutes by scientific method.

2. Identify any topic from classes III-V science. Write 5 behavioural objectives. Construct one multiple choice test item for each objective.
3. "I heard and I forgot. I saw and I remembered. I did and I understood". This is a research finding. Keeping this into consideration, what will be your role as a primary school teacher?
4. (a) List the abilities which are expected to be developed through EVS.

   (b) What is the role of improvised equipments/low cost apparatus in science teaching?

   or

   How can you utilise community resources in science teaching? Explain giving examples.
5. Why science kit is essential for EVS? Explain giving examples.

   or

   Explain the terms 'continuous and comprehensive evaluation'. In what way it is useful at elementary level?

Paper No. 8

Teaching of Science

Time : 3 hrs. ***M. Marks : 70***

All questions are to be attempted. Write to the point.

1. Write 10 behavioural objectives to teach the topic "Characteristic of living things".
2. What are the various stages of cognitive development as suggested by Piaget? How can we evolve teaching strategies to suit the Primary School Children keeping these stages in mind?
3. "The different parts of a plant have different functions." What are the roles of a teacher as an organiser and as a facilitator to teach this concept?
4. Why environmental studies is essential at primary level? Explain the objectives of environmental studies.

5. Write down the different steps of scientific method in proper sequence.
6. Write down the six objectives of science teaching at primary level.
7. (i) What is child-centred approach in teaching?
   (ii) What is the role of teacher in child-centred approach?
   (iii) Discuss limitations of child-centred approach.
   (iv) What are your suggestions to overcome these limitations?
8. (i) How will you identify slow learners in your class?
   (ii) What is the impact of science on our society?
   (iii) Define minimum levels of learning?
   (iv) What is peer-group learning?
   (v) What are the uses of improving science equipment in teaching science?
   (vi) What is integrated approach in science teaching?

Paper No. 9

Time : 3 hrs. ***M. Marks : 70***

All questions are to be attempted. Write to the point.

1. E.V.S. is the study ....
2. Evaluation is a ....
3. The main objective of the present examination system is ....
4. Low cost teaching aid is a necessity for a country like ours because ....
5. Improvisation of apparatus means ....
6. M.L.L. stands for ....
7. The main function of teaching aid in the teaching-learning process is ....
8. Scientific Attitude can be developed by ....
9. Community resources are ....

10. To learn science is to .... science and there is no other way to learn science—"Kothari"
11. What are the various objectives of teaching EVS at primary level? Give a brief account.
12. Give various steps involved in a scientific method of teaching.
13. What are the various abilities which can be developed during EVS teaching?
14. What is the importance of primary science kit in EVS teaching? Give example.
15. Take a suitable topic from EVS (Science) taught by you and prepare 5 questions at the application level along with relevant answers.
16. Why is a child centred method better than any other method of teaching? Explain.
17. What are the advantages and disadvantages of long answer type questions? Describe in brief.
18. "Evaluation is better than Examination". Explain.
19. What is a peer group learning? What are its advantages?
20. Why was the concept ofMLL introduced by NPE-1986? Whatis its importance in the teaching learning process?
21. Prepare a lesson plan for about 40 mts to teaching any EVS (Science) classes (III-V).
22. What are the various stages of cognitive development in children? Give examples.
23. What are the various approaches to teach EVS (Science)? Which approach is better? Why?
24. What do you understand by problem solving method in teaching EVS (Science)? Take any problem and provide steps to solve it.

Paper No. 10

Time : 3 hrs. ***M. Marks : 60 Note :***

All questions are compulsory.

1. What is nature of science? Describe its social, cultural and ethical aspects.

2. List the abilities which are expected to be developed through EVS (Science) teaching.
3. What is the role of improvised equipments/low cost apparatus in science teaching?
4. How can you utilize community resources in science teaching? Explain giving examples.
5. Explain the term continuous and comprehensive evaluation. In what way it is useful at elementary level?
6. "The different parts of a plant have different functions." What are the duties of a teacher as an organiser?
7. What is scientific method? Write down its different steps in proper sequence.
8. Write down five objectives of science teaching at primary level.
9. 'Air has weight'. Make a lesson plan to teach this concept in Class III in a period of 30 minutes by scientific method.
10. Write 10 behavioural objectives to teach the topic "characteristics of living things".

Paper No. 11

Time : 3 hrs. ***M. Marks : 60***

Note : *All questions are compulsory.*

1. Construct five Multiple Response type test items based on the topic mentioned in question number 9 or the concept mentioned in question number 10 of this paper.
2. Help in evaluating the pupils' achievement at different times, help in diagnosing the pupils' difficulties in learning and a mechanism for improving teaching are said to be three major functions of evaluation. Discuss giving examples selecting a topic of your choice from primary science syllabus.
3. Environmental studies is not a new subject in our school syllabus. It is a new approach. Discuss.
4. Keeping in view the different roles of science teacher, write outlines of a plan to take children to a field trip for teaching a 'suitable lesson' from primary science syllabus.

5. There is a close relationship between the scientific attitude and the scientific way of working. Illustrate through an example.
6. Name any five core components included in the school curriculum. Write statement for minimum levels of learning corresponding to each core component.
7. "Water is a valuable resource." Assuming this concept as a unit, divide it into five lessons. Name the lesson and write its objective in brief.
8. Discuss the suitability of content based approach and process based approach for teaching of primary science, giving suitable examples.
9. Make a lesson plan to teach in class IV in a period of 30 minutes, "the sun rises in the East and sets in the West". How does it happen?
10. "For good health, children of 6-11 age group should eat a variety of food." Write 10 statements of objectives making essential learning outcomes clear for the concept stated.

Paper No. 12

Time : 3 hrs. ***M. Marks : 70***

Note : *All questions are compulsory.*

Part 'A'

1. Name any two problems arising due to harmful impact of science on society.
2. Give two advantages of using a primary science kit.
3. Write any two points of difference between examination and evaluation.
4. Name any two community resources which can serve as teaching aids in science.
5. What are concepts?
6. Give any two limitations in the implementation of child centred approach.
7. What are behavioural objectives?

8. Which stage of cognitive development do the primary school pupils belong?
9. Under what condition is the 'peer group learning' useful?
10. Name the psychologist who propounded the various stages of mental development.

Part 'B'

11. What are the steps involved in the scientific method?
12. Define minimum levels of learning in science.
13. What is meant by concept mapping?
14. What is meant by ethical aspects of science?
15. What is process approach in science? Why is it needed in science teaching?
16. What is meant by improvised apparatus? Write two advantages of improvisation in science teaching.
17. What is the significance of community resources in environmental studies?
18. What is the importance of questioning technique in the teaching of science?
19. What is the importance of excursions in the teaching of science?
20. What is meant by scientific attitude?

Part 'C'

21. Select a topic of your choice from sciençe syllabus of classes III to V and make a lesson plan to teach this topic in a period of forty minutes by 'Problem Solving Method'.
22. Select a topic of your choice from the science syllabus of classes I to V. Write four behavioural objectives for this topic and construct one multiple choice test item for each one of the four objectives.
23. What is meant by an integrated approach to the teaching of science? What are its objectives?

or

Discuss the significance of environmental studies in the primary education and the abilities that can be developed through it.

24. Write short notes on any two of the following :
    (a) Activity based teaching.
    (b) Stages of mental development.
    (c) Objectives of science teaching at the primary level.
    (d) Social importance of science.

Paper No. 13

Time : 3 hrs. ***M. Marks : 60***

General Instructions:

(i) All questions are compulsory.

(ii) Question numbers 1 to 8 are short answer questions of 5 marks each.

(iii) Question numbers 9 and 10 are long answer questions of 10 marks each.

1. List any five important aspects of the content of 'science for all'.

2. (i) What are the four important steps of scientific method? Write the steps in sequence.
   (ii) Differentiate between objectives and learning outcomes. Give one example of each.

3. What are the three main requirements for stating behavioural objectives? Choose any three categories of cognitive domain and write one behaviour objective for each.

4. Explain the role of science teacher as an activity facilitator.

or

Explain the role of science teacher as an organiser.

5. (i) Environmental studies should be taught in an integrated form (including both social science and general science) at classes I and II level. Justify the statement giving one reason.

(ii) List any six abilities which can be developed among children by teaching science through environment.

6. (a) Write the learning areas associated with the following statements ofMLLs in Environment studies (EVS) :

(i) Understands important functions of human body, such as digestion, respiration etc. (class III).

(ii) Knows three states of matter—solid, liquid and gaseous. (class IV)

(iii) Appreciates the importance of science in our daily life. (class V)

(b) Explain the way in which you can use a fused electric bulb as magnifying lens.

7. Write five points favouring the use of science kit at primary level.

or

'Name five places in Delhi where field trips can be arranged for meaningful learning in Environmental studies (science). What preparation will you do before going on a field trip? (write only five points).

8. What is the difference between continuous evaluation and comprehensive evaluation? How will you do continuous comprehensive evaluation?

9. Identify a topic of your choice from Environmental studies (Science) class V and construct multiple choice type questions—one for testing knowledge objective, three for comprehension and one for application objective.

10. Select a topic in Environmental studies (science) class IV and explain how you will teach it by child centred method?

or

Select a topic in Environmental studies (science) class III and explain how you will teach it by problem-solving method.

Paper No. 14

Time : 3 hrs. *M. Marks : 40*

General Instructions :

(i) All questions are compulsory.

(ii) All questions carry equal marks.

(iii) Answer the questions to the point.

(iv) Unnecessary details are not required.

1. (i) Write two main considerations for introducing Environmental Studies (EVS) in primary education.

   (ii) Explain conceptual approach in teaching science.

2. What are the advantages of child centred activity based teaching-learning method? What things should be taken care of while applying this method?

3. Explain the term 'behavioural objective'. Choose any three categories of cognitive domain and write one behavioural objective for each.

4. For the development of the following major competency/learning area in Environmental Studies (Science) for Class IV, suggest five sub-competencies. "The pupil develops skill in gathering and classifying information about living things from one's environment and drawing simple inferences".

5. Prepare a lesson plan for a topic of your choice from Environmental Studies (Science) Class III.

   or

   Prepare a lesson plan for a topic of your choice from Environmental Studies (Science) Class IV.

6. Explain the role of Environmental Studies (Science) teacher as a content planner.

   or

   Explain the role of Environmental Studies (Science) teacher as an organiser.

7. (i) List six experiments from Environmental Studies (Science) which you can do with the help of primary science kit.

   (ii) How can you use a fused electric bulb as magnifying lens? Explain.

8. Identify a topic of your choice from Environmental Studies (Science) Class IV and construct multiple choice type questions—one for testing knowledge objective, three for comprehension and one for application objective. (Key is not required).

Additional Reading

Bhaskara Rao, Digumarti (1994). *Scientific Aptitude,* New Delhi: Ashish Publishing House. ISBN 81-7024-658-X.

Bhaskara Rao, Digumarti (1995). *Animal Kingdom.* New Delhi: Discovery Publishing House. ISBN 81-7141-274-2.

Bhaskara Rao, Digumarti (1995). *Batracology.* New Delhi: Discovery Publishing House. ISBN 81-7141-279-3.

Bhaskara Rao, Digumarti (1997), *Scientific Attitude.* New Delhi: Discovery Publishing House. ISBN 81-7141-308-0.

Bhaskara Rao, Digumarti (1996). *Scientific Attitude vis-à-vis Scientific Aptitude.* New Delhi: Discovery Publishing House. ISBN 81-7141-308-0.

Bhaskara Rao, Digumarti, Editor (1996). *Encyclopaedia of Education for All,* 5 Volumes. New Delhi: APH Publishing Corporation. ISBN 81-7024-759-4 (set).

Vol. I *Education for All: The World Conference.* ISBN 81-7024-760-8.

Vol. II *Education for All: The EPA-9 Summit.* ISBN 81-7024-761-6.

Vol. III *Education for All: Quality Education for All.* ISBN 81-7024-762-6.

Vol. IV *Education for All: Planning and Monitoring.* ISBN 81-7024-763-4.

Vol. V *Education for All: The Indian Scenario.* ISBN 81-7024-764-0.

Bhaskara Rao, Digumarti, Editor (1996). *Global Perceptions on Peace Education,* 3 Volumes. New Delhi: Discovery Publishing House. ISBN 81-7141-319-6.

Bhaskara Rao, Digumarti, Editor (1996). *National Policy on Education*. 2 Volumes. New Delhi: Anmol Publications Pvt. Ltd. ISBN 81-7488-323-1.

Bhaskara Rao, Digumarti, Editor (1997). *Care the Child*, 2 Volumes. New Delhi: Discovery Publishing House. ISBN 81-7141-394-3.

Bhaskara Rao, Digumarti, Editor (1997). *Education for the 21st Century*. New Delhi: Discovery Publishing House. ISBN 81-7141-389-7.

Bhaskara Rao, Digumarti, Editor (1997). *Reflections on Scientific Attitude*. New Delhi: Discovery Publishing House, ISBN 81-7141-319-6.

Bhaskara Rao, Digumarti, Editor (1997). *Success Story of a Primary Education Project*. New Delhi: APH Publishing Corporation. ISBN 81-7024-850-7.

Bhaskara Rao, Digumarti, Editor (1997). *World Food Summit*. New Delhi: Discovery Publishing House. ISBN 81-7141-386-2.

Bhaskara Rao, Digumarti, Editor (1998). *Adolescence Education*. New Delhi: Discovery Publishing House. ISBN 81-7141-432-X.

Bhaskara Rao, Digumarti, Editor (1998). *Community and School Nutrition Education*. New Delhi: Discovery Publishing House. ISBN 81-7141-435-4.

Bhaskara Rao, Digumarti, Editor (1998). *District Primary Education Programme*. New Delhi: Discovery Publishing House. ISBN 81-7141-396-X.

Bhaskara Rao, Digumarti, Editor (1998). *Earth Summit*, 2 Volumes. New Delhi: Discovery Publishing House. ISBN 81-7141-435-4.

Bhaskara Rao, Digumarti, Editor (1998). *National Policy on Education: Towards an Enlightened and Humane Society*, New Delhi: Discovery Publishing House. ISBN 81-7141-426-5.

Bhaskara Rao, Digumarti, Editor (1998). *Reforming School Education*. New Delhi: Discovery Publishing House. ISBN 81-7141-403-6.

Bhaskara Rao, Digumarti, Editor (1998). *Teacher Education in India*. New Delhi: Discovery Publishing House. ISBN 81-7141-406-0.

Bhaskara Rao, Digumarti, Editor (1998). *World Summit for Social Development*. New Delhi: Discovery Publishing House. ISBN 81-7141-420-6.

Bhaskara Rao, Digumarti, Editor (2000). *Education for All: Achieving the Goal*, 3 Volumes, New Delhi: APH Publishing Corporation. ISBN 81-7648-152-1.

Vol. I *The Global Consensus*. ISBN 81-7648-155-6.

Vol. II *Mid-Decade Review Reports of Regional Seminars*. ISBN 81-7648-154-8.

Vol. III *Issues and Trends*. ISBN 81-7648-155-6.

Bhaskara Rao, Digumarti, Editor (2000), *International Encyclopaedia of AIDS*, 11 Volumes in 13 Parts. New Delhi: Discovery Publishing House. ISBN 81-7141-6 (Set).

Vol. 1 *Introduction to HIV/AIDS*. ISBN 81-7141-523-7.

Vol. 2 *HIV/AIDS—Issues and Challenges*, 2 Parts. ISBN 81-7141-524-5.

Vol. 3 *HIV/AIDS—Socio Economic Realities*. ISBN 81-7141-524-3.

Vol. 4 *HIV/AIDS—Law Ethics and Human Rights*, 2 Parts. ISBN 81-7141-526-1.

Vol. 5 *AIDS and NGOs*. ISBN 81-7141-527-X.

Vol. 6 *AIDS and Home Care*. ISBN 81-7141-528-8.

Vol. 7 *STD Case Management*. ISBN 81-7141-529-6.

Vol. 8 *HIV/AIDS Prevention and Care—Teaching Modules for Nurses and Midwives*. ISBN 81-7141-530-X.

Vol. 9 *HIV Prevention Education for Education for Educational Institutions*. ISBN 81-7141-531-8.

Vol. 10 *Instructional Modules for AIDS Education*. ISBN 81-7141-532-6.

Vol. 11 *School Health Education to Prevent AIDS and STD—A Package for Curriculum Planners*. ISBN 81-7141-5338-4.

Bhaskara Rao, Digumarti, Editor (2000). *International Encyclopaedia of Science and Technology Education*, 11 Volumes. New Delhi: Discovery Publishing House. ISBN 81-7141-548-2 (Set).

Vol. 1 *Science and Technology Education*. ISBN 81-7141-568-7.

Vol. 2 *Science Education in Developing Countries*. ISBN 81-7141-570-9.

Vol. 3 *Organisational Structure of Science*. ISBN 81-7141-570-9.

Vol. 4 *Science Education in Asia and the Pacific*. ISBN 81-7141-571-7.

Vol. 5 *Science and Technology Education for All*. ISBN 81-7141-572-5.

Vol. 6 *Values, Ethics, Talent and Girls in Science and Technology Education*. ISBN 81-7141-573-3.

Vol. 7 *Popularization of Science and Technology Education*. ISBN 81-7141-574-1.

Vol. 8 *Science, Power and Society*. ISBN 81-7141-575-X.

Vol. 9 *Information Technology*. ISBN 81-7141-576-8.

Vol. 10 *Teacher Training in Science and Technology Education*. ISBN 81-7141-577-6.

Vol. 11 *Teacher Training in Science and Technology: A Curriculum Framework*. ISBN 81-7141-578-4.

Bhaskara Rao, Digumarti, Editor (2001). *Distance Education in Different Countries*. New Delhi: APH Publishing Corporation. ISBN 81-7648-229-3.

Bhaskara Rao, Digumarti, Editor (2001). *Decentralised Management of Education (Management of Education in Panchayati Raj and Municipal Bodies)*. New Delhi: Discovery Publishing House. ISBN 81-7141-617-9.

Bhaskara Rao, Digumarti, Editor (2001). *Electrochemistry for Environmental Protection*. New Delhi: Discovery Publishing House. ISBN 81-7141-619-5.

Bhaskara Rao, Digumarti, Editor (2001). *Global Educational Studies*. New Delhi: Discovery Publishing House. ISBN 81-7141-616-0.

Bhaskara Rao, Digumarti, Editor (2001). *Global Synthesis of Educational Assessment*. New Delhi: Discovery Publishing House. ISBN 81-7141-613-6.

Bhaskara Rao, Digumarti, Editor (2000). *International Encyclopaedia of Human Rights*. 7 Volumes in 13 Parts. New Delhi: Discovery Publishing House. (Royal Size). ISBN 81-7141-567-9 (Set).

Vol. 1 *International Instruments of Human Rights*, 2 Parts. ISBN 81-7141-595-4.

Vol. 2 *Regional Instruments of Human Rights*. ISBN 81-7141-604-7.

Vol. 3 *Human Rights and the United Nations*, 2 Parts. ISBN 81-7141-605-5.

Vol. 4 *Fact Files of Human Rights*, 3 Parts. ISBN 81-7141-605-3.

Vol. 5 *Study Stories of Human Rights*, 3 Parts. ISBN 81-7141-607-3.

Vol. 6 *International Meetings on Human Rights*, 2 Parts. ISBN 81-7141-608-X.

Vol. 7 *Professional Training in Human Rights*. ISBN 81-7141-609-8.

Bhaskara Rao, Digumarti, Editor (2001). *Jomtein Decade of Education*. New Delhi: Discovery Publishing House. ISBN 81-7141-618-7.

Bhaskara Rao, Digumarti, Editor (2001). *Nuclear Materials: Issues and Concerns*, 2 Volumes. New Delhi: Discovery Publishing House. ISBN 81-7141-611-X.

Bhaskara Rao, Digumarti, Editor (2001). *World Conference on Education for All*. New Delhi: APH Publishing Corporation. ISBN 81-7141-274-9.

Bhaskara Rao, Digumarti, Editor (2001). *World Conference on Higher Education*, New Delhi: Discovery Publishing House. ISBN 81-7141-610-1.

Bhaskara Rao, Digumarti, Editor (2001). *World Conference on Science*. New Delhi: Discovery Publishing House. ISBN 81-7141-612-8.

Bhaskara Rao, Digumarti, Editor (2003). *Inspiring Experience in Teacher Education*. New Delhi: Discovery Publishing House. ISBN 81-7141-656-X.

Bhaskara Rao, Digumarti, Editor (2003). *International Studies in Education*, 3 Volumes, New Delhi: Discovery Publishing House. ISBN 81-7141-647-0.

Bhaskara Rao, Digumarti, Editor (2003). *Military Conversion: Impact on Science and Technology*, New Delhi: Discovery Publishing House. ISBN 81-7141-578-4.

Bhaskara Rao, Digumarti, Editor (2003). *United Nations Millennium Summit*. New Delhi: Discovery Publishing House. ISBN 81-7141-632-2.

Bhaskara Rao, Digumarti, Editor (2003). *World Assembly on Aging*. New Delhi: Discovery Publishing House. ISBN 81-7141-637-3.

Bhaskara Rao, Digumarti, Editor (2004). *World Conference on Human Rights*. New Delhi: Discovery Publishing House. ISBN 81-7141-661-6.

Bhaskara Rao, Digumarti, Editor (2003). *World Education Forum*. New Delhi: Discovery Publishing House. ISBN 81-7141-639-X.

Bhaskara Rao, Digumarti, Editor (2004). *Education Employment and Human Resource Development*. New Delhi: Discovery Publishing House. ISBN 81-7141-681-0.

Bhaskara Rao, Digumarti, Editor (2004). *Successfully Schooling*. New Delhi: Discovery Publishing House. ISBN 81-7141-677-2.

Bhaskara Rao, Digumarti, Editor (2004). *European Education and Teachers*. New Delhi: Discovery Publishing House. ISBN 81-7141-702-7.

Bhaskara Rao, Digumarti, Editor (2004). *Teachers in a Changing World*. New Delhi: Discovery Publishing House. ISBN 81-7141-694-2.

Bhaskara Rao, Digumarti, Editor (2004). *Learning to Live Together*, 4 Volumes. New Delhi: Discovery Publishing House.

Vol. 1 *International Conference on Learning to Live Together.*

Vol. 2 *Globalisation and Living Together.*

Vol. 3 *Curriculum for Learning to Live Together.*

Vol. 4 *Science Education for the Contemporary Society.*

Bhaskara Rao, Digumarti (2004). *International Guidelines on Open and Distance Education*, New Delhi: Discovery Publishing House.

Bhaskara Rao, Digumarti, Editor (2004). *Adult Learning in the 21st Century*. New Delhi: Discovery Publishing House.

Bhaskara Rao, Digumarti, Editor (2004). *Educational Practices: Research and Recommendations*. New Delhi: Discovery Publishing House.

Bhaskara Rao, Digumarti, Editor (2004). *Chernobyl: Never Again*. New Delhi: APH Publishing Corporation.

Bhaskara Rao, Digumarti, Editor (2004). *Virology and Immunology*. New Delhi: APH Publishing Corporation.

Bhaskara Rao, Digumarti, C.A.P. Swami and B.S.V. Dutt (1997). *Self-Evaluation in Student Teaching*. New Delhi: Discovery Publishing House. ISBN 81-7141-374-9.

Bhaskara Rao, Digumarti and B.S.V. Dutt, Editors (2003). *Education: Programmes and Policies*. New Delhi: APH Publishing Corporation. ISBN 81-7648-470-9.

Bhaskara Rao, Digumarti and D. Naresh Kumar (2004). *School Teacher Effectiveness*. New Delhi: Discovery Publishing House.

Bhaskara Rao, Digumarti and D. Sridhar (2002). *Job Satisfaction of School Teachers*. New Delhi: Discovery Publishing House. ISBN 81-7141-652-7.

Bhaskara Rao, Digumarti and Digumarti Pushpa Latha (1994). *Achievement in Biology*. New Delhi: Discovery Publishing House. ISBN 81-7141-264-5.

Bhaskara Rao, Digumarti, C. Sridevi and K. Vijaya (1995). *Achievement in Social Studies*. New Delhi: Discovery Publishing House. ISBN 81-7141-281-5.

Bhaskara Rao, Digumarti and Digumarti Pushpa Latha (1995). *Achievement in English*. New Delhi: Discovery Publishing House. ISBN 81-7141-283-1.

Bhaskara Rao, Digumarti and Digumarti Pushpa Latha (1994). *Achievement in Science*. New Delhi: Discovery Publishing House. ISBN 81-7141-280-70.

Bhaskara Rao, Digumarti and Digumarti Pushpa Latha (1995). *Achievement in Mathematics*. New Delhi: Discovery Publishing House. ISBN 81-7141-278-5.

Bhaskara Rao, Digumarti and Digumarti Pushpa Latha, Editors (1998). *International Encyclopaedia of Women*. 5 Volumes. New Delhi: Discovery Publishing House. ISBN 81-7141-410-9.

Vol. 1 *Status of World's Women*. ISBN 81-7141-494-X.

Vol. 2 *Women, Education and Empowerment*. ISBN 81-7141-498-1.

Vol. 3 *Women Challenges and Advancement*. ISBN 81-7141-497-4.

Vol. 4 *Women and Family Health*. ISBN 81-7141-497-4.

Vol. 5 *Women and International Action*. ISBN 81-7141-498-2.

Bhaskara Rao, Digumarti, Digumarti Pushpa Latha and Digumarti Harshitha, Editors (2001). *Biological Warfare*. New Delhi: Discovery Publishing House. ISBN 81-7141-597-0.

Bhaskara Rao, Digumarti, Digumarti Pushpa Latha and Digumarti Harshitha, Editors (2001). *Women as Educators*. New Delhi: Discovery Publishing House. ISBN 81-7141-602-0.

Bhaskara Rao, Digumarti and Digumarti Harshitha, Editors (2001). *Education in India*. New Delhi: APH Publishing Corporation. ISBN 81-7141-207-2.

Bhaskara Rao, Digumarti, Digumarti Pushpa Latha and Digumarti Harshitha, Editors (2001). *Assessing Learning Achievement*. New Delhi: Discovery Publishing House. ISBN 81-7141-601-2.

Bhaskara Rao, Digumarti, Digumarti Pushpa Latha and Digumarti Harshitha, Editors (2001). *Energy Security*. New Delhi: Discovery Publishing House. ISBN 81-7141-598-9.

Bhaskara Rao, Digumarti, Digumarti Harshitha and K.R.S.S. Rao, Editors (1999). *Advanced Biotechnology*. New Delhi: Discovery Publishing House. ISBN 81-7141-516-4.

Bhaskara Rao, Digumarti and K.R.S. Sambhasiva Rao, Editors (1996). *Current Trends in Indian Education*. New Delhi: Discovery Publishing House. ISBN 81-7141-311-0.

Bhaskara Rao, Digumarti and K. Vijaya (1995). *A Text Book of Evaluation*. Ambala Cantt: The Associated Publishers.

Bhaskara Rao, Digumarti and N.V.M. Mohana Rao (2002). *Problems of Mentally Handicapped Children*. New Delhi: Discovery Publishing House. ISBN 81-7141-645-4.

Bhaskara Rao, Digumarti and S. Chandra Mohan (2002). *Sports Management*. New Delhi: APH Publishing Corporation. ISBN 81-7648-467-9.

Bhaskara Rao, Digumarti and Sk. Johni Basha (2004). *Teachers' Population Education Awareness*. New Delhi: APH Publishing Corporation.

Bhaskara Rao, Digumarti, V.V. Rao, V.V. Lakshmi and V.V. Krishna, Editors (1999). *Status and Advancement of Women*. New Delhi: APH Publishing Corporation. ISBN 81-7648-169-6.

Babu, P.C., Author and Digumarti Bhaskara Rao, Editor (2004). *Flowers of Wisdom*. New Delhi: Discovery Publishing House. ISBN 81-7141-695-0.

Bhagya Lakshmi, Lingineni, Author and Digumarti Bhaskara Rao, Editor (2000). *Reading and Comprehension*. New Delhi: Discovery Publishing House. ISBN 81-7141-543-1.

Bhuvaneswara Lakshmi, Gadde, Author and Digumarti Bhaskara Rao, Editor (2000). *Attitude Towards Science*. New Delhi: Discovery Publishing House. ISBN 81-7141-541-6.

Devraj, T.A.S., Author and Digumarti Bhaskara Rao, Editor (1997). *Trace Analysis of Uranium and Thorium*. New Delhi: Discovery Publishing House. ISBN 81-7141-375-7.

Durga Rani, K., Author and Digumarti Bhaskara Rao, Editor (2000). *Educational Aspirations and Scientific Attitudes*. New Delhi: Discovery Publishing House. ISBN 81-7141-555-55.

Dutt, B.S.V. and Digumarti Bhaskara Rao (2001). *Empowering Primary Teachers*. New Delhi: Discovery Publishing House. ISBN 81-7141-615.2.

Ediger, Marlow and Digumarti Bhaskara Rao (1996). *Science Curriculum*. New Delhi: Discovery Publishing House. ISBN 81-7141-321-8.

Ediger, Marlow and Digumarti Bhaskara Rao (2000). *Teaching Mathematics Successfully*. New Delhi: Discovery Publishing House. ISBN 81-7141-552-0.

Ediger, Marlow and Digumarti Bhaskara Rao (2001). *Teaching Science Successfully*. New Delhi: Discovery Publishing House. ISBN 81-7141-600-4.

Ediger, Marlow and Digumarti Bhaskara Rao (2001). *Teaching Social Studies Successfully*. New Delhi: Discovery Publishing House. ISBN 81-7141-596-2.

Ediger, Marlow and Digumarti Bhaskara Rao (2002). *Philosophy and Curriculum*. New Delhi: Discovery Publishing House. ISBN 81-7141-631-4.

Ediger, Marlow and Digumarti Bhaskara Rao (2002). *Improving School Administration*. New Delhi: Discovery Publishing House. ISBN 81-7141-633-0.

Ediger, Marlow and Digumarti Bhaskara Rao (2002). *Elementary Curriculum*. New Delhi: Discovery Publishing House. ISBN 81-7141-658-6.

Ediger, Marlow and Digumarti Bhaskara Rao (2003). *Language Arts Curriculum*. New Delhi: Discovery Publishing House. ISBN 81-7141-657-8.

Ediger, Marlow and Digumarti Bhaskara Rao (2004). *Teaching Language Arts Successfully*. New Delhi: Discovery Publishing House. ISBN 81-7141-678-0.

Ediger, Marlow and Digumarti Bhaskara Rao (2004). *Teaching Mathematics in Elementary Schools*. New Delhi: Discovery Publishing House. ISBN 81-7141-687-X.

Ediger, Marlow and Digumarti Bhaskara Rao (2004). *Teaching Science in Elementary Schools*. New Delhi: Discovery Publishing House. ISBN 81-7141-709-4.

Ediger, Marlow and Digumarti Bhaskara Rao (2004). *School Curriculum and Administration*. New Delhi: Discovery Publishing House. ISBN 81-7141-709-4.

Ediger, Marlow and Digumarti Bhaskara Rao (2004). *Modern Elementary School*. New Delhi: Discovery Publishing House.

Ediger, Marlow and Digumarti Bhaskara Rao (2004): *Relevancy in Elementary Curriculum*. New Delhi: Discovery Publishing House. ISBN 81-7141-751-5.

Ediger, Marlow and Digumarti Bhaskara Rao, (2004). *Teaching Social Studies in Elementary Schools*. New Delhi: Discovery Publishing House.

Ediger Marlow, B.S.V. Dutt and Digumarti Bhaskara Rao (2004). *Teaching English Successfully*. New Delhi: Discovery Publishing House. ISBN 81-7141-707-8.

Harshitha, Digumarti and Digumarti Bhaskara Rao, Editors (2004). *Educational Innovations*. New Delhi: Discovery Publishing House.

Indira Devi, Author and J. Prasanth Kumar and Digumarti Bhaskara Rao, Editors (2004). *Values in Language Text Books*. New Delhi: Discovery Publishing House.

Jayasree, Kandi, Author and Digumarti Bhaskara Rao, Editor (1999). *Correlates of Socialisation*. New Delhi: Discovery Publishing House. ISBN 81-7141-517-2.

John Babu, Chikati, Author and T.J.R. Prasad, G.M. Madhukar and Digumarti Bhaskara Rao, Editors (1996). *Problem Solving in Mathematics*. New Delhi: APH Publishing Corporation. ISBN 81-7648-273-0.

Lalitha, T., Author and K.S. Prabhakaram, D.S.N. Sastry and Digumarti Bhaskara Rao, Editors (2004). *Educational Philosophic Beliefs*. New Delhi: Discovery Publishing House. ISBN 81-7141-765-5.

Madhu Bala, Jampala, Author and Digumarti Bhaskara Rao, Editor (2004). *Adjustment Problems of Hearing Impaired*. New Delhi: Discovery Publishing House.

Marja, Talvi and Digumarti Bhaskara Rao, Editors (1996). *Educational Leadership and Social Changes*. New Delhi: Discovery Publishing House. ISBN 81-7141-320-X.

Nirmala Jyothi, M., Author and Digumarti Bhaskara Rao, Editor (2003). *Non-detention Systems in School Education*. New Delhi: Discovery Publishing House. ISBN 81-7141-654-3.

Prabhakaram, K.S., Author and Digumarti Bhaskara Rao, Editor (1998). *Concept Attainment Model in Mathematics Teaching*. New Delhi: Discovery Publishing House. ISBN 81-7141-424-9.

Prasanth Kumar, J., Author and Digumarti Bhaskara Rao, Editor (1998). *Effectiveness of Distance Education System*. New Delhi: Discovery Publishing House. ISBN 81-7141-437-0.

Prasanth Kumar, J., Author and G. Sundara Rao and Digumarti Bhaskara Rao, Editors (2000). *Open University Student Support Services*. New Delhi: Discovery Publishing House. ISBN 81-7141-550-4.

Ramatulasamma, K., Author and Digumarti Bhaskara Rao, Editor (2002). *Job Satisfaction of Teacher Educators*, New Delhi: Discovery Publishing House. ISBN 81-7141-655-1.

Rama Krishnaiah, D., Author and Digumarti Bhaskara Rao, Editor (1998). *Job Satisfaction of College Teachers*, New Delhi: Discovery Publishing House. ISBN 81-7141-438-9.

Rama Kumar Ratnam, M., Author and Digumarti Bhaskara Rao, Editor (1998). *Dukka: Suffering in Early Buddhism*. New Delhi: Discovery Publishing House. ISBN 81-7141-653-5.

Rathaiah, Lavu and Digumarti Bhaskara Rao, Editors (1996). *International Innovations in Education*. New Delhi: Discovery Publishing House. ISBN 81-7141-359-5.

Ramesh, Ganta and Digumarti Bhaskara Rao, Editors (1998). *Environmental Education: Problems and Prospects*. New Delhi: Discovery Publishing House. ISBN 81-7141-423-0.

Rathaiah, Lavu and Digumarti Bhaskara Rao (1997). *Achievement Correlates*. New Delhi: Discovery Publishing House. ISBN 81-7141-385-4.

Reddy, Sudhakar Y., Author, and Digumarti Bhaskara Rao, Editor (2003). *Creativity in Adolescents*. New Delhi: Discovery Publishing House. ISBN 81-7141-659-4.

Reddy, M.S., Author and Digumarti Bhaskara Rao, Editor (2004). *Creativity in College Students*. New Delhi: Discovery Publishing House. ISBN 81-7141-697-7.

Radramamba, B., Author and Digumarti Bhaskara Rao, Editor (2003). *Problems of Teaching*. New Delhi: APH Publishing Corporation. ISBN 81-7648-462-8.

Sanjeeva Rao, P.C., Author and Digumarti Bhaskara Rao, Editor (1996). *A Text Book of Geology*. New Delhi: Discovery Publishing House. ISBN 81-7141-313-7.

Satya Narayana V., Author and Digumarti Bhaskara Rao, Editor (2001). *Physical Education, Social Attitudes and Leadership Qualities*. New Delhi: Discovery Publishing House. ISBN 81-7141-593-8.

Srinivasulu Reddy, M., and K.R.S. Sambasiva Rao, Authors and Digumarti Bhaskara Rao, Editor (1999). *A Text Book of Aquaculture*. New Delhi: Discovery Publishing House. ISBN 81-7141-482-6.

Srinivasa Rao, Mandalapu, Author and Digumarti Bhaskara Rao, Editor (2004). *Achievement Motivation and Achievement in Mathematics*. New Delhi: Discovery Publishing House. ISBN 81-7141-674-8.

Vanaja, M. Author and Digumarti Bhaskara Rao, Editor (1999). *Inquiry Training Model*. New Delhi: Discovery Publishing House. ISBN 81-7141-515-6.

Vanaja. M. and N. Sneha Latha, Authors and Digumarti Bhaskara Rao, Editor (2004). *Student Shyness*. New Delhi: APH Publishing Corporation.

Valeri V. Koustiouk, Author and Digumarti Bhaskara Rao, Editor (2002). *A Text Book of Cryogenics*. New Delhi: Discovery Publishing House. ISBN 81-7141-642-X.

Valeri V. Koustiouk, Author and Digumarti Bhaskara Rao, Editor (2004). *Refrigeration and Environment*. New Delhi: APH Publishing Corporation.

Veena Kumari, Balusu and Digumarti Bhaskara Rao (1996). *Operation Black Board*. New Delhi: Ashish Publishing Corporation. ISBN 81-7024-711-X.

Veena Kumari, Balusu, Author and Digumarti Bhaskara Rao, Editor (2000). *Psycho-Social Correlates of Achievement*, New Delhi: Discovery Publishing House. ISBN 81-7141-547-4.

Vanaja, M., Author and Digumarti Bhaskara Rao, Editor (1999). *Inquiry Training Model*. New Delhi: Discovery Publishing House. ISBN 81-7141-515-6.

Venkata Rao, P. and Digumarti Bhaskara Rao (1989). *A Text Book of Zoology—Junior Intermediate*. Guntur: Vignan Publishers.

Venkata Rao, P. and Digumarti Bhaskara Rao (1989). *A Text Book of Zoology—Senior Intermediate*. Guntur: Vignan Publishers.

Venugopala Rao, K., Author and Digumarti Bhaskara Rao, Editor (2000). *Teacher Morale in Secondary Schools*. New Delhi: Discovery Publishing House. ISBN 81-7141-551-2.

Vidya, C., Author and Digumarti Bhaskara Rao. Editor (1996). *A Text Book of Nutrition*. New Delhi: Discovery Publishing House. ISBN 81-7141-309-9.

Vidya Bharathi, D., Author and Digumarti Bhaskara Rao, Editor (2000). *Educational Philosophies of Swami Vivekananda and John Dewey*. New Delhi: APH Publishing Corporation. ISBN 81-7648-309-9.

Books in Telugu Language

Bhaskara Rao, Digumarti (1986). *Dhrushya Sravana Bodhanapakaranalu* (Audio Visual Teaching Aids). Guntur: Nagarjuna Publishers.

Bhaskara Rao, Digumarti (1993). *Jeevasashtra Bodhana* (Teaching of Biology). Guntur: Nagarjuna Publishers.

Bhaskara Rao, Digumarti (1995). *Vignanasasthra Bodhana* (Teaching of Science) Guntur: Nagarjuna Publishers.

Bhaskara Rao, Digumarti (1997). *Vidya Manovignana Seshtram* (Educational Psychology). Guntur: Creative Press.

Bhaskara Rao, Digumarti (1998). *DSC Study Material*. Guntur: Nagarjuna Publishers.

Bhaskara Rao, Digumarti (1998). *Upadhyayudu Vidya*. (Teacher and Education). Guntur: Nagarjuna Publishers.

Bhaskara Rao, Digumarti (1998). *Vidya Drukpadalu* (Prespectives of Education). Guntur: Nagarjuna Publishers.

Bhaskara Rao, Digumarti (1999). *EdCET Teaching Aptitude*. Guntur: Nagarjuna Publishers.

Bhaskara Rao, Digumarti (2001). *Bharata Samajamulo Upadyayudu Vidya* (Teacher and Education in Emerging Indian Society). Guntur: Nagarjuna Publishers.

Bhaskara Rao, Digumarti (2001). *Bhoutika Sastra Bodhana Paddathulu* (Methods of Teaching Physical Science). Guntur: Nagarjuna Publishers.

Bhaskara Rao, Digumarti (2001). *Jeeva Sastra Bodhana Padhathulu* (Methods of Teaching Biology). Guntur: Nagarjuna Publishers.

Bhaskara Rao, Digumarti (2001). *Vidya Manovignana Sastram* (Educational Psychology). Guntur: Nagarjuna Publishers.

Bhaskara Rao, Digumarti (2003). *Patsala Yajamanyam/Paripalana* (School Management and Administration). Guntur: Nagarjuna Publishers.

Bhaskara Rao, Digumarti (2004). *Vidya Sanketika Sastram mariyu Computer Vidya* (Educational Technology and Computer Education). Guntur: Nagarjuna Publishers.